A2 Music
Study Guide

Edexcel

Paul Terry and
David Bowman

R·

Rhinegold Education

239–241 Shaftesbury Avenue
London WC2H 8TF
Telephone: 020 7333 1720
Fax: 020 7333 1765

www.rhinegold.co.uk

Music Study Guides
(series editor: Paul Terry)

GCSE, AS and A2 Music Study Guides (AQA, Edexcel and OCR)
GCSE, AS and A2 Music Listening Tests (AQA, Edexcel and OCR)
GCSE Music Study Guide (WJEC)
GCSE Music Listening Tests (WJEC)
AS/A2 Music Technology Study Guide (Edexcel)
AS/A2 Music Technology Listening Tests (Edexcel)
Revision Guides for GCSE (AQA, Edexcel and OCR), AS and A2 Music (AQA and Edexcel)
Revision Guides for AS and A2 Music Technology (Edexcel)

Also available from Rhinegold Education

Key Stage 3 Elements
Key Stage 3 Listening Tests: Book 1 and Book 2
AS and A2 Music Harmony Workbooks
GCSE and AS Music Composition Workbooks
GCSE and AS Music Literacy Workbooks
Romanticism in Focus, Baroque Music in Focus, Film Music in Focus, Modernism in Focus,
The Immaculate Collection in Focus, *Who's Next* in Focus, *Batman* in Focus, *Goldfinger* in Focus,
Musicals in Focus

Rhinegold also publishes Choir & Organ, Classical Music, Classroom Music, Early Music Today,
International Piano, Music Teacher, Opera Now, Piano, The Singer, Teaching Drama,
British and International Music Yearbook, British Performing Arts Yearbook, British Music Education Yearbook,
Rhinegold Dictionary of Music in Sound

Other Rhinegold Study Guides

Rhinegold publishes resources for candidates studying Drama and Theatre Studies.

First published 2009 in Great Britain by
Rhinegold Education
239–241 Shaftesbury Avenue
London WC2H 8TF
Telephone: 020 7333 1720
Fax: 020 7333 1765
www.rhinegold.co.uk

You should always check the current requirements of the examination, since these may change.
Copies of the Edexcel Specification may be obtained from Edexcel Examinations at
Edexcel Publications, Adamsway, Mansfield, Notts. NG18 4FN
Telephone 01623 467467, Fax 01623 450481, Email publications@linneydirect.com
See also the Edexcel website at www.edexcel.com

Edexcel A2 Music Study Guide (2010–2012)
British Library Cataloguing in Publication Data.
A catalogue record for this book is available from the British Library.
ISBN 978-1-906178-73-4
Printed in Great Britain by Headley Brothers Ltd

Contents

The details of the A2 Music examination are believed to be correct at the time of going to press, but readers should always check the current requirements for the examination with Edexcel, since these may change. The Edexcel music specification can be downloaded from www.edexcel.com.

The authors

David Bowman and Paul Terry have co-authored many books in support of A-level music, including study guides for Rhinegold Publishing and the books *Aural Matters*, *Aural Matters in Practice* and *Listening Matters* published by Schott.

Paul Terry has taught music from primary to postgraduate level. He was a music examiner for nearly 30 years and has worked as a consultant for several examination boards. He also served as a member of the Secondary Examinations Council and its successor the Schools Examinations and Assessment Council. He was chief examiner for the Oxford and Cambridge Schools Examinations Board (now part of OCR) and he was a chief examiner for London Examinations (now part of Edexcel). In addition to the books listed above, Paul has written *Musicals in Focus* for Rhinegold Publishing and is co-author with William Lloyd of *Music in Sequence*, *Classics in Sequence*, *Rock in Sequence*, and *Rehearse, Direct and Play*, published by Musonix Publishing.

David Bowman was for 20 years director of music at Ampleforth College and was a chief examiner for the University of London Schools Examination Board (now Edexcel) from 1982 to 1998. He now spends more time with his family, horses and dogs. In addition to the titles listed above, David's publications include the *London Anthology of Music* (University of London Schools Examinations Board), *Sound Matters* (co-authored with Bruce Cole, published by Schott), *Analysis Matters* (two volumes, published by Rhinegold) and many analytical articles for *Music Teacher*. He is a contributor to the *Collins Classical Music Encyclopedia*, edited by Stanley Sadie, and is the author of the *Rhinegold Dictionary of Music in Sound*.

Acknowledgements

The authors would like to thank Dr Hugh Benham for his comments on the opening chapters of this book and Adrian Horsewood of Rhinegold Publishing for his invaluable work on the volume. We are also grateful to the following for permission to use printed excerpts from their publications:

Stravinsky *Pulcinella* Suite © Copyright 1924 by Hawkes & Son (London) Ltd. Revised version: © Copyright 1949 by Hawkes & Son (London) Ltd. U.S. copyright renewed.

Shostakovich String Quartet No 8 © Copyright 1960 by Boosey & Hawkes Music Publishers Ltd for the UK, British Commonwealth (excl Canada), Eire & South Africa

Shostakovich Symphony No 1 © Copyright 1925 by Boosey & Hawkes Music Publishers Ltd for the UK, British Commonwealth (excl Canada), Eire & South Africa

Shostakovich Symphony No 5 © Copyright 1939 by Boosey & Hawkes Music Publishers Ltd for the UK, British Commonwealth (excl Canada), Eire & South Africa

John Cage: Sonatas and Interludes, Edition Peters No. 6755 © 1960 by Henmar Press Inc., New York. Reproduced by permission of Peters Edition Limited, London

Shostakovich Preludes and Fugues Op. 87 © Copyright 1975 by Boosey & Hawkes Music Publishers Ltd for the UK, British Commonwealth (excl Canada), Eire & South Africa

Auric: *Passport to Pimlico* © Georges Auric. Reproduced by kind permission of Madame Michèle Auric

Planet of the Apes, music by Jerry Goldsmith © 1968 Warner Tamerlane Publishing Corp. Warner/Chappell North America Ltd. Reproduced by permission of Faber Music Ltd. All Rights Reserved.

West End Blues, words and music by Joe 'King' Oliver and Clarence Williams © 1928 (50%) B Feldman & Co Ltd and (50%) Redwood Music Ltd. Reproduced by permission of International Music Publications Ltd (a trading name of Faber Music Ltd) and Faber Music Ltd. All Rights Reserved.

Black and Tan Fantasy, by Duke Ellington and Bubber Miley © 1934 EMI Mills Music, Inc. Copyright Renewed and Assigned to EMI Mills Music, Inc. and Famous Music LLC in the U.S. All Rights Reserved. Used by Permission of Alfred Publishing Co., Inc.

Niall Keegan: *Tom McElvogue's (jig)* and *New Irish Barndance* © Copyright 1994 Niall Keegan. Used by permission of Niall Keegan and Nimbus Records. All rights reserved. International copyright secured.

Introduction

Course overview

A2 Music consists of three units, which follow on from the three units that you studied for the AS exam:

Unit 4: Extended Performance

This unit accounts for 30% of the marks for A2 Music. You will have to perform a balanced programme of pieces of your choice lasting between 12 and 15 minutes. Any instrument (or voice) can be used, and you may perform as a soloist and/or with a small ensemble. Your programme can be presented at any time before the end of the course, but it must consist of a single performance – you are not allowed to assemble a portfolio of pieces presented on different occasions. However, you can repeat the *entire* programme (although not individual pieces from it) on another occasion if you and your teacher are not happy with your first attempt. Your programme will be recorded and marked by your teacher, and the recording will be sent to an Edexcel examiner who will check the mark that you have been awarded.

Unit 5: Composition and Technical Study

This unit accounts for 30% of the marks for A2 Music and is based on a choice of briefs that will be set by Edexcel at the start of your course. You have to complete two tasks under controlled conditions: two compositions, or two technical studies, or one of each. The work is then recorded, and scores and recordings sent to an Edexcel examiner for marking.

Unit 6: Further Musical Understanding

This unit accounts for 40% of the marks for A2 Music. You will study two groups of set works, as well as techniques for answering questions on unfamiliar music. At the end of the course you will sit a two-hour exam paper in three sections:

➢ In Section A you will have to answer questions on recordings of music that will be unfamiliar, although the excerpts played will be related to the set works you have studied

➢ In Section B you will have to answer two questions on one of the groups of set works

➢ In Section C you will have to answer an essay question about three pieces from the other group of set works.

You will be allowed to refer to an unmarked copy of NAM throughout the exam. Your answers to this paper will be sent to an Edexcel examiner for marking.

The set works change each year and are not the same as those you studied for AS Music. They are all taken from the *New Anthology of Music*, referred to as NAM in the rest of this book.

NAM is published by Peters Edition Ltd, ISBN 978-1-901507-03-4 (with a set of four CDs, ISBN 978-1-901507-04-1), and is available from Edexcel publications (see page 2), or from the publisher (www.editionpeters.com) or from any music retailer.

Getting started

This book will help you prepare for the exam by providing tips and advice for performing and composing, along with detailed notes on the set works that you will need to study. Explanations of technical terms printed in **bold type** can be found in the glossary at the end of the book. If you need further help with these, or with other terminology you encounter during the course, we recommend that you consult the *Rhinegold Dictionary of Music in Sound* by David Bowman. This not only gives detailed explanations of a wide range of musical concepts, but also illustrates them using a large number of specially recorded examples on CD, enabling you to hear directly how theory relates to the actual sounds of music.

The *Rhinegold Dictionary of Music in Sound* by David Bowman is published by Rhinegold Publishing, ISBN 978-0946890-87-3.

As with AS Music, you will have little more than 24 weeks in which to complete your composing and performing coursework, and to prepare for Unit 6, so it is essential to be well-organised from day one of the course.

Planning is the secret of success. Choosing music and beginning practice for performing need to get under way as soon as possible, as does preparation for Unit 5. Work for Unit 6 needs to continue throughout the course and be completed in time to allow for revision and the working of several mock papers in the weeks before the actual exam.

Take responsibility for your own progress, using this book as a starting point for your studies, and remember that by meeting deadlines you can avoid the stress of a huge workload in the final weeks of the course.

It is worth repeating the advice we gave in our AS Music Study Guide, because it applies equally to A2 Music.

Firstly, it will help enormously if you try to spot connections between the music you hear, the music you play and the music you compose. Understanding the context and structure of music will increase your enjoyment when listening, inform your performing and illuminate your composing. Composing, performing, listening and understanding are all related aspects of the study of music, and this integration of activities is an important aspect of the course you are taking.

Secondly, try to broaden your musical experience by learning new pieces, taking part in group activities, improvising on your instrument to create different moods and new sounds, and listening to as wide a range of music as you can, both recorded and live. Don't just listen to comfortably familiar music – look for opportunities to broaden your understanding of new types and styles of music by listening to broadcasts and tracks available on the internet, and by going to concerts. This will help to increase your musical understanding and build your confidence as a musician. It should also help to make your year of studying A2 Music highly enjoyable.

Good luck!

Unit 4: Extended Performance

What, when and where

You are required to give a performance that lasts between 12 and 15 minutes. It doesn't matter if you run a little over this limit, but if the total playing time is less than 12 minutes your mark will be reduced.

Your entire programme must be performed in a single continuous session – you are not allowed to assemble a recording of pieces given on different occasions. If you are not satisfied with your performance, you are allowed to repeat it on a later occasion, but you must present the complete programme again – you cannot repeat just selected items.

You may perform on any instrument (including singing). You can include pieces played on different instruments if you wish, but there is no advantage in doing so. It is best avoided unless you really do play two instruments to an equally good standard.

Throughout this chapter the word 'instrument' includes the voice.

You can perform as a soloist (with accompaniment, if appropriate) and/or as a member of a group of up to five performers. Any style of music is acceptable, but read the notes about 'difficulty level' on the next page.

Your performance can take place in class, or as part of a concert either within your school or in the wider community. Your teacher will advise what is the best type of occasion for you. It can take place at any time during the course until the date when marks have to be sent to Edexcel (usually about the middle of May). Again, your teacher will advise on a suitable date.

It is a good idea to have several practice runs at formal performance during the course. Performing for at least 12 minutes is demanding for all musicians, especially wind players and singers, and the added strain of being recorded and assessed will almost certainly make you a little tense. You will be far less anxious if you have experienced performing the full programme to others before the actual assessment day.

Remember that the final assessment should not be left until the end of the course – you will be busy revising and completing coursework for all your subjects by then, and will have little time in which to focus on doing your best in performing. Choose a date with your teacher that is early enough to allow time for at least one later performance in case you should be unwell or not ready for the planned occasion.

Choosing a programme

Plan your programme carefully. It should be well-balanced, with variety of style, mood and tempo. Playing a succession of similar slow movements, for example, would not be a good idea.

You can present a single substantial work providing that it lasts for at least 12 minutes and includes sufficient variety within itself. However, most people present a group of shorter pieces. If you wish, these could be linked by a common theme, such as:

➢ A set of dance movements in different styles

➢ Songs by different composers that are all settings of words by Shakespeare

➢ A group of jazz standards played in contrasting styles.

A popular way of achieving contrast is to perform music from several different periods (such as Baroque, Classical, Romantic and Modern) or in several different styles (such as covers of popular songs from four different decades). If your pieces all come from the same stylistic period, it is particularly important that they are varied in tempo and character.

Choosing the right music for your programme is very important. You are not allowed to include pieces that you played for the AS performing unit, but other works that you know well are likely to be a better choice than pieces that you are currently in the process of learning (unless you are really sure that you will have totally mastered them well before the assessment).

The music you choose should allow you to show technical and expressive control as a performer as well as an understanding of the music. Remember that some types of music, such as technical studies, easy arrangements and certain styles of pop music, tend to focus on a limited range of techniques and so may not give you much chance to show what you can do as a performer. Music that offers some contrasts in mood and the opportunity to show different types of technical skill is likely to serve you best.

The same considerations apply if you choose to include your own composition(s) – the music needs to give you the scope to show a good range of performing skills, which may be difficult if it is technically quite simple.

Think carefully about the order of the programme. A good plan is to start with a short piece that you know really well to give you confidence. Follow this with something that is longer and/or more demanding – don't leave difficult works to the end, when you are likely to start feeling tired. Finish with a short, bright work – perhaps a favourite 'party piece' that has been successful in the past – to bring your programme to a sparkling conclusion.

Difficulty level

Edexcel expects the pieces performed for this unit to be of about Grade 6 standard, although they do not have to come from the lists of pieces specified for grade examinations. Your teacher will be able to advise you on the difficulty level of specific pieces. In addition, the A2 Music section of the Edexcel website includes a booklet listing the difficulty levels of many different pieces.

A little extra credit is available if you give a good performance of music that is of a higher standard than Grade 6. If you present an item that is of a lower standard than Grade 6, it will not be possible to get the maximum marks available for that piece.

Whatever your technical standard it is better to choose music that you can perform with confidence than to attempt a difficult work which stretches your technique to its limit. Difficult pieces that are marred by hesitations or even breakdowns are likely to score far fewer marks than more modest pieces played really musically. The exam reports issued each year by Edexcel have consistently warned that many candidates choose over-ambitious programmes. Try not to fall into this trap yourself, but remember that a *little* adrenalin arising from performing a piece which is a challenge, but not an insuperable obstacle, may bring out your best work, providing that you are well prepared.

Note that you can omit repeats in your performance and shorten long sections that consist purely of accompaniment, but it is not acceptable to cut passages because they happen to be too difficult or to stop in the middle of a movement because it is too long. In such cases it would be better to choose a different work.

Accompaniment

If the music is intended to have an accompaniment (as will be the case for most music apart from that for piano and other chordal instruments) then it must be played with the accompaniment.

Try to work with an accompanist who can rehearse with you regularly, or at least on several occasions before the day. Even the most skilful accompanist will be unable to let you sound your best if the first time you perform together is at the actual performance.

Unless you are performing in an ensemble, the accompaniment should normally be played by just one person on a contrasting instrument. This will usually be a piano but other combinations are allowed – for example, a flute solo could be accompanied on an acoustic guitar or a jazz saxophone solo could be supported by a double bass. You can use a pre-recorded (or sequenced) backing if it is appropriate for the style of music, provided that your own part is performed live and can be clearly distinguished. This is often a good option for electric guitarists and rock drummers.

Ensemble performing

You can, if you wish, perform as a member of an ensemble for this unit. If you choose to do so, note that there mustn't be more than five performers in the group, including yourself, and your own part must be clearly audible and not doubled by anyone else. Suitable ensembles include wind trios, string or vocal quartets, and small rock groups. You can include both solo and ensemble items in your programme if you wish, but there are no additional marks available for doing so and it could prove more difficult to organise the necessary resources.

> A useful book which gives many ideas for getting the best out of ensemble performing of all kinds is *Rehearse, Direct and Play* by William Lloyd and Paul Terry, published by Musonix (www.musonix.co.uk).

Scores

You will have to submit a photocopy (not the original copy) of the music you perform for this unit. Only your own part is required, not the accompaniment or the parts for others in the case of an ensemble.

If your performance is improvised, as often occurs in jazz and rock music, you will still need to submit something on paper that will allow your work to be followed. If a score in conventional stave notation is not available this could be a lead sheet, chord chart, track sheet, table or diagram, together with a description of what is being attempted in improvised passages.

Similarly, if you perform your own composition(s), make sure that the score is as detailed as possible, and accurately reflects your performance.

Preparation

Having chosen and studied your piece(s) with your teacher, and practised to a standard that you feel is acceptable, it is essential that you try out the music under performance conditions – not to your instrumental teacher, parents or anyone else who has heard you working on the music week by week, but to someone who is able to hear the performance fresh. This could be a visiting relative, your fellow students, or another teacher at your school or college.

A small slip or two in this trial performance should not concern you greatly, but if you find that you often hesitate in the more difficult passages, it is an indication that you may have chosen something which might be too difficult. This means that you will need to decide if the work is viable or whether it would be better to make a more realistic choice.

In planning the run-up to the performance allow much more time than you think you are likely to need. Illness may curtail practice time and other commitments may prevent adequate rehearsal with accompanists or other members of an ensemble.

Try to have a run-through of the music in the venue in which you will be performing. If it is a large hall you will probably find that you need to project the sound and exaggerate the contrasts much more than when practising at home. Conversely if you are playing a loud instrument (brass or electric guitar, for example) in a small room, you will almost certainly need to limit louder dynamics.

Decide where you are going to sit or stand and check that the lighting is adequate but not dazzling. If you have an accompanist make sure that you have good eye contact without having to turn away from your listeners. If the piano is an upright, it may take some experimentation to find the best position. If you play an instrument that needs tuning before you start, plan how you are going to do this and remember that tuning is not necessarily something that all accompanists are able to help with.

Whether the piece is accompanied or not, spend some time trying out the opening in various ways. For pieces with a tricky start it can be easier to set the right speed by thinking of a more straight-forward phrase from later in the piece and establishing a mental image of the right tempo from that.

The performance

On the day make sure you leave time for a warm-up. Check that you have to hand any extra equipment you might need (mutes, guitar foot-stools, spare strings and so on). If you require a music stand, check that you know how it is adjusted and secured – collapsing music stands are good for comedy acts but they can seriously undermine your confidence in a performance.

At the performance, there must be an audience of at least one person, in addition to the performer(s) and the teacher assessing your work, but there can be more if you wish. If there is to be an audience of any size, practise walking on stage and setting up, and plan how you will react to applause. Listeners will be disappointed if you shamble on at the start and rush off at the end. Audiences need plenty of time to show their appreciation: a hurried nod in their direction as you leave will appear clumsy, if not downright rude. If there is no printed programme, announce each piece in a positive and friendly manner before you perform it.

Expect to be a little nervous but remember that the more experience you can get of performing to others during the course, the more natural and enjoyable it will become. Blind panic will only normally set in if the music is under-rehearsed or too difficult and this, as we have explained, can be avoided by selecting suitable music and preparing it thoroughly.

How is the performance marked?

Each piece (or movement) that you perform is awarded up to eight marks in each of the following categories:

1. Quality of outcome: security and effectiveness, interpretation and communication; reaction to other parts in an ensemble; sufficient minimum length

2. Accuracy of pitch and rhythm

3. Continuity: fluency and control of tempo

4. Tone and technique, including any specific matters that are appropriate, such as bowing, intonation, pedalling

5. Phrasing, articulation and dynamics.

In the case of improvisation, marks in category 2 are awarded for the use of the stimulus in the performance; marks in category 3 are awarded for the coherence of the work (structure and balance), and marks in category 5 are awarded for use of instrument or voice (including appropriate range of timbre and management of texture).

The mark out of 40 for each piece is balanced against an overall mark for its total impression, and the total is adjusted if the piece is above the standard Grade 6 difficulty level.

Each piece is marked in the same way, and then an average mark out of 40 for the entire group of pieces is calculated. Finally, a mark out of 10 is added to reflect the quality of the performance as a whole, including the suitability and order of the pieces to provide a coherent yet contrasting programme. The complete unit is therefore marked out of 50.

A good mark requires technically secure performing, although the occasional well-covered slip that can happen in even the best-regulated performances should not be a matter of great concern. However, if your performance lacks fluency and coordination, perhaps being marred by stumbles, poor intonation or inability to maintain the correct speed, it is unlikely to be awarded a satisfactory mark. You can avoid this danger by choosing simpler music in which you have mastered the technical challenges and can therefore concentrate on communicating a really musical performance with good tone, effective and appropriate contrasts, and a sense of the style of the music.

It will help if you have a clear image of what you are trying to put across in your performance. You might, for instance, wish to convey rhythmic energy, a dreamy atmosphere, elegant phrasing, dramatic contrasts or subtle blends. Focus on expressive detail throughout the music. Rather than thinking of a passage as merely 'happy', try to decide if you mean boisterous, contented, frivolous, celebratory, cheeky or just cheerful. If it is 'sad', do you mean tragic, doom-laden, nostalgic, angry or solemn? Then try to evoke the moods you intend in your interpretation of the piece, whether it be the glittering ballroom of a minuet, the moonlit night of a nocturne or the smoky languor of a blues club. Never be content with merely 'getting the notes right'.

Unit 5: Composition and Technical Study

Requirements

For this unit you have to submit two pieces of work, which can be either:

➤ Two compositions (from different areas of Study), or

➤ Two technical studies, or

➤ One composition and one technical study.

Edexcel will set briefs for compositions and tasks for technical studies. You have to complete your submissions in time to send to an examiner in May of your examination year. The final writing-up of your work has to be completed under controlled conditions.

The composition briefs

If you are intending to submit two technical studies, turn to page 28.

Edexcel will set four composition briefs in September at the start of your A2 course. Each is linked to one of the two areas of study (Instrumental Music and Applied Music) that also form the focus of your work for Unit 6. Here are the main choices (we will look at detailed examples later):

➤ Instrumental Music **Topic 1: Development and contrast**
A composition in which you will need to devise and vary short motifs in order to develop a longer structure.

➤ Instrumental Music **Topic 2: Exploiting instruments**
A composition in which you will need to write technically challenging music for acoustic instruments.

➤ Applied Music **Topic 3: Music for film and television**
A composition to accompany the events in a given scene.

➤ Applied Music **Topic 4: Music, dance and theatre**
A composition intended primarily for the world of dance.

Your composition should be about three minutes long and, unless directed otherwise in the brief, you are allowed to write it in any style and for whatever resources you wish, including parts for voices. However, be aware that marks are awarded for your use of forces and textures: it may prove difficult to achieve credit for a range of textures if you write for very slender resources, such as an unaccompanied flute.

If you submit two compositions, each must be about three minutes in length and each **must** come from a *different* area of study – in other words, you must choose either Topic 1 or 2 for the first piece, and either Topic 3 or 4 for the second.

Note that if you submit two pieces, each must last about three minutes. You should not submit a six-minute package made up of one long work and one much shorter one.

Once the work is finished you will have to submit a detailed score, either hand-written or computer-printed. Stave notation should be used if this is the convention for the style that you have chosen.

However, other forms of notation are acceptable if they are sufficiently detailed and more usual for the type of music you have created. For example, a pop or jazz composition might be presented as a lead sheet (melody and chord symbols); an electronic piece might be shown as a detailed track diagram, or a work in an experimental style might be notated as a prose score (a detailed table of instructions) or in graphic form.

Whatever type of score you decide upon, it is important to show as much musical detail as possible. For instance, if you use guitar tab, indicate the rhythms you want and add a few words to show the style – the same applies if you use guitar grids (or frames, as they are sometimes called) for the chords.

For more on guitar tab and guitar grids, see the *AS Music Literacy Workbook* by Rebecca Berkley (Rhinegold, 2009).

You will also have to submit a recording of the composition on audio CD or MiniDisc. This can either be of a live performance or it can be a studio-based recording. If the necessary resources are not available, you are allowed to submit a recording of an arrangement or a synthesised version. Whatever route you take, try to ensure that the recording matches the score as closely as possible. Although the quality of the recording is not assessed, it plays a valuable role in showing the examiner what you intend, especially if your score doesn't consist of detailed stave notation.

You do *not* have to submit a sleeve note for your A2 composition(s), as you did for the AS Composing unit.

Regulations about preparatory work done outside of controlled conditions have changed since the publication of the original specification. New information can be found on the music section of the Edexcel website in a document entitled 'Further Guidance'. Although this refers to AS Unit 2, it also applies to A2 Unit 5.

It is important to spend time practising your general composing skills before starting on the brief, and to continue to do so while working on it. Your score for the brief itself has to be completed under controlled conditions, for which you are allowed 14 hours (not 15 hours, as at AS). You are allowed 28 hours in total for completing the scores if you choose to submit two compositions.

Additional time is allowed for recording the work, but if you then need to make any changes to the score, these must be completed under controlled conditions, within whatever is left of your 14 hours. It is therefore best not to leave the recording until all your supervised time has been used up.

Research and preparation for the brief, including listening to and studying relevant music, does not have to be done under controlled conditions, but your teacher is required to check that any rough drafts or sketches that you use when working on your final score are your own work.

Your submissions for this unit need to be completed in time to send to the examiner by the specified date, which is likely to be in the middle of May.

Getting started

Once you have chosen a brief, you can do some valuable research and planning before starting to use up your supervised time on the actual process of composing. Listen carefully and analytically to plenty of relevant music and start to gather information about the resources you intend to use.

It is important to study as many models as you can for the brief you choose, as this will provide you with a variety of ideas on how to go about structuring and developing your own piece. There may be suitable works to study in NAM, which you are allowed to consult while working on your own piece. Other ideas for related listening are included in the sample briefs later in this chapter, but obviously you will need to find pieces that are relevant to your own chosen brief.

When studying other music it is important to realise that you are not expected to write in the style of any specific composer. You should instead be looking at the ways in which composers:

➤ Begin and end a piece

➤ Establish and develop ideas

➤ Create specific moods

➤ Introduce contrasts (of key, mood, timbre or texture)

➤ Design material to suit the characteristics of the instruments and voices concerned

➤ Use structure – not just a form, such as theme and variations, but also how the music is paced to include areas of tension and relaxation, and points of climax

➤ Unify their music, so that it sounds like a satisfying whole rather than a succession of unrelated ideas.

Getting the right balance between unity and diversity is one of the most important tasks for a composer. Too much repetition and the piece will sound boring. Too many new ideas and it will not gel. Careful listening to a broad range of relevant music will show you how composers throughout the ages have evolved many different solutions to this problem.

Resources

You will need to decide on the resources you are going to use for your piece. If other performers are to be involved it is best to write for people who will be available to work with you during the whole composing process, so other students in your group would be the obvious choice.

Start by planning how the characteristics of the instruments and/ or voices might best be exploited. Try to identify the skills (and weaknesses) of each performer so that you can use their individual strengths in your composing. You could discuss what sorts of things are easy and what are difficult for each instrument or voice – although improvising, both separately and together, is often much quicker and more productive than using words.

Your research should also include the ranges and characteristics of the instruments and/or voices you intend to use. Reread pages 14–19 of the *Edexcel AS Music Study Guide* for a discussion of some of the matters to consider when writing for different types of instrument.

Understanding the composition brief

In this section we shall look at an example of each of the four types of brief, and discuss how it might be tackled.

Instrumental Music Topic 1 **Development and contrast**

The focus of this brief will be a composition in which you have to create a musical structure by developing and/or varying a musical idea. Here is an example of the type of brief that could be set:

Compose a piece in which two or more themes are developed and contrasted. You could use a conventional structure, such as rondo form, but you are free to adopt whatever structure you wish for the piece.

The key to successfully developing a musical idea is to begin with something very short but rhythmically distinctive. Perhaps the most famous example is the first movement of Beethoven's 5th Symphony, in which the opening four-note motif develops into some 500 bars of music. At the start it is announced *ff* in octaves, but there is an immediate contrast in dynamic and texture as Beethoven recasts the motif as a succession of quiet imitative entries:

Beethoven, Symphony No. 5 (i)

Straight after this passage Beethoven fills in the interval of a falling 3rd, but keeps the rhythm the same, and then alternates this new version of the opening motif with its own inversion (in which the intervals rise rather than fall), forming the dialogue between upper parts shown in (a) *below*.

The brevity of the motif allows it to be developed into figures that cascade down diminished 7th chords (b) and punctuate the music with perfect cadences at climactic moments (c):

After 58 bars Beethoven introduces what at first might appear to be a contrasting theme:

However, it begins with a new version of the opening motif, which is then expanded by the addition of extra notes and is accompanied by the familiar rhythm of the opening motif at its cadence.

Short motifs are often repeated when they first appear. In the next example, by Mendelssohn, a one-bar motif using notes from the tonic chord is repeated to form a two-bar unit. This is then balanced by two bars that outline chord V^7 to complete a four-bar phrase:

A repeated motif can be varied in:

➢ Dynamic (the repeat could be a quieter, like an echo),

➢ Register (it could appear in a different octave, perhaps even in the bass), or

➢ Timbre (it could be assigned to a different instrument).

Repeating a motif is a good thing to do after its first appearance, but repetition is not development. Once an idea has been established, it needs to develop – in other words, to change in pitch or rhythm (or both). One of the simplest means of development is sequence. Here, a three-note motif is repeated and then extended to two bars. After the crotchet rest, this opening is repeated a step lower to form a two-bar sequence:

This is called a diatonic sequence because all of the notes have been kept within the same key. If *every* note had moved down a tone, the last two pitches would have been E♭–C.

A diatonic sequence is good for establishing the key at the start of a composition (notice how the one above suggests chords I and V^7) but an exact sequence can be more useful later in a piece to give a sense that the music is developing and moving forward, since it opens up the possibility of modulating to a different key:

An exact sequence like this is known as a real sequence. This particular example is a modulating sequence that begins in A major and then moves a step higher to B minor.

Another way of developing a motif into a tune is to increase the size of one or more of its intervals (a process known as melodic augmentation). Often, as here, one pitch serves as an 'anchor' to which the tune frequently returns:

It is often possible to make a number of changes to a motif without losing its identity, providing it has a strong basic shape. The next

example shows just a few of the ways in which the opening motif from Mendelssohn's *Hebrides* Overture is developed later in the movement:

This works so well because the ear notices the rhythm of a motif at least as clearly as its pitches, which is why it is worth spending time devising rhythmically strong main ideas in your own work. In the following example, the pitches of (b) are only loosely related to those in (a), and yet the distinctive rhythm ensures that we hear it as a development of the opening tune:

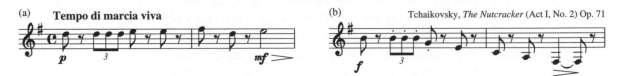

There are many other ways to develop an idea, but we will end by looking at just two other common methods. The first is more like variation rather than true development, because it simply involves decorating a melody. Nevertheless, if you closely compare the second bracketed phrase *below* with the first, you can see that some of the original notes have also been subtly nudged into different places in the bar to achieve a very elegant sense of development of the opening phrase:

The second is a process known as fragmentation, in which a part of a melodic idea is detached and then developed in its own right. Here, a two-bar motif is repeated in sequence (bars 3–4) and then bar 4 is developed in a sequence of its own (bar 5–6):

Later in the movement, Beethoven fragments this material still further, isolating just the turn-like triplet figure:

You may have noticed that almost all of the advice on this topic has focused on development rather than contrast. This is because unifying a composition, so that all of its sections sound as though they belong to the same piece, is the more difficult task. Writing contrasting passages is relatively easy, but they need to have a logical relationship with what has gone before, and not sound as if a totally different piece has interrupted your work. Remember that contrast achieved through changes of key, instrumentation and texture can be more effective than introducing *totally* new musical material. Think about making connections and carefully plan the transition from one section to the next.

Studying pieces such as those from which the examples in this section have been taken should form an important part of your research. You will pick up many tips on how to develop ideas and how to link contrasting sections, in whatever style you choose to write. Be aware that if you write in a style such as minimalism, in which repetition plays an important role, it is essential that your musical ideas constantly grow and mutate – simple repetition will not be enough for a topic based on development and contrast.

Exploiting instruments

Instrumental Music Topic 2

The title of this topic refers to making the best possible use of the instrument(s) for which you write by bringing out their most effective musical qualities. It is an extension of Composing Topic 2 ('Composing idiomatically for instruments') in AS Music, so you should find the advice given on pages 14–19 and 20–21 of the *Edexcel AS Music Study Guide* useful as a starting point.

Like the AS task, electronic pieces are not suitable for this topic, although you are allowed to submit a synthesised recording if suitable live players are not available. However, if you do this, take great care to check that your work is playable on the acoustic instrument(s) concerned.

The composition brief you receive from Edexcel will indicate the main requirements, which may involve writing some technically challenging material – although it could ask you to demonstrate other qualities of the instrument, such as maintaining a lyrical line or making use of particular instrumental techniques. Here is an example of the type of brief that could be set:

Compose a fantasy for one melody instrument accompanied by piano, or for two or three melody instruments. It should exploit the potential of the chosen forces and include contrasting sections (for example, a lyrical opening leading to a solo cadenza, and rounded off with a brilliant finale).

A fantasy (or *fantasia* in Italian) is, in the sense used here, a piece which simply follows the composer's imagination or fancy, and doesn't have a set form. A cadenza is an extended solo, usually unaccompanied, sometimes improvised, and often placed towards the end of a movement.

Composers have used a wide variety of titles for display pieces, including pictorial descriptions (such as 'The Flight of the Bumble Bee'). Some common terms for various types include:

Toccata (from the Italian *toccare*, meaning 'to touch') – a fast piece designed to show off rapid finger movement

Study (or, in French, *étude*) – a piece designed to show off one or more particular aspects of technique, such as staccato tonguing on a wind instrument or double-stopping on a string instrument

Impromptu ('unprompted') – a piece without a set form, often intended to sound as though it is improvised

Capriccio – another type of piece without a set form, in which the composer seems to follow his own caprice or whim

Perpetuum mobile ('perpetual motion') – a piece based on a fast and continuous stream of notes, sometimes with repeats arranged so that it seems never to reach a definite stopping place.

Of course, if an unusual term appears in the brief, you will have plenty of time to research its meaning before starting work on your composition.

Your research should also include detailed study of works in which instrumental technique plays an important role, such as:

Bach's Toccata and Fugue in D minor for organ
The Toccata from Widor's Organ Symphony No. 5
Chopin's 'Raindrop' Prelude, Op. 28 No. 15 for piano
Chopin's 'Revolutionary' *Étude*, Op. 10 No. 12 for piano
Alkan's *Le festin d'Ésope*, Op. 39 No. 12 for piano
Paganini's Caprice in A minor, Op. 1 No. 24 for solo violin
Ian Clarke's *Zoom Tube* for solo flute
Berio's *Sequenza IX* for solo clarinet
Arban's Variations on 'The Carnival of Venice' for solo cornet
Tárrega's *Recuerdos de la Alhambra* for acoustic guitar
Joe Satriani's album 'One Big Rush' for electric guitar
Rimsky-Korsakov's 'The Flight of the Bumble Bee'
    (arranged for various instruments).

When planning your own composition, think carefully about the techniques that you could explore. These include using the full range of the instrument, perhaps contrasting the tone colours that are available in different registers. Various types of articulation could be explored, as well as different types of melodic patterns, and the use of specific techniques, such as pizzicato, mutes, piano pedalling, electronic effects for the guitar and so on.

If the brief doesn't suggest a structure, variation form can be useful for this topic. Whatever you use, remember that the composition needs to work well as a piece of music, with a sense of development and points of climax and repose – it should be more than just a showcase for a succession of different techniques.

For reasons of space, we can only give a few suggestions for study here. When conducting your own research, try entering into a web search engine 'virtuoso music for' followed by the name of the instrument concerned – this is likely to produce a wide range of resources, including technically challenging music in styles as diverse as gypsy music and Indian music, as well as pieces from the jazz, rock and classical repertoire.

Applied Music Topic 3   Music for film and television

The brief for this topic will focus on writing music for the moving image. It could specify a piece (known as an underscore) suitable to accompany a given scenario, or it might ask for a title theme and perhaps a succession of short extracts to be used in a documentary or other type of television programme.

The brief will consist of a simple written description – you won't be provided with visual images on DVD. Similarly, you are not required to synchronise your music to any type of visual image or to submit video clips with your work. However, where the brief involves writing music for a given scenario, you are encouraged to add comments to your score to show where the music is designed to illustrate specific visual images. Here is an example of the type of brief that could be set:

Compose music to underscore a short film about the effects of global warming on an idyllic Pacific island. It starts with pictures of holiday-makers on sun-drenched beaches, then cuts to a simulation of the disasters that occur when the sea level rises. It ends with pictures of the islanders leaving their tropical paradise for ever.

In this topic, the structure of the music is likely to be dictated by the scenario in the brief, so you will not necessarily need to think in terms of conventional musical forms. Our example suggests a three-part structure that might begin with warm, exotic colours, leading to passages of great turbulence, and rounded off by a sad and nostalgic section.

Although a brief like this is likely to result in a work of changing moods to reflect the visual images, it is important not to let your composition become a series of unconnected episodes or sound effects. Think how you might be able to use a small number of motifs that can change as the drama unfolds but that also serve to unify the work as a whole. Some of the suggestions on developing motifs on pages 16–18 should help in giving you ideas.

Research for this topic could include the six film and television extracts in NAM, although if you read the notes on these later in this book you will see that some are arrangements based on film music rather than extracts from the actual film underscore. Other famous pieces of film music to explore include:

Psycho (1960). Bernard Hermann's score for this classic horror film uses only strings, paralleling director Alfred Hitchcock's decision to restrict his palette to black and white film. The 'shower scene' is famous for the way in which terror is portrayed by screechingly dissonant violins rather than by precise images of the murder.

For more on film music, including discussion of a number of famous soundtracks, see *Film Music in Focus* by David Ventura (Rhinegold, 2008).

The Magnificent Seven (1960), with a score by Elmer Bernstein (unrelated to Leonard Bernstein) that is highly typical of the music that has become associated with the epic American western.

The Good, the Bad and the Ugly (1966). Another classic western, but Ennio Morricone's style is very different from Elmer Bernstein's, having a modal main theme, unusual instruments such as the ocarina and harmonica, wordless voices and whistling.

Jaws (1975). John Williams' score for this thriller is famous for a simple two-note ostinato that represents the killer shark. Williams uses this motif persistently to signal approaching danger and avoids using it when there is a false alarm of a shark attack. But having thus conditioned his audience, later scenes in which the huge jaws surge up from the water become even more frightening because they occur without any musical warning.

Chariots of Fire (1981) with music by Vangelis is an early example of a soundtrack written for entirely synthetic sounds.

Batman (1989) has a dark and dramatic score by Danny Elfman that also reveals the composer's love of musical irony. Batman himself is associated with a five-note motif in a minor key, while major-key music accompanies the evil Joker, whose death is preceded by a macabre roof-top waltz.

The Da Vinci Code (2006). Hans Zimmer's sombre score draws on a wide variety of resources, ranging from the combination of electric violin and acoustic cello in the title sequence to massive choral effects that underpin the religious overtones in this controversial murder mystery.

When you study film music, observe how composers react to a variety of stock dramatic situations such as love scenes, tragedy, comedy, horror, chases and fights. Also take note of how music can be used to 'paint' pictures of different types of landscape and seascape in various moods – tranquil, stormy, bathed in sunlight or threatened by storms – and how they sometimes draw on features of older music to suggest an historical period. Pay special attention to the ways in which composers move from one mood to another, since this is something you will almost certainly have to do in your own composition.

Applied Music Topic 4   Music, dance and theatre

This brief is potentially very wide-ranging, since it could involve writing music for:

➢ Social dancing (from classic ballroom dancing, through salsa and other Latin-American dances to modern night-club styles involving the use of music technology)

➢ Performance in a theatre – which could mean formal ballet, contemporary dance, or a dance sequence for a musical or an opera (possibly including voices, if you wish)

➢ Performance in a concert or for playing for pleasure at home, based on dance styles but not intended for actual dancing.

The brief is likely to give you reasonable flexibility, although it is worth noting that Edexcel's sample brief for this topic requires the composition to show the influence of a non-Western style. This could be Asian-inspired Bhangra or a Latin-American style such as the tango, but there is nothing to stop you exploring some more unusual enthusiasm, such as African ritual dance, dance for the classical Chinese theatre or the Hawaiian sacred dance known as hula. Providing it is well executed, examiners are always likely to enjoy the work of candidates who explore beyond the obvious!

Whatever is set by Edexcel, you will have plenty of time between receiving the brief and starting on your own work to research any unusual requirements. Here is an example of the sort of brief that could be set:

Compose a piece of dance music based on the idea of conflict and resolution. It could be designed as a number to appear in a musical or modern opera, or it could be intended for professional dancers to present in a dance studio or at an arts festival.

A brief like this can be realised in a number of ways. No particular style is mentioned, so you could write a piece of electronic music for the dancers to use as a backing track. This would be fine for use in a dance studio, but in the theatre live musicians are normally employed. If the work is intended to form part of a contemporary opera, you might choose to write in a dissonant Modernist style, or perhaps in a gentler Postmodernist or Minimalist style. However, if the dance is to form part of a musical, a lighter, possibly rock-based, style would be more appropriate.

Much dance music, especially for social dancing, has a clearly defined beat, with phrases of equal lengths, and often quite a lot of repetition. Structures are generally simple – for example, verse and chorus form or various types of rondo, such as ABACABA – and variety is often achieved by thinning out the texture in some sections rather than by introducing highly contrasting material. However, professional dancers are used to much more complex rhythm patterns, allowing composers to be more adventurous.

As with the other topics, preparation should include the study of relevant examples. For dance music, these could include:

Stravinsky's three early ballet scores (*The Firebird*, *Petrushka* and *The Rite of Spring*), along with his Neoclassical score for *Pulcinella*, excerpts of the concert suite from which can be found in NAM 7.

Prokofiev's ballet *Romeo and Juliet*, one number from which ('The Dance of the Knights') has become well known through its use as the title music for the television series 'The Apprentice'.

The Three-Cornered Hat by Manuel de Falla, much of it inspired by flamenco and the many other types of Spanish folk music that influenced the work.

Witty French ballet music, such as Satie's *Parade*, Milhaud's *Le Boeuf sur le Toit* and Poulenc's *Les Biches* (all revealing a rich mix of influences from music hall and circus music to Latin-American styles, ragtime and early jazz).

Copland's *Rodeo*, which incorporates cowboy tunes, dances in unusual rhythms and the popular 'Hoe Down' in barn-dance style.

Britten's *The Prince of the Pagodas*, which is influenced by Balinese gamelan music.

'Still Life' at the Penguin Café – a ballet with an ecological message about endangered species and a witty score by Simon Jeffes that reflects Latin rhythms, elements of folk and pop music, and aspects of minimalism.

Dance has played an important role in many musicals. In some cases dance numbers are included as an excuse to add to the colour and spectacle of the show, but dance is more effective when it forms an integral part of the plot. An early example is Richard Rodgers' *On Your Toes* (1936), in which the story about classical ballet meeting the world of jazz enabled dance to be introduced in a way that enhances, rather than interrupts, the drama.

Most of Rodgers' later musicals include dance numbers, notably *Oklahoma!* (1943), in which dance is used to further the action and develop the audience's understanding of the characters and their motivation. In addition to songs that develop into dance routines and a big set-piece Barn Dance in Act 2, the first act ends with a 15-minute 'dream sequence' in which premonitions of the future are acted out in modern ballet.

Production numbers centred on dance can be found in many musicals over the following decades, including Frederick Loewe's *My Fair Lady* (1956), Jerry Bock's *Fiddler on the Roof* (1964) and John Kander's *Cabaret* (1966), while in Marvin Hamlisch's *A Chorus Line* (1975), dance is used as the main vehicle to convey the action in almost every important scene. After this, dance gave way to impressive technical effects in many of the 'mega musicals' of the last quarter of the 20th century, but it is central to works such as Elton John's *Billy Elliott: the Musical* (2005).

In the 21st century, musicals based on back catalogues of pop songs have become popular, the most famous being *Mamma Mia!* (2001), which uses the hits of ABBA. These works, known as 'compilation musicals' or 'jukebox musicals', tend to have a slender plot, but are filled out with bright dance sequences in the style of pop videos.

The musical most closely associated with dance is undoubtedly Leonard Bernstein's *West Side Story* (1957). Bernstein had already written for contemporary dancers in his ballet *Fancy Free* and its spin-off, the musical *On the Town* (both 1944). He worked with the same choreographer (Jerome Robbins) on *West Side Story*, in which much of the drama is conveyed in dance. Instead of an overture, the work opens with a prologue in which the tension between rival gangs is conveyed in mime choreographed to music. The 'Dance at the Gym' forms a showcase of challenge dances between the rivals, and the casting of one of the gangs as Puerto-Rican immigrants gave Bernstein the opportunity to base various song-and-dance numbers on the rhythms of popular Latin-American dances.

If the brief allows you to write music intended for social dancing, there could be a number of options. The main types of ballroom dance in use today include the waltz, foxtrot and quickstep as well as Latin-American styles such as the tango, samba, rumba, paso doble and cha cha. In Latin nightclubs, salsa is the most popular style, along with dances such as the lambada and the merengue. In other nightclubs, dance music could range from disco and hip-hop to styles such as house, techno and trance.

Other types of social dance include styles that have developed from folk music and which often involve group dances rather than partner dances. In country and western, for example, the line dance and the square dance are the two standard forms. Many communities maintain their own local dance traditions, such as the reels, jigs and strathspeys of Scottish country dancing, or Bhangra, which began as Punjabi folk music but which is now often heard in a more westernised form in Britain.

In general, all such dances have a characteristic speed, metre and rhythm pattern which needs to form a prominent feature of your own composition, and some have their own characteristic instrumentation.

Research to identify the main features of any dance style you are interested in can usefully begin on the internet, where recorded examples are also often available for study.

Working the composition brief

Writing the final score must be done under controlled conditions and within the 14 hours allowed, although you can (and should) practise general composing skills, research your chosen brief, study relevant music and make preliminary drafts outside this time. Remember that developing ideas and varying the texture will help you to achieve that really good mark you hope for.

Developing ideas

However good your main idea is, it needs to be developed so that the listener feels that the music is taking them on a journey. Too much repetition can easily become boring, but a constant stream of new material will sound confusing. Take time to explore your ideas in depth rather than introducing too much new material.

As well as striking the right balance between unity and diversity, plan clear areas of tension, relaxation and climax in your work. Study the methods used in music that you enjoy, and then apply the principles you discover to your own style of composing.

> Some minimalist and riff-based music is highly repetitive. If you choose one of these styles, think carefully about how you can achieve variety and a sense of development in your work. Be prepared to write a piece longer than the basic three minutes if you feel that greater length is needed in order to include these important features.

Varying the texture

A good variety of texture will enhance almost any style of music. If the tune is always allocated to the same instrument, accompanied by sustained chords in the other parts, the piece is likely to be dull to listen to and boring to play. Give all your resources a share in thematic material, and remember that presenting a tune in different octaves, or giving it to two instruments in unison or in octaves, will help create variety. Make accompaniments more interesting by basing them on distinctive rhythmic patterns and including the occasional melodic motif to complement the main tune.

If your piece is for four instruments, try giving one of them a rest in some sections, or alternate one pair of instruments with a different pair, and include a few totally unaccompanied phrases. Don't forget that each instrument can be used in different parts of its range for variety and that the use of well-contrasted dynamics and articulation will also make your work more interesting.

If you are writing a piece for solo instrument and piano, remember that the pianist can carry the tune in some sections, and doesn't have to be limited to accompaniment. Even if the piece is for piano alone, remember that the tune could sometimes be in the bass, or it could be presented in bare octaves (without chords), and that passages for both hands in the treble clef (or both in the bass clef) can offer a very effective contrast.

Other ways to maintain variety include splitting a long melody between different instruments and adding a countermelody or other point of contrapuntal interest. If phrase-endings on a long note cause the pace to flag, consider adding a link (or 'fill') to propel the music forward, or, alternatively, see if the start of the new phrase could overlap with the end of the previous one.

Plan the pacing of your work carefully. For example, a climax can be supported by thickening the texture, increasing the harmonic rhythm (perhaps over a dominant pedal) and introducing greater rhythmic activity, as well as by much more obvious means such as ascending to a high note and getting louder.

Above all, though, remember that *rests* are the key to achieving good variety of texture. If all of your players are occupied in every bar and there are few rests, there is unlikely to be enough variety of texture in your composition.

How is composition marked?

The mark scheme is basically the same as that used for composing at AS, although expectations will be higher at A2 than at AS in each of the mark categories listed below. If you submit two compositions, each will be marked in a similar way.

The examiner will give a mark for overall impression created by the piece, and will balance this against marks for five of the six categories below – the first three, plus whichever two of the last three are most appropriate for the composition concerned:

1. Quality of ideas and outcome. To do well, your composition needs to sound convincing and complete, with some exciting musical ideas. If it is less than three minutes in length, you risk receiving a low mark in this category.

2. Coherence. To do well, your composition needs to have a well thought-out structure, with a balance of unity and diversity, so that the work is neither over-repetitive nor so full of unrelated ideas that it fails to hang together.

3. Forces and textures. To do well, you need to write effectively and sympathetically for the resources you have chosen and you need to include a good variety of texture.

4. Harmony. To do well, your work should show a good grasp of harmonic progressions and treatment of dissonance (including a wider range of chords and perhaps more sophisticated use of modulation than was expected in the AS composing unit).

5. Melody. To do well, your melodies should be distinctive and have a good shape, with real sense of direction, and your part-writing should flow well.

6. Rhythm. To do well, your rhythms need to be imaginative and well controlled in all parts of the texture. Aim for a good balance between repetition to help unify the piece and variety to help differentiate contrasting sections.

As in the AS composing unit, you will be awarded marks for *two* categories out of harmony, melody and rhythm. This suggests that the full mark range would not be available for music with neither melody nor harmony, such as a piece for drum kit. If you are planning such a work, try to include melody and/or harmony parts, either for tuned percussion or for another instrument.

Using a computer

Some people find that developing compositions at a MIDI workstation can be a good way of working, even if the piece is destined for eventual performance by live musicians. Sequencer systems can also be useful to produce an approximation of a performance for recording purposes if live instrumentalists are unavailable.

However, the advice we gave in the *Edexcel AS Music Study Guide* also applies to composing at A2. MIDI software can give you little or no warning that what you write could be unplayable by live musicians – string chords which sound good on a synthesizer may be impossible on a violin, wind parts without breathing points that are no problem for a computer are unlikely to be possible for humans, and untransposed trumpet parts that descend into the bass clef will leave your trumpeter bewildered.

If you are using a sequencer to develop a piece for live players it will therefore be wise to try out ideas with the performers at an early stage.

Another potential drawback of computer-based composing is the ease with which 'copy and paste' can add extra sections to a piece. In music, repeated sections are frequently varied in some way – perhaps by being in a different key, or by having a different ending, or by being decorated in various ways, or by having changes made to the instrumentation and texture. Too many unaltered repeats runs the risk of a low mark for 'coherence'.

The score

Your score may be fully notated or, if appropriate to the style of the music, it could take the form of a lead sheet, chord chart, track diagram or annotated graphic. Whatever format you use, it should be clear and detailed, with numbered pages clipped together in the right order. Bar numbers, either at the start of each system or every ten bars, are a helpful addition to any score.

If the piece includes a number of different instruments, make sure the staves are labelled with instrument names at the start of every system, although abbreviations can be used after the opening. If you write the score by hand, it will help the layout if you leave a blank stave or two between systems. Remember that you can use conventional repeat signs in the score to avoid copying out identical sections of music.

Whatever type of score you submit, you should include full and clear directions to show how you want the music performed. However, there is nothing to be gained by using lots of Italian terms (English is perfectly acceptable) or by peppering the music with a random selection of dynamics and phrase marks. All markings should relate clearly to the music.

Computer-generated scores

Using a computer to produce a score can give neat results if you have a good understanding of music notation and the software concerned. However, music notation programs can produce very inaccurate scores if left to their own devices. You need to be able to evaluate the results of what you see and adjust the settings if note lengths, rests, ties, beams or accidentals don't follow the normal conventions. Similarly, the use of incorrect clefs is likely to lead to the appearance of too many leger lines. Take particular care that the software correctly handles parts for instruments that are written an octave higher than they sound (such as the guitar, bass guitar and double bass).

An amusing example of how software can mislead rather than help can be seen in the anonymous 'Owed Two a Spell Chequer':

Eye have a spelling chequer
It came with my pea sea
It plane lee marques four my revue
Miss steaks eye can knot sea …

The entire poem can be found at en.wikipedia.org/wiki/Spell_checker

Remember to add phrasing, articulation and dynamics, and check that staves are labelled with instrument names (not track numbers) or are identified as parts for sequenced sounds if you are writing an electronic studio piece.

You also need to know how your software handles repeats. It may well print the music out again in full, when what is really required is a repeat sign or a *da capo* direction, perhaps with first- and second-time bars for different endings.

Remember that an entirely electronic piece is not suitable for Topic 2 (Exploiting instruments).

Finally, check that the layout of the score is clear throughout. The stave size should be set to allow for a reasonable number of bars per page, and there should be more than one system per page unless you are writing for a very large ensemble. Staves that contain only rests for an entire system can be omitted to save space – just printing two or three bars per page is a waste of paper and the examiner will find your work hard to follow if pages of the score have to be turned every few seconds. However, make sure that staves and systems are not so close together that leger lines or other symbols overlap.

The recording

Whichever brief you choose, the recording can be mocked up using sequenced and synthesised sounds if the musicians required are not available. Although the quality of the recording is not assessed, it plays a valuable role in showing the examiner what you intend, especially if your score is not in full stave notation.

The recording is made outside the 14 supervised hours allowed for completing the score. Remember that if you make changes at this stage, you won't get extra time for revising the score, so don't leave recording until after all your supervised time has been used up.

The technical study tasks

The Edexcel specification states that the Technical Study tasks will be made available in September, at the start of your A2 course. However, check this with your teacher, as the date could possibly change.

The technical studies are very different from the composing briefs, although there are a number of overlaps between the two skills. Each technical study involves completing a passage in a specified style, and so a thorough knowledge of harmony and the style concerned is required, as well as a good sense of melodic line and skill in part-writing. The three briefs are.

> **Topic 1: Baroque counterpoint**
> The brief will consist of an exercise in two-part counterpoint for instruments from the Baroque period, in which you have to complete a bass part (with figuring) to harmonise the given melody in some bars, and to write a melody to fit the given figured bass in others.

> **Topic 2: Chorale**
> The brief will consist of a chorale in four-part harmony, with some passages printed in full but with only the melody given elsewhere. You have to complete the harmonisation by adding parts for alto, tenor and bass voices.

> **Topic 3: Popular song**
> The brief will consist of an exercise in ballad style, in which you will have to add a melody (without words) to fit the given bass part and chord symbols in some sections, and to supply a bass part and chord symbols to harmonise the given melody in others.

Completing your coursework has to be done under controlled conditions. You are allowed a maximum of three hours for each technical study, during which time you are allowed to try out your work on a keyboard or computer equipped with headphones. The finished task is submitted as a score – no recording is required.

The specification states that technical studies will be issued in September (although you should check with your teacher that this remains the case). However, it is likely that you will only start work on the actual task(s) quite late in your course, as much time will first be needed to master the techniques involved and to work a number of preparatory exercises. These techniques would take an entire book of their own to explain, but fortunately a very good one is available: the *A2 Music Harmony Workbook* by Hugh Benham (Rhinegold, 2008) contains full information about each of the three briefs, along with tips, working methods and many preparatory and practice exercises.

> Remember that you can choose two technical studies (and no composition) or two compositions (and no technical study), or one composition and one technical study.

> The *AS Music Harmony Workbook* by the same author will also be useful if you feel unsure about the basics of keys, chords and part-writing.

How are technical studies marked?

The examiner will give a mark for an overall impression of the work, and will balance this against marks for the following five elements:

1. Chords and keys. To do well, you need convincing harmonic progressions and a good understanding of modulation and the appropriate treatment of dissonance.

2. Realisation of, and adding, a figured bass (topic 1) or chord symbols (topic 3). To do well, this must be done accurately.

3. Sense of line. To do well, your melodic writing needs to have a good shape and a sense of purpose.

4. Part-writing. To do well, the individual lines in your work need to flow convincingly and without technical errors.

5. Style. To do well, you need to capture the characteristics of the specified style securely and creatively.

> In the case of Topic 2, marks in category 1 are awarded for chords and keys in the first half of the study and marks in category 2 are awarded for chords and keys in the second half.

Unit 6: Further Musical Understanding

Part A will take about 30 minutes, including the preliminary five minutes for reading the paper. It is suggested that you keep to less than 40 minutes for Part B and less than 50 minutes for Part C, in order to leave a little time for checking your answers at the end.

Requirements

This final unit is about listening to music and showing that you understand how it works. At the end of the course you will sit a two-hour exam paper, marked out of 90 and consisting of the three parts described *below*.

Part A is based on music that will almost certainly be unfamiliar, but that will be related in some way to works in NAM that you have studied. The music for this part will be played to you on CD. Parts B and C are based directly on the works from NAM that you will have studied. You will be able to refer to an *unmarked* copy of NAM during the exam.

Part A: Aural awareness (28 marks)

At the start of the exam you will have five minutes to read through the entire paper, after which the music for Part A will be played to you on CD. There are two main questions in this section.

Question 1 will involve comparing two excerpts of music. They will be played three times each (in the order A–B, A–B, A–B) and there will be no score to follow.

You will have to answer a series of short questions that will focus mainly on similarities and differences between the two extracts. These are likely to refer to resources (instruments and/or voices) and ask for comparisons in the way they are used. For example, you could be required to spot that one extract features a triadic melody for bassoon beneath a tremolo in the upper strings, while the other features a stepwise melody for saxophone supported by sustained chords from the brass.

In addition, you will be asked to place the music into its context, usually by suggesting the type of work from which it is taken, the name of a likely composer and the probable date when it was written (for more about this, see *below*).

Question 2 will consist of a single extract heard five times (with pauses between playings), for which there will be a skeleton score. You will have to:

➢ Notate a short section of the music you hear, such as a couple of bars of melody or bass

➢ Identify some chords (which could include chromatic chords such as the diminished 7th, augmented 6th and Neapolitan 6th)

➢ Recognise certain standard chord progressions (such as cadence patterns and the circle of 5ths)

➢ Identify one or more modulations to related keys (the relative minor or major, the dominant and its relative minor or major, and the subdominant and its relative minor or major).

Again, you are likely to be asked to suggest the type of work from which the extract is taken, and to name a likely composer and date when it was written.

Identifying specific features of the music is a skill that will be familiar from AS Music Unit 3, although now you will be working with unfamiliar extracts rather than with set works that you have studied. As with the part of question 2 that requires you to notate a short passage, you will need plenty of practice throughout the course on tests of this sort.

Practice listening papers are available from the publishers of this book, but you can also do much to help yourself by listening to music analytically whenever you get the chance. When you hear something unfamiliar, try to identify the type of ensemble and the instruments you hear – can you recognise any special effects such as muted brass or pitch bends on a guitar? Is the music in a major or minor key, or is it modal or atonal? What is the metre and is there anything particularly noticeable about the rhythm, such as dotted patterns, triplets or syncopation? How would you describe the shape of the melody? Is it diatonic or chromatic, and does it include any particular features such as wide leaps or appoggiaturas? What sorts of texture can be heard?

Detailed listening needs real concentration – it is not something that can be done while reading a magazine or texting – but the more you practise, the easier it will become. At the same time, try to widen your knowledge of repertoire. A good way to do this is to dip into Radio 3 or Classic FM's morning and teatime broadcasts and try to identify the music being played – check your answer when the presenter identifies the piece after it has finished.

At first, this may seem difficult, but try to link features of the music you hear with other pieces that you know or are studying. There are various 'markers' that can help identify musical styles and periods. For example, if you hear a harpsichord and the melodies seem to be formed by spinning out short motifs to create long musical paragraphs, there is a good chance that the piece will be Baroque. Equally, if the rhythms seem irregular and the harmonies very dissonant, it is likely to be 20th-century.

Never rely on a single point of identification – you need to operate as a musical detective and sift *all* of the evidence to see which features support your conclusion and which perhaps contradict it.

As you build up a knowledge of different types of repertoire, identification will become easier, but be aware that at A2 you will usually be expected to identify quite narrow periods, such as early Baroque, mid-Baroque or late Baroque. However, remember that the music in Section A will be related in some way to the set works you have studied. If you know these thoroughly, it should help you make connections. For example, if your set works include NAM 23 (the short piano pieces by Schumann, written in 1838), then one of the extracts could be from a song by Schumann, dating from the same decade. Remember that you will have an unmarked copy of NAM in the exam, in which you could quickly check any stylistic features of the recorded extracts that seem familiar.

Practice listening tests for this paper are available from Rhinegold Publishing: www.rhinegold.co.uk

You can listen to Classic FM live on the radio (100–102 FM), or on the internet at www.classicfm.co.uk.

You can listen to BBC Radio 3 live on the radio (90.3–92.3 FM) or on the internet at www.bbc.co.uk/radio3.

Both websites allow you to listen to programmes for up to seven days after they were broadcast and they identify the music currently being played.

Part A has to be answered first because that is when the CD will be played. The remaining questions can be tackled in whatever order you prefer, but keep an eye on the clock or you may run out of time – a sure way of missing valuable marks.

Part B: Music in context (26 marks)

This section will contain three questions on the group of set works from the 'Applied music' area of study that you have worked on during the course. You have to answer two of these, either in short notes or in continuous prose, spending about 20 minutes on each. Questions are likely to ask you to identify technical features of the music that contribute to its style, purpose or emotional impact. Sample questions are included at the end of the discussion on each of the set works later in this book, and some important points about writing answers are given *below*.

Part C: Continuity and change in instrumental music (36 marks)

In this section there will be two questions about the set works from the 'Instrumental music' area of study that you have worked on during the course. These will not be the same instrumental pieces that you studied for AS. You have to answer one of these questions by writing an essay, which will need to be completed in a little under 50 minutes.

Each of the questions will ask you to compare and contrast one or more musical features of *three* works. This could involve writing about form, texture, tonality, harmony, melody, metre and rhythm, or the resources used, showing what has remained similar over time, and what has differed. Sample questions are included at the end of the discussion on each group of instrumental works later in this book.

Analytical writing about music

At this level, examiners will hope to see that you can present clear and reasoned arguments in a logical way, supported by factual evidence and the accurate use of technical terminology. Although this may seem daunting at first, most of these skills are similar to those in any A-level subject where technical writing is involved and will be useful in later life whenever you have to write a report, an analysis, a proposal or any other similar document.

There are two important conventions in analytical writing that you should try to observe. Firstly, slang and colloquial expressions are never used, so we would always write 'Brahms varies the rhythm' rather than 'Brahms mucks around with the rhythm'.

Secondly, value judgements on how you perceive the worth of the music or its composer are normally avoided, so we wouldn't write something like 'Debussy's orchestration is better than Wagner's' or 'Mozart, the greatest Classical composer, created this masterful sonata …'. In fact, personal opinion in technical writing is seldom useful (unless a question actually asks you for it – even then, you should back up opinion with evidence). So, avoid expressions like 'Indian raga doesn't make sense to me'. A useful rule of thumb is to avoid personal pronouns (as in expressions such as 'I think', 'in my opinion' or 'you will see') and instead to write in a detached and objective style, since your subject should be the music itself rather than your reaction to it.

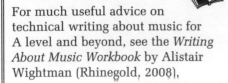

For much useful advice on technical writing about music for A level and beyond, see the *Writing About Music Workbook* by Alistair Wightman (Rhinegold, 2008).

So, what *will* help you gain an outstanding mark? In each of the Part B questions you need to make nine clear and relevant points (plus 18 in the essay for Part C), supported by references to precise locations in the score wherever possible. These references should take the form of bar numbers, along with beat numbers and the name of the part(s) concerned, if necessary. Don't waste time writing out the music, as examiners have their own copies of NAM.

Supplying evidence to support your points is one of the best ways to accumulate marks. You can save a lot of time if you know the score of each work thoroughly so that you can find examples to illustrate your arguments quickly.

Here are some other points to bear in mind:

1. Check that you *really* understand the question. It is likely to include technical terms such as tonality and texture that are often confused in the panic of an exam. Revise the information about the elements of music on pages 44–48 of the *Edexcel AS Music Study Guide* if you are at all unsure about such terms.

2. Only include points that are relevant to the question. If it asks about the style and texture of the music, you will get no marks for listing the instrumentation or writing about the composer and his other works, even if what you say is true.

3. Group your points in a logical way. If the question asks about tonality and instrumentation, deal with each separately and try to draw out conclusions. For tonality you could show how keys are defined by cadences in the piece, how the modulations are all to related keys, how the return of the final section is signalled by a section of dominant preparation, and how the ending is marked by a series of perfect cadences in the tonic – remember to give a location for each example you mention. This is far better than just listing events without analysis (e.g. 'It starts in G major, and modulates to D major, B minor, E minor' etc.).

4. Quotations of what other people have written about the music are best avoided. Examiners want to discover what you know about the music, not how well you can memorise quotations.

5. Be concise, avoid repeating yourself and keep to the facts. Words that we often use in speech while the brain ticks over, such as 'actually', 'basically' or 'generally' are seldom necessary in written exam answers.

If you find written English difficult, remember that you can answer the Part B questions in short note form or as a list of bullet points. If you do this, make sure that your meaning is totally clear and unambiguous and remember the importance of giving an example (with location) of each point you make.

In Part C, an essay is essential, but don't dive in too quickly. First check that you have chosen the title about which you feel most confident – you don't want to get halfway into the essay before realising that the other choice would have been better.

Then spend a few minutes planning what to include. If you start without a plan, you are likely to miss points, repeat yourself and fail to deal with matters in a logical order, so a few minutes making a plan is time well spent. It can be quite simple. Let's make a plan for an essay in which you have to compare and contrast rhythm and melody in three works which we will call A (from the Baroque period), B (from the Classical period) and C (a 20th-century work):

1. Introduction. Establish the context by naming the style and/or dates of the three works concerned.

   There is no need to copy out the question or to 'set the scene' with lots of background detail.

2. Body of the essay. Compare and contrast aspects of the rhythm in works A, B and C, and then deal with the melodic writing in the three works.

   It is usually clearer to deal with each element separately in questions of this type. There is no point in simply describing the rhythms and melodies in each work. Concentrate on important features. For example, work A might feature dotted rhythms and hemiolas, work B might have many simple repeated rhythms, while work C might contain unusual metres, changing time signatures and syncopation. Then deal with important aspects of melody in a similar way.

3. End with a conclusion that summarises your main points and that ties in with your opening paragraph.

   Here, we might observe that the dotted rhythms and hemiolas of work A are characteristic of many Baroque pieces, the simple quaver accompaniments supporting a more florid melody in B are typical of the Classical period, and that the irregular metres and rhythms of C are a feature of many early 20th-century works.

> When writing about dates, be careful not to confuse years with centuries. We live in the 21st century, but the years begin with 20, not 21. Similarly, 1750 is in the 18th century, not the 17th century.

Make sure that you practise writing timed essays before the actual exam. Running out of time is a common way of losing marks, so try not to let that happen to you.

Finally, don't apologise! If you get really stuck, remember that you will get no marks for writing something like 'I don't know much about this piece' or 'I was absent when we studied this work'. Nor will you get marks for paraphrasing points that you've already made. Have a go – after all, you will have the score in front of you and careful observation of the music will almost certainly produce some extra marks that you might otherwise have lost.

In the rest of this book we discuss all of the set works for exams between 2010 and 2012 inclusive. For each year we deal with the instrumental works first, with an exercise after each one so that you can check your understanding of the text. At the end of these sections there are essay questions on comparisons and contrasts between the works, similar in style to those in Section C of the paper. The applied music works are then discussed, again with an exercise after each one, and at the end of these sections there are some sample questions in the style of those you will encounter in Part B of the paper. The glossary at the end of the book can be used to look up the meaning of terms printed in **bold**.

Set works for 2010

If you are taking A2 Music in summer 2010, you have to study the seven pieces of instrumental music *below*, plus the five pieces of applied music in the section starting on page 60.

Instrumental music

The pieces for this area of study span musical periods from the Baroque to the middle of the 20th century:

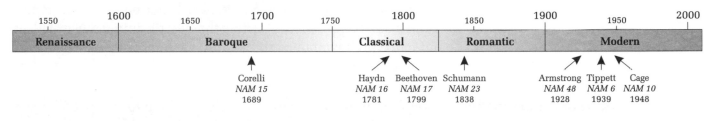

Trio sonata in D, movement 4 (Corelli)

Arcangelo Corelli was an Italian violinist and composer whose published works were widely distributed and influential in the development of instrumental music in the late Baroque period.

NAM 15 comes from a collection of 12 trio sonatas by Corelli published in 1689. The term trio refers to the three melodic lines printed in the score, but normally four players are required for a trio sonata. The two treble staves are for solo violins, but the lowest stave, known as a **figured bass** because of the numbers and other symbols printed below it, is labelled for violone *and* organ.

The violone was any sort of low-pitched bowed string instrument (the part is usually played on a cello today, as on CD2). The figuring below the bass part indicates the type of chords to be improvised by the organist in order to fill out the texture between the high violin parts and the much lower bass notes. This practice is known as 'realising' the figured bass.

The music on the lowest stave is known as a **continuo** part, and is found in almost all Baroque music that requires more than one performer. Although the instruments used can vary, a continuo part normally needs at least one bass instrument to play the notes as written and one chordal instrument, such as a harpsichord, lute or organ, to realise the figured bass.

Most of the 12 trio sonatas that make up Corelli's Opus 3 have four movements, in the order slow–fast–slow–fast. NAM 15 is the last movement of the second sonata in the collection. The whole set are sometimes described as church sonatas, perhaps because of the use of the organ as a continuo instrument. It is certainly possible that they could have been played during church services, but it is just as likely that they would have been performed for entertainment in the palaces of the nobility, where a small organ suitable for continuo playing could generally be found.

Context and forces

> NAM 15 (page 200) CD2 Track 4
> Fitzwilliam Ensemble

> If possible, try to perform NAM 15 with your fellow students. If you don't have violinists available it would work very well on two flutes. Experiment with different ways of realising the figured bass, using a piano or a soft pipe-organ voice on a synthesizer.

> You may see this work described as a *sonata da chiesa* – Italian for a church sonata.

Corelli's string writing is idiomatic. This means that each part is conceived in terms of the instrument for which it is written – one of the reasons why Corelli's work was so influential. Although he doesn't use the extremes of the violin's range, the first-violin part in bars 34–35 does require the use of third position (with the left hand higher up the fingerboard), and both violin parts exploit the contrast between lively rhythms and sustained notes.

Structure

Although not labelled as such, NAM 15 is in the style of a gigue, a dance in fast compound time, often used by Corelli and many other Baroque composers to conclude a multi-movement composition (see page 83). Like the gigue in NAM 21, this piece is in **binary form**, its two sections being indicated by repeat marks.

Binary form is often depicted as ‖:A:‖:B:‖, but note that the letters A and B don't represent contrasting themes: the initial musical ideas and mood are maintained throughout each movement, as they are in much Baroque music.

Harmony and tonality

Corelli's **diatonic** harmony and cadences help to clarify the binary structure. The movement starts in D major and then modulates to a perfect cadence in the dominant key of A major in bars 10–11, where it remains until the first double bar. The longer B section passes through several related keys before returning to the tonic in the closing bars:

Bar	9		20	22	26	29	32	34	36		43
‖: D major		A major :‖	‖: A major	D major	B minor	E minor	A major	G major		D major	:‖

The harmony is **functional** – that is, it defines the keys we have identified, chiefly through the use of perfect cadences. Most of the chords are root-position or first-inversion triads, seasoned with dissonant suspensions that usually resolve by step to a consonant note. Thus nearly every 7 in the figured bass (which indicates a 7th above the bass) is followed by 6 – the resolution of the dissonance above the same bass note.

Rhythm

We noted earlier that the movement contains rhythmic variety, especially in the violin parts. The dotted crotchet pulse is enlivened further by the following rhythmic features in bars 26–27:

The first is the **cross-rhythm** in bar 26, where the tie across the middle of the bar results in the first violin sounding as though it is in $\frac{3}{4}$ while the lower parts remain in $\frac{6}{8}$ time. The second is the **hemiola** in bar 27 that results in all three parts sounding as though they are in $\frac{3}{4}$ time. Notice how the position of the chord changes in bar 27 reinforces the effect of this rhythmic disruption. An added delight is the **syncopation** caused by the first violin's tie that joins these two bars.

Texture

The movement has a **contrapuntal** texture. It begins like a **fugue**, based on the subject heard in the first two bars. This is followed by a real fugal answer played by the second violin ('real' because it is exactly the same melody as the subject, 'answer' because it sounds a 4th below the subject). The third entry comes in the bass at bar 6. At the start of the B section the fugal subject is heard in free **inversion**. The imitative second-violin and bass parts now enter only a bar apart, forming the fugal texture known as **stretto**.

Most of the melodic material in the movement derives from the quaver and semiquaver motifs in the subject. Although the imitative entries are shared among all three parts, the bass takes on a more functional role after bar 23 (especially in bars 35–38).

The texture is mainly widely-spaced, with the two violin parts often crossing, and placed high above the bass (as in bar 12). The wide gap (which is filled by the organ) is known as a **polarised texture** and is a feature of much baroque music.

Exercise 1

1. Why are four people usually needed to play a trio sonata?

2. Explain the purpose of the figures and other symbols printed below the bass part.

3. What type of dance is reflected in the style of NAM 15?

4. What is a polarised texture?

5. Identify the location of an inverted **pedal** in the second-violin part.

6. At the start of bar 18 the violins create tension by being a tone apart. What is this device called?

7. Complete the blanks in the following: The first violin part in bar 20 is an .... of the melody in bar 1. It is .... by the second violin in bar 21 and by the violone in bar 22.

8. What type of instrument is a violone?

9. Where in bars 28–35 is there a hemiola?

10. Corelli's violin writing is often described as 'idiomatic' and his harmony as 'functional'. Explain what is meant by each of these terms.

String quartet 'The Joke', movement 4 (Haydn)

Context and forces

For much of his life Haydn was director of music to the Hungarian Prince Esterházy at a magnificent palace 50 kilometres south-east of Vienna. Here he had musicians at his disposal to supply the court with a huge variety of music, ranging from operas, church music and orchestral works, to intimate pieces of chamber music in which the prince himself often took part as one of the performers.

NAM 16 (page 202)	CD2 Track 5
The Lindsays	

Haydn established the string quartet as the most successful and long-lasting of all **genres** of chamber music. The combination of two violins, viola and cello proved ideal. The instruments blend superbly well and can offer full four-part harmony, without the support of a continuo, in a wide variety of textures. By the time Haydn wrote the movement in NAM 16 he had completed at least 30 string quartets, gradually developing a style in which all four instruments are treated as equally important. He had also settled on a four-movement format, typically in the order fast – slow – minuet – finale. The last of these is usually the fastest of the four movements and is often (as here) cast in the form of a jolly **rondo**.

In 1781, after Haydn had completed the six quartets published as his opus 33, he wrote to potential purchasers describing them as 'written in a new and special manner'. Although this statement was perhaps just a marketing ploy, the way in which Haydn provides musical interest in all four parts was certainly a feature that would appeal to the increasing number of amateur musicians who were playing string quartets at home, purely for their own pleasure.

These works are also lighter in style than some of Haydn's earlier quartets and often deliberately humorous. NAM 16 is the finale of the second quartet of the set. It is nicknamed *The Joke* for reasons that will become apparent, but all six quartets contain many appealing features, including melodies that are frequently folk-like in their dancing simplicity.

Structure

As in many of Haydn's finales, the form of NAM 16 is a **rondo**, a structure in which a main section in the tonic, called the refrain, alternates with contrasting sections, usually in related keys, called episodes. It is unusual in that the refrain gets shorter each time it appears, and that the second episode is in the tonic key. Although we've used the letters A, B and C to show the structure, the themes in these sections are closely related and so sound very similar.

The refrain (A) has a structure called **rounded binary form** because material from the first section comes round again near the end. Its first section is eight bars long and concludes with a perfect cadence in the tonic, E♭ major. It is repeated. The second section (B, bars 8–28), remains in E♭, but is distinguished from A by:

➤ A slower **harmonic rhythm** at the start (V for two bars, then I for two bars) and a more sustained style of accompaniment

➤ Prominent **appoggiaturas** at the ends of the third and fourth two-bar phrases (bars 14 and 16)

➤ A long dominant **pedal** (bars 16–28) supporting some chromatic colouring (A♮ and G♭, both resolving by step, one to the root and the other to the fifth of chord V).

These final bars of B form a **dominant preparation** for the exact repeat of A in bars 28–36 (the 'rounding' of the binary form), after which the entire second section is marked to be repeated (see *left*).

The first episode (C, bars 36–70) focuses on A♭ major in bars 36–47 and F minor in bars 48–53, but neither key is established with a root-position tonic chord. Haydn then returns to E♭ major for bars

Bars	Section	Key
0–36	‖: A :‖: BA :‖	E♭ major
36–70	C	A♭, Fm, E♭
71–107	ABA	E♭ major
107–140	C¹	E♭ major
140–172	A (Adagio) A¹	E♭ major

54–70. The **harmonic rhythm** speeds up after the last pedal resolves to chord I of E♭ major (bar 59). This progression includes a sequential rise from tonic to submediant (I–IV–II–V–III–VI in bars 59–61), creating tension which is released when VIIb of V (the second chord of bar 63) resolves to another dominant pedal of E♭ major in bars 64–60.

The entire rounded binary structure of the refrain (ABA but without any repeats) then returns in bars 71–107.

The second episode (bars 107–140) is a modified repeat of the first episode, so we'll call it C[1]. It stays in the tonic key throughout, and ends with yet another another dominant pedal (bars 128–140).

The final refrain is shorn of its B section. It starts with a repeat of just section A in bars 140–148, but then Haydn surprisingly adds a short Adagio that begins with a melodramatic dominant major 9th (bars 148–149) and ends with another perfect cadence in the tonic key.

Section A returns, but it is now chopped up into its constituent two-bar phrases by silences (see *right*). The perfect cadence in bars 165–166 seems to be the end – Haydn follows it with three bars of silence to tempt a premature round of applause, but he's playing a joke. Suddenly the refrain starts up again! Before the audience has time to work out what's going on, it fizzles out after only two bars – another joke, since that really is the end.

Nearly all of the thematic material derives from motifs in the opening theme of the refrain. which is underpinned by strongly functional harmony:

Harmonic sequence

In the theme itself motif *y* is inverted (*y¹ above*) then repeated to form the rising scale in bar 6. In bars 9–13 chromatic notes are added to both motifs, and in bars 22–24 the middle note of motif *x* is shortened to produce playful slurred quavers. This new version of *x* is then repeated to form the chromatic **sequence** in bars 24–27.

Many more manipulations of this material occur throughout the movement – try to spot some for yourself.

The nickname for this work should be 'the jokes' for there's more than one. For example, at bar 16 the cello begins a dominant **pedal** that lasts for 13 bars, creating expectancy for a terrific musical event. What actually follows is the tiny eight-second musical squib of the refrain (bars 28–36).

The central episode begins with another dominant pedal, this time in the key of A♭ major (bars 36–47). But instead of resolving to chord I in bar 41 the music gets stuck on chord Ic, not once, but four times. Every time this happens chord Ic is marked *sf*, as though Haydn were venting his fury at being unable to find the root

G.P. in bar 155 and later stands for General Pause. This indicates that everyone is silent in these bars, not that there is necessarily any pause in the pulse. The figure 3 along with the rests in bar 167 indicates that the last of these general pauses extends through three complete bars.

The jokes

position. Haydn then moves down to F minor with a similar lack of success (bars 48–53). Having failed to establish either key, he gives up and returns to E♭ major and, after two abortive attempts (bars 55 and 57), Haydn at last achieves a perfect cadence in bars 58–59. To celebrate his success he uses motif *y* in a rising sequence which leads to … another dominant pedal (bars 64–68)!

By the time we get to the second episode, 54 out of 107 bars have featured prolonged dominant pedals so it is a relief to hear a tonic pedal (bars 107–111) and what sound like some conclusive perfect cadences (bars 120–123). But Haydn hasn't finished – he continues to another dominant pedal (bars 128–141) and some fun with a truncated version of motif *x*. A total silence and melodramatic appoggiaturas (bar 139) lead to a dominant 7th (note the pitch of the viola in bar 140). After another dramatic silence that catchy refrain sneaks in yet again.

Could this be the end? No! A loud dominant 9th ushers in the Adagio almost as if we're in for an extra slow movement, just when we thought it was all over. But all movement stops and the wretched refrain starts up yet again. But this time it is in its death throes – chopped into pieces by the general pause that interrupts every two bars. After the silence has expanded to a total of more than four bars (a long time when you are trying not to giggle) Haydn pulls his last rabbit out of the hat in the shape of the first two bars of the movement which, we now discover, already contain the perfect cadence with which the work abruptly ends.

The score   Note that the viola part is in the alto C clef throughout, and that the *sf* accents in bars 41 and 43 are emphasised by **double-stopping** in the first violin part. Notice also that since Corelli published his trio sonatas, nearly a century earlier, composers were including much more performance detail in their scores, including dynamic and articulation marks (staccatos, slurs and *sforzandi*).

Style   NAM 16 is typical of the Classical style in many of its features. **Periodic phrasing** – pairs of equal-length phrases sounding like questions and answers – is seen in the example printed on the previous page. This also shows the Classical preference for clear harmonic progressions, centred on chords I and V^7, with regular cadences to define keys. Progressions such as II–V^7–I in bars 35–36 are a feature of the style, as are appoggiaturas, both chromatic (B♮ in bar 161) and diatonic (G in bar 165). Finally, the texture of melody-dominated **homophony** (although with plenty of interest in the accompanying parts) is typical of much Classical music.

Exercise 2

1. In harmony, what is a pedal? In which bars does a pedal occur (a) in the viola part, and (b) in the violin 1 part? How do these differ?

2. What is double-stopping? Where is it used on page 206 of NAM?

3. What is meant by harmonic rhythm? In what way is the harmonic rhythm in bars 9–28 different from that in the first eight bars?

4. Which note in the first-violin part of bar 5 is chromatic?

5. In a rondo, what is the difference between the refrain and an episode?

6. Explain the precise meaning of the letters G.P. and the figure 3 in bars 167–169.

7. What term describes the way in which Haydn's use of harmony is similar to that of Corelli?

8. In NAM 15, Corelli depended on a continuo instrument to fill out the harmony. Why did Haydn not need to use a continuo instrument in this work?

Septet in E♭, movement 1 (Beethoven)

Although this Septet (a work for seven players) is another example of chamber music, it is on a much larger scale than the previous two pieces we have studied, making it more suited to performance in a small concert hall than a private room. The complete work has six movements, of which NAM 17 is the first, and it requires three wind instruments as well as four strings.

Context and forces

| NAM 17 (page 207)   CD2 Track 6 |
| Berlin Philharmonic Octet |

When reading the score, notice that composers of the Classical period, such as Haydn and Beethoven, supplied many more detailed performance directions than Baroque composers such as Corelli. Also note that:

➢ The clarinet in B♭ sounds a tone lower than printed

➢ The horn in E♭ sounds a major 6th lower than printed

➢ The double bass sounds an octave lower than printed

➢ The viola part is printed in the alto C clef, in which the middle line of the stave represents the pitch of middle C.

Beethoven wrote the work at the end of 1799 and it received its first public performance in April 1800 at a concert in the Royal Imperial Court Theatre, Vienna, where it shared the programme with the premiere of his first symphony. The Septet was well received and it proved to be Beethoven's most popular work for some years to come.

The movement begins with a slow introduction that moves from the opening tonic chord of E♭ major to chord V in bar 8. Notice the dramatic contrast between the loud **tutti** opening and the solo violin figures. The four violin notes starting after the rest in bar 8 will dominate much of the rest of the movement. Bars 8–10 are repeated in the tonic minor (E♭ minor, bars 10–12). The major mode returns for the ornate violin melody that ends on a dominant-7th chord (bars 17–18), decorated with a very characteristic clarinet arpeggio.

Introduction

The Allegro con brio that follows the introduction is in **sonata form**, the most common structure for first movements in the Classical period. It is based on the idea of juxtaposing the tonic key with a related key (usually the dominant or relative major) in the first section – often with contrasting themes in each key, as occurs here. Tonal conflict becomes more apparent in the middle section, in which the thematic material is developed through a wider range of keys, but this conflict is resolved in the final section, which is centred entirely on the tonic key:

Sonata form

Bars	18	53	111	154	188	233
	Exposition		**Development**	**Recapitulation**		**Coda**
	1st subject	2nd subject		1st subject	2nd subject	
Keys	E♭ major	B♭ major	Various	E♭ major	E♭ major	E♭ major

Exposition

The first subject starts with a version of the four-note motif we noticed in the introduction, treated in **sequence** in bars 18–21. The whole of the ten-bar violin melody is repeated on the clarinet, supported by a **syncopated** accompaniment in the strings.

The harmony is generally simple and **diatonic**, although decorated with chromatic notes such as those in bar 26. The **harmonic rhythm** is often slow, speeding up towards the cadences. This is evident in the first subject (bars 18–29) in which the first four bars are all harmonised with chord I, then the chords change every bar in bars 23–26, then every half bar in the next two bars.

The second subject, which starts at bar 53 in the dominant key of B♭ major, initially has a very different character: a **homophonic** texture of three-part strings, at first in minims although when this four-bar phrase is repeated by wind (bars 56–60) the lively quavers are added in the string parts. Another second subject theme appears in bars 61–68, shared between violin and clarinet doubled by bassoon; this is also immediately repeated in a different scoring. Finally Beethoven introduces a third idea (also part of the second subject) – the staccato chordal phrase in bars 86–88. This is repeated in sequence and (in bar 90) at the original pitch but with varied harmony. A **cadential** $^6_4$ (in the typically Classical progression Ic–V–I) concludes the second subject in bars 97–98.

Bars 98[3]–111 form a **codetta** that reinforces the establishment of the dominant key. The one-bar phrase at the start of this section (based on the four-note motif) will later assume considerable importance. It is repeated in sequence over a reiterated tonic pedal (B♭ played by horn then double bass until bar 106). The exposition ends with three perfect cadences (bars 107–111).

Development

The development of ideas from the exposition begins with the opening of the first subject and a rapid modulation to C minor. In this key the melody from the codetta is heard on the clarinet (bars 116–120). The same theme is then heard in sequence on the horn and the music starts to modulate through a wider range of keys, as is usual in a development section.

At bar 125 Beethoven draws on another earlier idea (from bar 40) which alternates with the codetta theme until a dominant pedal in bar 140 heralds the imminent return of the tonic key. Over the pedal the codetta theme is combined with a new version of the minim motif from bar 53. Our four-note motif then appears in rising sequence (bars 148–151), climbing up a chord of V[7] (cellos in **dialogue** with viola and woodwind).

Recapitulation

The recapitulation starts with a rescored repeat of bars 18–30, but a sudden modulation to A♭ major in bars 166–172 leads to more development of earlier material until, at bar 182, Beethoven returns to E♭ major for a repeat of bars 47–98 in the tonic key.

Coda

The coda begins at bar 233 with a repeat of the codetta, but it is greatly expanded by further development of the four-note motif (starting in the cello at bar 249). This accompanies a variation of the codetta theme played on the horn, together with a syncopated dominant pedal on the violin. At bar 258 the two melodies swap positions, the four-note motif now in the treble and the codetta theme in the bass, the latter imitated by woodwind in bar 260. Arpeggios and scales lead to a conclusive cadence in E♭ major (bars 276–277). The movement ends with a new trill figure, compressed in rhythm to increase excitement from bar 285, and harmonised by no fewer than nine perfect cadences in the last 11 bars.

Texture

One of the features that made the Septet so popular when it first appeared is its lively variety of texture. Let's choose some of the most diverse passages and describe them as concisely as possible.

➢ Bars 1–4: tutti chords flank the **monophonic** texture of bar 2

➢ Bars 8–11: alternation of three-part strings and tutti chords

➢ Bars 12–14: melody-dominated **homophony** (tune in violin accompanied by wind and cello, with melodic fragments in the viola)

➢ Bars 47–49: an **antiphonal** exchange between wind and strings

➢ Bars 111–115: **melody in octaves** with harmony sketched in by horn and double bass

➢ Bars 221^3–231^1: a **homorhythmic** texture in which the three-part string chords alternate with the tutti chords

➢ Bars 254–257: **two-part counterpoint** (clarinet and horn in octaves against lower strings in octaves) plus a tonic **pedal** in bassoon and violin

➢ Bars 258–264: **imitation** (the part for cello and bass is imitated by oboe and bassoon in bar 260, which in turn is imitated by cello and bass in bar 262) plus a **countermelody** for violin. The violin and bass parts in bars 258–261 form a contrapuntal inversion of the clarinet and bass parts in the previous four bars

➢ Bars 274–277: a duet for clarinet and bassoon above sustained string chords.

Style

The Classical style of the work is apparent in Beethoven's use of mainly diatonic chords, decorated with melodic chromaticism, and in clear cadence points that define keys. Equally typical of the Classical style is the **periodic phrasing** that prevails throughout most of the movement. This is created by pairs of equal-length phrases that sound like questions and answers. For example, the melody of bars 116–136 consists entirely of sequential pairs of two-bar phrases. At the start of this passage two of these phrases form a four-bar phrase that ends with a perfect cadence in C minor (clarinet, bars 116–120). This is answered by a four-bar phrase from the horn (bars 120–124) that ends with a balancing perfect cadence in A♭ major. The frequent melodic exchanges between instruments are also typical of the dialogue technique used by composers of the Classical era.

1. On what chord does the movement begin?

2. Compare bars 2 and 4.

3. In bars 161–164 the key is E♭ major. Which of these bars are diatonic and which include chromatic writing?

4. What is the name of the ornament in the violin part of bar 163?

5. What precisely is meant by 'a syncopated dominant pedal' in the description of the coda, *above*?

6. Compare bars 53–56 with bars 188–191. What is the main difference between these two passages?

7. To what extent are the cello and double bass parts independent in this movement?

8. Which two instruments have most of the melodic interest?

9. Give an example of **double-stopping** on page 207 of NAM.

Kinderscenen, Nos. 1, 3 and 11 (Schumann)

Context

NAM 23 (page 258) CD2 Tracks 13–15
Alfred Brendel (piano)

The Romantic period in music was an age of extremes, with works ranging from opera, choral and orchestral music on a huge scale, through extremely difficult solo music for virtuoso professionals, to modest songs and piano pieces for amateurs to enjoy at home.

The set of musical miniatures for the piano entitled *Kinderscenen* (Scenes of Childhood), written by the German composer Robert Schumann in 1838, was clearly designed for the domestic market. Works of this type are called character pieces (or characteristic pieces) and are intended to express intense emotional experiences in the most intimate manner. They were extremely popular – Romantic composers could hardly keep up with the demand.

Although Schumann wrote the music first and gave each of the 13 pieces an individual title later, he always intended *Kinderscenen* to be a set of reminiscences of childhood that would be played by adults, unlike his *Album for the Young*, written for his seven-year-old daughter (and for all young pianists) to play.

Schumann's titles deliberately encourage us, as we listen or play, to allow memories to float across our minds: images of distant lands and people, a game of blind man's bluff and spooky childhood experiences. These programmatic interpretations are typical of much Romantic music and are quite different from the absolute music of NAM 17, where Beethoven makes no suggestions about how anyone should experience his sonata-form movement – its elegant patterns and musical architecture stand on their own and can be enjoyed in as abstract a fashion as the listener wishes.

Even more characteristic of early Romanticism is the fragmentary, suggestive nature of many of the pieces in *Kinderscenen*. Thus the melody of 'Von fremden Ländern und Menschen' ends inconclusively on the mediant rather than the tonic, and the accompaniment runs on through the final bar, as though the pianist had intended to stop but instead drifted off into a romantic daydream.

The reverse happens in 'Fürchtenmachen' in which the music slides in as though it had been going for some time and had only just become audible. This effect is enhanced by the chromatic writing in the first two bars which disguises the tonic key.

The first eight bars are repeated at the end, after a six-bar middle section, forming the pattern ‖:A:‖:BA:‖ – this is similar to the type of binary form that we saw in NAM 15, except that the second section is rounded off by a return of the opening material, as we saw in the **rounded binary form** of the refrain in NAM 16.

The melody is simple, repetitive and entirely diatonic – features reflecting the style of the innocent German folk songs that so pleased the growing middle classes of the early Romantic period. But while the many repetitions of the opening two-bar phrase and the short **sequence** in bars 9–12 give the *impression* of a children's song, this is an adult's recollection of childhood, so do not be surprised by sophisticated chromatic harmonies such as the diminished-7th chord in bars 1 and 3, the juxtaposition of the unrelated triads of B major and G major in bar 12, and the artful left-hand **countermelody** based on a **circle of 5ths** in bars 9–12.

Schumann's piano textures are also far from childlike. Notice the way the broken chords are shared between the hands, the contrast between the legato melody and semi-staccato bass at the start, the two-part **counterpoint** between the outer parts in bars 9–14, and subtle nuances such as the sustained notes in inner parts (bars 5–6 and 14). Other points to note are:

➤ The balanced **periodic phrasing** (2+2+4 bars in the first section, shown by the phrase marks) – typical of Schumann's style but also typical of music from the preceding Classical period (as we saw in NAM 17)

➤ An A section that does not modulate and that is repeated almost exactly when it returns in bars 15–22

➤ A central B section (bars 9–14) that is melodically distinct from section A and that makes only fleeting reference to a different key (E minor)

➤ Triplet figuration in the middle part that continues throughout the piece.

The combination of a simple diatonic melody with subtle and sometimes ambiguous harmonic touches, in a texture of melody-dominated **homophony**, is typical of Schumann in his dreamy romantic mode. The effect is enhanced by the frequent rhythmic blurring caused when the dotted patterns coincide with triplets, often tempting the performer to use **rubato** (encouraged by the ritardando followed by a pause in bars 12–14).

By 1838 the piano could be found in middle-class homes throughout western Europe, and Schumann's idiomatic writing exploits some of its most characteristic features. The articulation of the

Von fremden Ländern und Menschen

The F♯ in bar 11, beat 2 (left hand) should have a down-stem to show that it is part of the bass counter-melody and is to be sustained as a crotchet – this stem is missing in some editions of NAM.

uppermost part as a song-like melody depends on the performer's ability to play it more loudly than the lower parts (despite the fact that the highest notes of the accompaniment must be played with the right-hand thumb). Although it is possible to give a *cantabile* rendition of the melody without the sustaining pedal, Schumann's romantic style demands the sustained resonance that can only be achieved through its careful use. The artful two-part counterpoint between the outer parts in bars 9–14, with continued harmonic filling, is typical of romantic textures that are enhanced by the sustaining power that pianos had by this time achieved.

Hasche-Mann

This is another rounded binary-form movement with tell-tale signs of Romanticism, such as the sudden intrusion of C major into the key of B minor in bars 13–15. Once again a constant rhythm, this time semiquavers, is heard in one part or another right through to the final bar.

The game of blind-man's bluff is evoked by scurrying semiquavers. The first two bars are repeated in sequence, creating a four-bar phrase which is then repeated in bars 5–8. Like the A section of 'Von fremden Ländern', these bars never move out of the tonic key (in this case B minor). The prominent flattened leading note (A♮) in bar 2 comes from the use of the descending melodic minor scale, but A♯ appears in the perfect cadences (V^7–I in B minor) in bars 4 and 8.

The rising sequence of bars 1–4 is balanced by a falling sequence in bars 9–12, which carries the music to the unexpected and un-related key of C major. Schumann avoids clearly defined tonal centres by the use of interrupted cadences in G major (bars 10–11) and E minor (bars 12–13). Like a disorientated, blindfolded child, the music seems to get stuck on a chord of C (bars 13–15). Indeed, we seem to be in the *key* of C major judging by the alternating C and G^7 chords above the double pedal on C and G. But in bars 15–17 the tonic key is regained by the appearance of chords V^7 and I of B minor, the home key.

The texture is again melody-dominated homophony, with a difficult leaping accompaniment for the left hand to suggest the jerky, lurching movements of the blindfolded child.

Fürchtenmachen

The ABACABA structure of this piece is known as symmetrical **rondo** form. The A section is called the refrain, while the other sections (B in bars 9–12, repeated in bars 37–40, and C in bars 21–28) are called **episodes**. Both contrast vividly with the refrain and Schumann emphasises this by marking episode B *schneller* (faster) in bars 9 and 37. On CD2 Alfred Brendel sensibly extends this idea to episode C at bar 21.

The refrain consists of two soothing four-bar phrases in G major. Both start with the type of chromatic harmony that disguises the true key and is typical of the Romantic style, but both end with clear imperfect cadences in G major. Notice how, when the opening four-bar melody is freely adapted to form the answering melody of bars 5–8, it starts in the left hand (bar 5) and then transfers to the right hand on the second quaver of bar 7.

Both episodes are characterised by syncopated chords. The first two bars of Episode B are in E minor (the relative minor) and are repeated in sequence a third lower (in C major, but ending on an ambiguous second-inversion chord of E minor).

There is no clear tonal centre in the second episode (C) – the shifting chromaticism gives it an unsettling effect – all part of Schumann's hazy recollection of childhood fear. In fact, the 'scare' seems to be no more than a brief flash-back, since the new rhythm pattern, off-beat *sforzandi* and loud dynamic all vapourise after only four bars. The remainder of the episode then wends its way back to the soothing mood of the refrain, while Schumann cleverly avoids an exact sequence when bars 25–26 are varied to form bars 27–28.

Further examples of Schumann's idiomatic piano writing can be seen in his use of a bass melody with right-hand accompaniment in bars 5–6 and 9–12, and in the sudden contrast of dynamic and off-beat accents in bars 21–24.

Exercise 4

1. Name the main key of each of the three pieces in NAM 23.

2. What term is often used to describe short Romantic piano pieces of this type?

3. Describe the texture *and* form of 'Von fremden Ländern und Menschen' using appropriate technical terms.

4. What type of scale occurs in bar 16 of 'Hasche-Mann'?

5. What does diatonic mean?

6. In a rondo, what is the difference between an episode and the refrain?

7. Explain what is meant by idiomatic instrumental writing, and give three examples of ways in which Schumann's piano pieces in NAM 23 are idiomatic.

8. What features of the music suggest that *Kinderscenen* was intended for adults, not children, to play?

West End Blues (Joe 'King' Oliver)

Although popular music has a long history, we know relatively little about it until the 19th century, when new industrial processes led to cheaper instruments and inexpensive sheet music at the very time when ordinary people first started to have enough time and money to spend on entertainment, either at home or in music halls and dance halls. By the end of the 19th century, popular music was becoming a profitable industry, spurred on by the invention of recording and later, in the 1920s, of radio.

Most commercial popular music was modelled on simple types of European art music in the 19th century, but after 1900 the main influence came increasingly from African-American music. This is first seen in ragtime, which developed in the midwest of the USA, its 'ragged time' reflecting the syncopated banjo playing of black Americans in the popular minstrel shows of the late 19th century.

Context

NAM 48 (page 461)   CD4 Track 7
Louis Armstrong (trumpet and voice) and his Hot Five:
  Jimmy Strong (clarinet)
  Fred Robinson (trombone)
  Earl Hines (piano)
  Mancy Carr (banjo)
  Zutty Singleton (drums)

Ragtime was only one of the sources of jazz – the improvisatory style of playing that developed in the sea port of New Orleans on America's southern coast in the early decades of the 20th century. Small bands – typically consisting of a clarinet, cornet, trombone, string bass, banjo or guitar, and percussion – would play anything from hymns to the popular songs of the day, adding blue notes, enlivening the rhythms with syncopation, and freely embellishing the original melodies.

Louis Armstrong

Louis Armstrong was born in New Orleans in 1901. By the age of 17 he was playing cornet in the leading jazz band in the city but by this time work was becoming scarce and, like many fellow musicians, he moved to Chicago in 1922 to join a band in which Joe 'King' Oliver (composer of *West End Blues*) played first cornet and Armstrong played second cornet. It was in Chicago that their music was first recorded and thus became internationally famous. Armstrong went on to form his own bands for a series of records made between 1925 and 1928, and it is from one of his 1928 recordings that the music on CD4 is taken.

Resources

The instrumentation of *West End Blues* is typical of early jazz, although at first the cornet was often preferred to the trumpet. It consists of a frontline (trumpet, clarinet and trombone) and a rhythm section (piano, banjo and drums).

In jazz of the New Orleans period there is considerable collective improvisation of the theme by all of the frontline instruments simultaneously, but in the later Chicago style of *West End Blues* there is more emphasis on solo improvisation, allowing each player to establish totally new melodic ideas over the common chord pattern (this is particularly evident in the piano solo, bars 43–54).

Some editions of NAM refer to a bass in the score of this work, but there is no evidence of this in the recording.

Early jazz bands often also included a plucked double bass, but this is absent in Armstrong's Hot Five recordings, perhaps because it was so difficult to pick up in the early days of gramophone recording (he partially solved this problem by using a tuba on the bass line in other recordings of this period).

In live performance drums would play a greater role than they do here, but again the limitations of recording often dictated that just quiet novelty effects had to be substituted. Here, the 'milk bottle sound' mentioned in bars 18–19 of the score is actually a percussion instrument of the time called a *bock-a-da-bock*. It consists of two metal discs about eight centimetres in diameter, mounted on sprung tongs, which the drummer cups in his hands to play.

Structure

In most jazz the underlying chord progression, called the changes, is the most important element, and forms the foundation for most of the improvised material. Each repetition of the chord pattern is known as a chorus. *West End Blues* uses the best-known of all changes, the 12-bar blues, which here takes the form:

The precise chords in a 12-bar blues can vary. For instance, the tenth chord (V^7 in bar 16) is often IV in other blues-based pieces.

bars	7	8	9	10	11	12	13	14	15	16	17	18
chord	E♭	E♭	E♭	E♭^{7}	A♭	A♭	E♭	E♭	B♭^{7}	B♭^{7}	E♭	E♭
	I	I	I	I^7	IV	IV	I	I	V^7	V^7	I	I

West End Blues is based on five choruses of this pattern, with a solo introduction and short **coda**, in the pattern shown *right*. Listen to it without following the music and see if you can hear the five repetitions of the 12-bar blues.

Did you notice that some of the original chords are changed? For instance, in the sixth bar of the trombone solo the chord is A♭ minor, not A♭ major. This is known as a **substitution chord** and is an important means of giving variety to the changes.

In many types of jazz, and in jazz-influenced pieces (including some pop music), individual beats are usually divided into uneven pairs of notes in a long–short pattern, known as **swing quavers**. The opening of the main theme, shown on the upper stave *right*, is played closer to the rhythm shown on the lower stave. The precise way to play swing quavers defies conventional musical notation, because much depends on the speed and rhythmic 'feel' of the piece concerned. In some transcriptions, swing quavers are shown as normal (undotted) quavers for simplicity. In swing style, pairs of quavers that are played evenly may be given staccato dots (as in bar 1 of NAM 48) or marked as 'straight 8s'.

There is no written-out arrangement (remember that NAM 48 is a transcription of what was improvised, not a score from which the music was played) but all of the players would have been familiar with the original melody and the chord pattern of a 12-bar blues. There is clearly collective agreement about what goes where, but also much spontaneity in decorating the basic material.

The example *below* shows the relationship between the start of Joe Oliver's original song and the beginning of the five choruses in the improvisation by Louis Armstrong and his Hot Five:

Form	
Intro	
Chorus 1	Theme (trumpet)
Chorus 2	Trombone solo
Chorus 3	Clarinet and voice
Chorus 4	Piano solo
Chorus 5	Theme (trumpet)
Coda	

Swing rhythm

Improvisation

Listening guide

Introduction

The introduction is one of the most famous moments in early jazz. It combines the cadenza (a **virtuoso** unaccompanied solo) found in many light-classical cornet pieces of the time with the type of brilliant high brass playing that Armstrong would have heard from the Mexican bands that visited New Orleans in his youth – and it forms a very novel way of starting a blues number.

Notice the rhythmic freedom of the passage, the **blue notes** (F♯/G♭ and D♭) and the way that Armstrong gives little hint of the E♭ tonality of the piece until bar 6, where he outlines a dominant 7th chord and the rest of the band enters on an augmented dominant triad (B♭–D–F♯). This chord is used not just for its colourful chromatic effect but also because the F♯ is the first note of the theme, and so provides the smoothest of transitions to the opening chorus.

It is only in bar 7, when the band so satisfyingly resolves these dominant chords to tonic harmony, that it becomes clear we are to hear a blues in E♭ major.

Chorus 1

The theme is presented by Armstrong on trumpet, with his familiar fast **vibrato**. It is characterised by the motif F♯–G–B♭, taken from bar 2 beat 2 of the original song, although Armstrong cleverly slips it in three times in all during his first phrase. This is probably a pre-arranged opening, since the clarinet mainly follows the trumpet in parallel 3rds during the first four bars.

> The blue 3rd of E♭ major is G♭, but it is enharmonically notated as F♯ when followed by G, the normal major 3rd.

Armstrong links this first phrase with the next, landing on the flat seventh in bar 10. The rest of the chorus moves further from the source, occasionally touching on a principal note or characteristic interval, but mainly becoming a free improvisation over the blues harmony. In bars 17–18 Armstrong recalls bars 2–3 on the way to a climactic top B♭, which he decorates with a fast lip trill to the C above (made by using the lips, not the valves).

To give prominence to Armstrong's solo, the clarinet and trombone mainly sustain harmony notes, with the latter often sliding up to the correct pitch (a technique known as a 'smear'). Piano and banjo accompany with detached chords in a style called **comping** – improvising simple block chords as a backing to a solo.

Chorus 2

A high trombone solo, accompanied by tremolo piano chords, staccato banjo chords and the curious percussion device called a *bock-a-da-bock*. Whereas the theme was elaborated in Chorus 1, here it is simplified, with the opening motif reduced to just two notes (a blue 3rd smeared into a major 3rd). As in Chorus 1, the rests in the original song are filled in with improvisation by the soloist. Notice the chord substitutions in bars 20, 24 and 26.

Chorus 3

An improvised call-and-response duet for clarinet and voice, the latter sung by Armstrong in the jazz style that he invented known as scat (singing to nonsense syllables). The clarinet is entirely in the low (chalumeau) register and is played with the fast vibrato typical of early jazz clarinettists.

The opening motif appears twice per bar at the start of this chorus, and in various transformations. For example, its upward 3rd is melodically augmented to a 4th by the clarinet (bars 31^4–32), a modification to which Armstrong responds just two beats later, decorating the interval with an expressive appoggiatura (at bar 32^3). The original motif is transposed and rhythmically varied by Armstrong in bar 34 and the clarinettist freely inverts the motif from the end of bar 34 onwards.

> It was Armstrong's ability to respond instantly to the other musicians around him, as well as his superb technique and enormous range of tone, that accounts for his reputation as one of the greatest jazz musicians.

Chorus 4

Another change in texture, this time to a brilliant piano solo in salon music style. The florid right-hand part is supported by a left hand which leaps between bass and harmony notes in a ragtime technique known as stride bass. The absence of the rest of the band in this chorus allows Earl Hines to freely substitute chords, and there are only the sketchiest references to the original melody.

Chorus 5 and coda

The full frontline returns for the final chorus, which begins with the greatest possible simplification – the first phrase, now an octave higher, is reduced to just its distinctive three opening notes, the last of which Armstrong sustains for almost four bars. As the $E\flat^7$ chord resolves to $A\flat$ he releases the tension with a sparkling cascade of notes, the repeated $B\flat$s bouncing off the $A\flat$ chord that supports them. The final phrase is left to the pianist, who plays descending chords over a dominant pedal which dissolve into a tiny coda played by the full band. This is based (as was often the case in the early blues) on a chromatic version of a plagal cadence, the nature of which will seem clearer if you read the chords as $A\flat m^7 - E\flat^6$.

The supremacy of the soloists in this Chicago-style jazz is obvious in the three central choruses. Even in the tutti choruses (1 and 5) Armstrong dominates the texture, the other frontline instruments mostly supplying sustained harmony notes, enlivened with the occasional melodic fragment.

Exercise 5

1. (i) What is meant by the term 'the changes' in jazz?

    (ii) What are the changes in *West End Blues*?

2. Using examples from the introduction, explain the difference between swing rhythm and straight rhythm.

3. On what type of chord does the band enter in bar 6?

4. Briefly describe the roles played by the clarinet and trombone in the first chorus of *West End Blues*.

5. Which aspects of *West End Blues* suggest that there must have been some pre-planning of improvised material?

6. What do you notice about the rate of harmonic change in most of this piece?

7. Why is the blue 3rd in this piece ($G\flat$) often notated as F♯?

8. Name an instrument that would normally have been heard in a live performance of this piece but that is missing from the recording on CD4.

9. Explain the meaning of the terms 'comping', 'scat' and 'stride bass'.

10. Which aspects of CD4, track 7, reveal the limitations of recording technology in 1928?

Concerto for Double String Orchestra, movement 1 (Tippett)

Context and forces

NAM 6 (page 120)   CD1 Track 6
Academy of St Martin in the Fields
Conducted by Neville Marriner

The English composer Michael Tippett wrote this work in 1939 for the South London Orchestra, a group formed in the 1930s to provide performance opportunities for unemployed professional musicians, particularly those who had worked in cinema orchestras in the days of silent film. He conducted them in the first performance of the work at Morley College, Lambeth on 21 April 1940, during the early months of the Second World War.

Although the term concerto usually refers to a work in which one or more soloists and an orchestra are heard together and apart, here Tippett uses it for a piece in which two identically-sized string groups are heard separately and in combination.

The players at his disposal would have been proficient, since the work is technically demanding, but Tippett requires few unusual effects. **Double-stopping** is required in only three bars, solo strings and extreme registers are both avoided, and special performance techniques are limited to a few pizzicato bass notes and a passage beginning at bar 113 marked *sul tasto poco a poco Naturale* (bowed over the fingerboard then gradually reverting to the normal bowing position).

Rather than employing unusual timbres, Tippett concentrates on the two elements that characterise this concerto – **counterpoint** and **syncopation**. However, although the score looks dense, Tippett often doubles his melodies at the octave above and/or below. Look carefully at the first eight bars and you will discover that they are in lean two-part counterpoint, with each part doubled in octaves and galvanised by syncopation. Throughout the movement, Tippett doubles important melodic lines in octaves to give them clarity and emphasis within the overall string sound.

Notice that the viola parts have an alto C clef, with a treble clef for higher passsages, and be aware that double basses sound an octave lower than written. Tippett includes bowing marks in some places: ⊓ indicates a down bow, and ⋁ means an up bow.

Tonality

Tippett sometimes uses modes as a substitute for tonality, but although the work is dissonant, it is not atonal. His use of modes and keys is shown in the diagram *opposite*, but they don't form a hierarchy of related keys as they do in NAM 15 and NAM 17.

Modality is usually associated with music of the Renaissance, but its use in modern music had fascinated a number of British composers in the early 20th century. Other indications of the influence of earlier music in the work include the archaic **phrygian cadence** (IVb–V in a minor key) in bars 20–21, the contrapuntal texture and several aspects of the structure discussed *opposite*.

Rhythm

Syncopation makes the music sound jazzy, but do you agree that at the start (and for most of the rest of the movement) there is no clear sense of a regular pulse, as in most types of jazz?

Instead we hear 'additive rhythms' of a type that composers such as Stravinsky and Bartók often used. In this type of rhythmic organisation there is a constant unit of time (the quaver in Tippett's concerto) which is too fast to be perceived as a pulse. These quavers are gathered into irregular units that deny a regular beat. At its simplest such units can produce the type of 3+3+2 rhythms that are found in Latin-American dances (as in bar 15 and other bars marked 'Beat 3').

At a more complex level, additive rhythms can ride rough-shod over the barlines, as in the melody in the second orchestra during the first four bars. It is the contrapuntal combination of two or more rhythmically independent strands that gives this movement its tremendous vitality and excitement.

Tippett's interest in music of the past is also reflected in the structure of the movement. On a small scale there is, embedded within the two contrasting contrapuntal strands of the first four bars, a number of motifs from which most of the rest of the movement is constructed – a method we saw in our study of Haydn's quartet. Take, for example, the oscillating two-pitch figure of the first four notes. In bars 8–12 it becomes a sequence (violins) that is imitated in **inversion** by violas and cellos. In bars 21–30 this syncopated figure becomes an accompaniment to a new motif (marked *scherzando* – jokingly). On a larger scale the two-note figure, and the motif introduced by the second orchestra in bar 1, help us recognise the start of a section (bars 1–20) that recurs in whole or in part in bars 68–71, 129–146 and 194–197, rather like the ritornellos in Baroque **ritornello form**.

But listen again and you will hear that these sections signal the starting points for something that seems more like the **sonata form** we encountered in our study of Beethoven's Septet. All of the main features of the form are present, with the important exception that Tippett doesn't use the related key centres that are such as vital part of Classical sonata form (see *right*).

The first section that we identified earlier (bars 1–20) corresponds with a 'first subject' and bars 33–67 serve as a 'second subject', although the latter is a step below the tonal centre of the first subject – a much more modal-sounding relationship than the conventional dominant key. In the 'development' (bars 68–128) Tippett does indeed manipulate motifs from the first part of the movement, but it is marked by a passage in which additive rhythms give way to simpler rhythms (sounding more like $\frac{2}{2}$ time) starting at bar 95. Look at the first-orchestra staves and compare the violin parts in bars 95–96 with the cello and bass parts two bars earlier. Do you see that the violins are playing the inverted theme in **augmentation** at bar 95? Now look at the cello and bass parts of bars 99–102. Can you say how this inverted theme has been changed again?

Eventually forward propulsion begins again and additive rhythms return in bars 107–112 until we reach the recapitulation. Almost the whole of the 'first subject' is repeated in bars 129–146 (compare them with bars 1–18) and the 'second subject' in bars 159–193 (which is a transposed and slightly modified repeat of bars 33–67).

The final section, beginning in bar 194, forms a coda in which a new lyrical cello melody (bars 202–208) is combined with earlier

Structure

Exposition (bars 1–67)
First subject (bars 1–20)
tonal centre A
Transition (bars 21–32)
aeolian mode on A and lydian mode on C, leading to …
Second subject (bars 33–67)
tonal centre G

Development (bars 68–128)
Unrelated tonal centres such as A (bars 68–75),
C# major (bars 80–89) and
Ab major (bars 107–112)

Recapitulation (bars 129–193)
First subject (bars 129–146)
tonal centre A
Transition (bars 147–158)
modified to maintain A as the chief tonal centre
Second subject (bars 159–193)
tonal centre A

Coda (bars 194–232)
more unrelated tonal centres but ending with a cadence that features the two chief tonal centres: G (now lydian in bars 228–231) and A (with a bare-5th chord in the last bar)

motifs, and the descending triadic figures of bars 15–16 are inverted to form the ascending figures in bars 210, 212 and 215. The movement concludes with a contrapuntal fireworks display that ends with a cadence on the note with which the movement began.

Exercise 6

1. In what way does NAM 6 differ from most works described as a concerto?

2. Why does Tippett use $\frac{8}{8}$ rather than $\frac{4}{4}$ as the time signature?

3. Compare the music played by the three lowest parts of the first orchestra in bars 5–6 with the music the first orchestra plays in bars 1–2.

4. How is the opening motif from bar 1 treated when it returns in bar 8?

5. What is the significance of the instruction 'Beat 3' in bar 15?

6. Explain the meaning of *sotto voce* (bar 148) and *cantando* (bar 213). Use a music dictionary or the internet to help if you are not sure.

7. What is unusual about the final chord?

8. Briefly mention some of the variety of string-orchestra textures that Tippett uses in this work.

Sonatas and Interludes: Sonatas I–III (Cage)

John Cage

NAM 10   CD1 Tracks 12–14
(page 166)
Joanna MacGregor (piano)

As a young American in the 1930s, Cage studied with Schoenberg (composer of NAM 40), and his own early works reflect something of his teacher's new ways of organising music without depending on tonality for structure. But it is rhythm that emerges as the predominant element in many of these works, most likely as a result of Cage's employment, from 1937 onwards, as musical director for various contemporary dance groups which were interested in exploring percussion-based music.

John Cage was not only an influential (if controversial) composer, but also one of the 20th century's great musical intellects. In a lecture given in the late 1930s, he anticipated the age of the synthesiser by 50 years, making the (then astonishing) claim that electrical musical instruments would eventually be able to produce any type of sound.

Cage was also greatly influenced by another of his teachers in those early years, the Californian **avant-garde** composer, Henry Cowell. Cowell pioneered the use of new piano techniques, such as chord clusters (large groups of adjacent notes, sometimes played with the whole forearm on the keyboard) and strumming the strings of the piano with the fingers.

Cage developed a similar interest in new sounds in his own music. *Imaginary Landscape No. 2* (1942), for example, includes parts for tin cans, a metal wastepaper bin and electric buzzers. Another work of 1942, *Credo In Us*, includes a part for radio (tuned to whatever happens to be on) or gramophone (set to play a randomly-selected recording of classical music), introducing the idea of arbitrary sounds that interact with Cage's own music.

The prepared piano

In 1940, the dancer Syvilla Fort asked John Cage to provide music for a new dance with an African theme. The intended venue did not have enough room for the composer's regular percussion group and so Cage came up with the idea of modifying the sounds of a piano by inserting objects between the strings, creating the type of one-man percussion ensemble that he was to use in a number of his compositions during the 1940s, including these sonatas.

The table of preparations on page 167 of NAM shows which pitches are altered and how. There are essentially three types of note:

1. Those with objects (described by Cage as 'mutes') between all of the strings that produce a given note, creating a percussive sound of no clear pitch

2. Those with objects between two out of three strings, resulting in a mixture of the original pitch with the prepared sound

3. Those without mutes and that therefore sound normally.

> In the table on page 167 of NAM, tone is the American word for note. When reading the table, you need to be aware that pianos have three strings per note, reducing to two in the lower register (and just one for each of the very lowest notes).

The **timbre** of the prepared sound is determined by the material from which the mute is made (metal, plastic or rubber) and it can be varied by using the *una corda* ('soft') pedal. This causes only two of the three strings per note to vibrate when a key is struck, thus either reducing or intensifying the effect of the mute.

Of the 88 notes on a typical piano, 45 need to be prepared for this work, the majority of which are from middle C upwards (Cage makes little use of the low register of the piano in NAM 10).

Although the table of preparations seems very specific, Cage later realised that the timbres produced also depend on the piano being used, and suggested that pianists should determine their own way of preparation and not necessarily follow his detailed instructions.

> While it is a good thing to get to know set works by performing them, in the case of NAM 10 you need to be aware that serious damage can be done to pianos by pushing objects between the strings. Resist the temptation to do so unless you have permission to use a suitable instrument in this way.

Although each movement in the Sonatas and Interludes is short, the entire work lasts over an hour because there are 16 sonatas and four interludes, arranged symmetrically as shown *right*.

Cage used the term sonata in the sense it was used by keyboard composers of the late Baroque period, such as Domenico Scarlatti, to mean a single-movement in binary form, in which each of the two sections are repeated. The repeated sections are clear to see in NAM 10, but there the similarity ends, because 18th-century composers used contrasts in tonality to define their structures, and this is not an option with the often indeterminate pitches produced by the prepared piano.

Instead, Cage turned to duration as the way to structure his music – an idea that possibly arose from his work with dancers. In his percussion piece, *First Construction (in Metal)* of 1939, we can see a simple version of the principle used in the sonatas of NAM 10. The piece starts with five phrases forming a unit of 4+3+2+3+4 bars. This numerical sequence then determines the proportions of the entire piece, which consists of 4+3+2+3+4 of these 16-bar units (see *right*). We will look at this in more detail when we discuss each individual sonata, but for now remember that we are talking about replicating patterns of *length*, not repeating precise rhythms.

Cage described such a nested structure as 'micro-macrocosmic' (the small-scale reflected in the large-scale). Today we would recognise it as the self-similar formation known as a fractal (seen in crystals, snowflakes and ferns), in which each sub-division of the structure resembles a miniature version of the whole.

Structure

> Sonatas I–IV
>   Interlude 1
> Sonatas V–VIII
>   Interlude 2
>   Interlude 3
> Sonatas IX–XII
>   Interlude 4
> Sonatas XIII–XVI

> ```
> 43234  43234  43234  43234 = 4 × 16
> 43234  43234  43234        = 3 × 16
> 43234  43234               = 2 × 16
> 43234  43234  43234        = 3 × 16
> 43234  43234  43234  43234 = 4 × 16
>     Total length of 256 bars = 16 × 16
> ```

Eastern philosophy

The Hindu theory of *rasa* (idealised emotional character) is described in Ananda Coomaraswamy's *The Dance of Šiva* (1924). There are four light moods (heroic, comic, wondrous and erotic) and four dark ones (fury, fear, disgust and sorrow). A ninth *rasa*, tranquillity, exists as a common tendency of the other eight. The purpose of a work of art is to balance these emotional states in order to achieve the tranquillity of the ninth *rasa*.

The analyses that follow are based on the score, since that is what you will use in the exam. However, the use of a prepared piano means that what you hear on the recording doesn't always correspond with the pitches that you see on paper.

When reading the score, note that the figure 8 above a treble clef indicates music to be played an octave higher than written, while 15 instructs the performer to play two octaves higher than written. The end of these transposed sections is indicated by the word *loco*, meaning 'place' (that is, in normal position).

During the 1940s, Cage became interested in Eastern philosophy, including Zen Buddhism and the Hindu theory of *rasa* (see *left*). He said that Sonatas and Interludes were intended to express the moods or emotions described by Coomaraswamy, but it is not known how Cage implemented the details of this plan. However, it seems likely that each movement expresses a single emotion, and that the entire collection of 20 pieces resolves towards the simple ('tranquil') proportions of its last four sonatas.

It is possible that the wide range of timbres in Sonata I reflects wonder, the dancing rhythms of Sonata II reflect mirth, and the sinuous contours of Sonata III are an expression of the erotic, but this is just speculation. What is clear, though, is that each sonata establishes its own mood. The first is mainly chordal, and includes chord clusters (groups of adjacent notes sounded simultaneously) in bar 10. The second is based on syncopated rhythms heard in **monophonic** and two-part textures, while the third features numerous speed changes as well as highly contrasting note lengths.

Another feature running through the first group of sonatas is the way in which the units of their micro-macrocosmic structures expand. As explained *below*, Sonata I is based on units of 28, II on units of 31 and III on units of 34 (Sonata IV, not in NAM, is based on units of 40 in regularly proportioned subdivisions of 3:3:2:2, thus offering the first signs of emerging tranquillity).

Despite the importance of Indian philosophy in John Cage's works of the 1940s, it is important to realise that the Sonatas and Interludes don't reflect the *sounds* of Indian music. In fact, you may well feel that the sound world of the prepared piano is closer to that of gamelan than Indian raga.

Sonata I

The durational proportions in all three sonatas are more complex than the example from *First Construction (in Metal)* shown on the previous page, although they follow similar principles. In Sonata I the durations are 4:1:3 (repeated) followed by 4:2 (repeated). Here they are at the micro level in the first seven bars:

The entire pattern of 28 crotchets equates to four double-dotted semibreves ($\circ.. = \circ + \downarrow + \downarrow = 7$ crotchets). Cage uses this seven-beat length as a multiplier from which to construct the entire sonata (forming its macro structure). In other words, seven-beat lengths are used in the pattern 4:1:3 (repeated) followed by 4:2 (repeated), as shown *left*.

Bar numbers	Duration in crotchets
1–7	4 × 7 = 28
8	1 × 7 = 7
9–12	3 × 7 = 21
1–7 (repeat)	4 × 7 = 28
8	1 × 7 = 7
9–12	3 × 7 = 21
13–19	4 × 7 = 28
20–26	2 × 7 = 14
13–19 (repeat)	4 × 7 = 28
20–26	2 × 7 = 14

The micro structure is not clearly articulated in bars 8–12, but you should be able to follow it in bars 13–19: look for the pattern of 4+1+3 4+1+3 4+2 4+2 crotchets (4 in bar 19, 1+3 in bar 20, and so on). Finally, the same proportions are used twice more in bars 20–26, but now in quavers rather than crotchets (4 quavers in bar 20, 1+3 quavers in bar 21, and so on). The last two-quaver unit falls in the second half of the final bar and so doesn't coincide with the start of a new note.

Although proportional durations dominate the sonata, there are also repetitions and developments of ideas used in a structural way. For example, bar 3 is a restatement of bar 1, while the two chords in bar 5 are repeated in compressed form in the first half of bar 6, followed by two more appearances of the first chord from bar 5.

In bar 13, the sustained B (left hand) leading to C (right hand) in the next bar sounds like a semitone because both notes are only partially muted, but when the semitone is inverted in bar 15 (E♭–D), it sounds like a distorted echo, because the E♭ is fully muted.

Bars 18–19 include a reference to the opening chords of the sonata and bars 20–21 are given a varied repeat in the next two bars. The entire progression of parallel chords creates a cadential effect, despite the fact that many of the notes are of indeterminate pitch. This is confirmed by the tiny coda, in which the right hand of bar 24 is subjected to varied repetition in bars 25–26.

Cage's references to bars 1 and 4 in the final section of the sonata seem a little like the way in which rounded-binary form movements (such as NAM 16 and NAM 23) end with material from their opening section, although the effect is totally different in this atonal work.

At the end, Cage achieves a sense of conclusion not only by using *ff* homophonic chords, but also by including a stepwise descent from F to C (in the bass of bars 24–26) that harks back to the fall from C to G in the lower part of bar 4. The rhythm of the melody in the final bars is also a reminder of the rhythm in bar 4.

Sonata II

Sonata II is based on a 31-crotchet unit, subdivided as follows at the micro level:

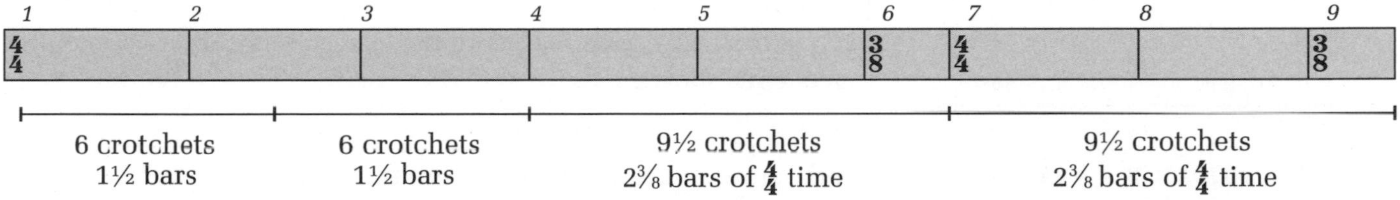
1
2
3
4
5
6
7
8
9
4/4
3/8
4/4
3/8
6 crotchets
1½ bars
6 crotchets
1½ bars
9½ crotchets
2⅜ bars of 4/4 time
9½ crotchets
2⅜ bars of 4/4 time

31 crotchets equates to 7¾ bars of $\frac{4}{4}$ time, and so Cage forms his macro structure from 7¾ permutations of the micro structure, in the pattern 1½ (repeated) followed by 2⅜ (repeated), as shown *right*. The first of these patterns is shown *above*. The second consists of 31 *quavers* (bars 10–14), to complete the first part of the binary form. The second part starts with two more 31-crotchet units (bars 15–32), and ends with a section in which Cage aims for ⅜ of the original 31-crotchet length. However, for rhythmic tidiness, he settles for a close approximation of 11½ crotchet beats rather than a mathematically exact 11⅝ crotchet beats.

Bar numbers	Duration in crotchets
1–9	1 × 31 = 31
10–14	½ × 31 = 15½
1–9 (repeat)	1 × 31 = 31
10–14	½ × 31 = 15½
15–32	2 × 31 = 62
33–37	⅜ × 31 ≈ 11½
15–32 (repeat)	2 × 31 = 62
33–37	⅜ × 31 ≈ 11½
Total:	7¾ × 31

The sums are complicated, but each of these sections is preceded by the useful visual clue of a double barline.

Notice that the multiplier in Sonata I was 7 (a double-dotted semibreve), while here 7¾ is the length of a quadruply-dotted semibreve.

The entirely monophonic opening starts with a six-beat idea in the right hand. When this is answered by a new idea in the left hand, Cage substitutes a rest for the crotchet in the middle of the rhythm. The rest falls on a strong beat and so launches the syncopation that dominates this sonata. The crotchet rest also causes the four-quaver figure that started on a strong beat in bar 2 (left hand) to start on a weak beat in bar 3, a device known as 'metrical displacement'.

Such jazz-like rhythms permeate much of this sonata. For example, the metrical displacement of the repeated figure in bars 7–8 is essentially the early-jazz device of 'secondary rag', in which a three-beat figure is repeated across the four-fold beat of quadruple time. A cascade of ragtime-like syncopation follows in the rhythmic repetitions of bars 10–14.

The material in the first nine bars derives from bars 1–2. A new idea appears with the start of two-part writing in bar 10, and Cage adapts this to announce the beginning of section two (bar 15).

The ostinato (A#–B) starting at bar 17^3 perhaps derives from the rising semitone at the start of the left-hand figure in bar 2, and the flurry of high-register activity, starting with the right-hand ostinato in bar 28, seems to derive from bar 5. However, while the pitches resemble earlier material, the different mutes in the upper range of the piano result in a brilliant wash of gamelan-like sound rather than any clear motivic link. Similarly, while the long left-hand descent in bars 30–31 may *look* like a scale, the mutes ensure that it doesn't *sound* like one. In this sonata, Cage seems to concentrate more on vivid contrasts in the dynamics and exhilarating rhythms, rather than on conventional musical development.

Sonata III   Sonata III is based on a micro structure of 34 crotchets (bars 1–8):

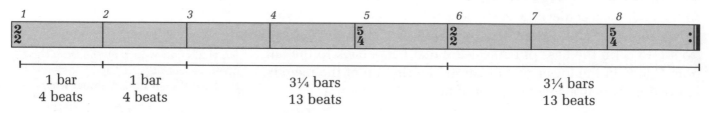

1 bar	1 bar
4 beats	4 beats

3¼ bars	3¼ bars
13 beats	13 beats

Further units start in bars 9, 17 and 25 (each preceded by a double barline), the last of which is 42½ (= 34 × 1¼) beats long. The proportions of this micro structure (1 : 1 : 3¼ : 3¼ in terms of $\frac{4}{4}$ bars) is once again mimicked in the macro structure of the entire movement, shown *left*.

Bar numbers	Duration in crotchets
1–8	**1** × 34 = 34
1–8 (repeat)	**1** × 34 = 34
9–32	**3¼** × 34 = 110½
9–32 (repeat)	**3¼** × 34 = 110½

The first section consists of three statements of the opening right-hand figure, in the second of which the final note is truncated to a crotchet. The left-hand part *looks* like a pedal, but preparation leaves the pitch unclear, and so it *sounds* more like a percussive reference point (momentarily shifting off the beat in bar 6) for the irregular note lengths in the melody. The latter sound even more irregular than they look because the recurring G# is heavily muted and so seems percussive rather than pitched.

The second section opens with a new idea in bar 9 (left hand). This is transformed into a fragment of a rising chromatic scale in bar 17, truncated to two notes in bar 18, and then greatly extended in bars 19–21. The last F of bar 21 is also the first note of a **retrograde** repetition of the previous 12 pitches, so the two-note chord in bar 24 is the same chord with which the pattern began in bar 19. A further variant appears in bars 25–26 and versions of the two-note chord (a 4th) are heard until the end of the work.

While all of this is going on in the left hand, the first three demi-semiquavers of the motif from bar 2 return in bar 13, augmented to eight times their original value. They are heard in retrograde order in bar 14 and extended into bar 15 by means of sequence. The left-hand of bars 14–15 repeats the ostinato accompaniment first heard in bars 11–12, but in bar 14 (only) it is transposed up a semitone.

Meanwhile, the right hand picks up the chromatic scale figure in bar 22. It begins in octaves with the left hand, but the tied A causes the right hand to lag by a beat, producing minor 9ths in bar 23 – once again, though, preparation ensures that these intervals often don't *sound* like consecutive octaves and 9ths, just as what looks like a chromatic scale on paper doesn't necessarily sound like one in performance. Be that as it may, the chromatic scale is inverted in the right-hand part of bars 27–28 (in other words, it now descends before ascending), and is subsequently joined with variants of the motif from bar 2 in the final system of the sonata.

Exercise 7

1. Name two composers who influenced Cage's early work.

2. In what sense are the movements in NAM 10 sonatas?

3. Explain how the concept of *rasa* applies to NAM 10.

4. What is meant by the terms augmentation and metrical displacement?

5. Why did Cage describe the structure of these works as 'micro-macrocosmic'?

6. Explain what is meant by una corda and why the use of this effect makes such a difference to these sonatas.

7. What is the main reason for rhythm, texture and dynamics seeming to be more significant than either melody or harmony when listening to NAM 10?

Sample questions

In Section C of the Unit 6 paper you will have to answer one of two questions about the instrumental works you have studied. Your response is expected to be an essay, written in continuous prose, and your clarity of expression, spelling and grammar will be taken into account in the marking.

Remember that it is important to give locations of each specific feature that you mention, but there should not normally be any need to write out music examples. You will be allowed to refer to an unmarked copy of NAM as you write.

Here are two essay topics to use for practice. Aim to complete each essay in 50 minutes.

(a) Compare and contrast the instrumental writing and textures in the three following works:

Corelli's Trio Sonata in D, Op. 3 No. 2, movement IV (NAM 15, pages 200–201)
Haydn's String Quartet in E flat, Op. 33 No. 2: movement IV (NAM 16, pages 202–206)
Beethoven's Septet in E flat, Op. 20: movement I (NAM 17, pages 207–230).

(b) Comment on the use of metre and rhythm in the three following works:

West End Blues, as recorded by Louis Armstrong and his Hot Five (NAM 48, pages 461–464)
Tippett's Concerto for Double String Orchestra: movement I (NAM 6, pages 120–138)
Cage's Sonatas and Interludes for Prepared Piano: Sonatas I, II and III (NAM 10, pages 166–170).

Applied music

Sonata pian' e forte (Giovanni Gabrieli)

Context

NAM 14 (page 194)   CD2 Track 3
His Majesty's Sagbutts and Cornetts
Directed by Timothy Roberts

Although Venice is a tiny city, situated on a group of islands in a lagoon at the head of the Adriatic, it accrued enormous wealth through its position on the trade route between Europe and the far east. As a result, Venetians were able to erect palaces and churches of the utmost splendour to line the banks of the city's canals, and to impress visitors with the scale of their entertainment and music.

Most magnificent of all was the palace of their elected leader (the Doge) and its chapel of St Mark (now a cathedral), where Giovanni Gabrieli was appointed organist in 1585. In the late Renaissance, it became famous for polychoral music, in which separate choirs of singers and instrumentalists were positioned in galleries around the building, to perform in **antiphony** – one group answering another in stereophonic 'surround sound', as in NAM 27.

The *Sonata pian' e forte* comes from a collection of works for eight to 15 instruments by Gabrieli, published in 1597, and is famous for being among the earliest works in which a composer indicated dynamic levels (*pian'* is an abbreviation of *piano*) and precise details of instrumentation. It is not known for what purpose the work was written, but its polychoral style, dictated by the acoustics of St Mark's, suggests that it may have been played during a service, or perhaps to accompany one of the magnificent state processions into the great church on special festivals.

The title of NAM 14 illustrates yet another meaning of the word sonata, which at this time simply meant a piece to be played (from *sonare*, to sound) as opposed to a cantata, which meant a piece to be sung (from *cantare*, to sing). The term sonata didn't imply any particular structure at this time.

Instruments and dynamics

The parts for trombones 1 and 2 use the tenor C clef. This indicates that the second line down on the stave is middle C. Thus the first note of the sonata is D a tone above middle C.

The *Sonata pian' e forte* is written for two four-part 'choirs' of instruments (coro I and coro II in the score). Both choirs contain three trombone parts and on CD2 each also includes a chamber organ (which can only just be heard). Gabrieli did not write parts for the organs, but by 1597 it was becoming common practice for an organ to be used to support music intended for the church.

The top part in coro I is for a cornett and should not be confused with the cornet, which is a brass-band instrument. The cornett is a wooden wind instrument with a mouthpiece similar to that of a brass instrument, but it has a softer tone than the trumpet.

The top part in coro II is labelled 'violin', but in the 16th century this could refer to several sizes of the violin family. In this sonata its range dictates that it could be played on a viola (in bar 28 it descends to D a perfect 4th lower than the modern violin's lowest note). A viola is used for this part on CD2.

Although specifying dynamics was highly unusual at this time, they follow a simple plan in which *piano* is mainly used when the choirs play separately and *forte* when they play together.

The texture is dominated by the dark sonority of the six trombones, instruments associated with solemnity and priestly ritual. The polychoral texture, with its use of opposition (bars 1–13 and 14–25), combination (bars 26–31), antiphonal exchanges (bars 37–40) and echo effects (bars 45–49) forms the main feature of the sonata.

Several other matters add to the solemnity of the music:

➢ The textures are never less than four-part (one complete choir)

➢ Although mostly contrapuntal, the only obvious imitation occurs in the last ten bars (e.g. the entries marked *forte* in bars 71–72)

➢ There is a preponderance of root-position triads, such as those in the **circle of 5ths** in bars 36–41

➢ The music is more **modal** than much secular music written at this time.

This last point requires explanation. The sonata is in the dorian mode, which can be found by playing an octave of white notes on the piano from D to D. The mode is here transposed to G, giving the notes G–A–Bb–C–D–E–F–G. However, accidentals are used to avoid awkward intervals, to form a **tierce de Picardie** at the end of important sections, and to construct cadences such as the **phrygian cadence** in bars 44–45 and the final plagal cadence.

Texture, style and harmony

By 1597, when this work was first published, the modal harmony of the Renaissance was starting to give way to the tonal harmony of the early Baroque.

Many of the important harmonic features of the music can be seen in the following quotation of bars 12^3–17:

1 passing dissonances
2 a suspension (and its resolution)
3 F♯ is outside the mode but it allows a perfect cadence on G
4 B♮ is a tierce de Picardie
5 a progression of modal root-position triads
6 two chords (IVb–V in D minor) that form a phrygian cadence.

Exercise 8

1. Why is St Mark's, Venice particularly significant to the context of this work?

2. How many suspensions are there in bars 22–25?

3. When both choirs first play together in bar 26 on what chord do they start?

4. What do you notice about the rhythm on pages 198–199 of NAM?

5. With what type of cadence does the sonata end? How is the final chord of this cadence modified?

6. Explain what is meant by (i) polychoral music, and (ii) a cornett.

'Thy hand, Belinda' (recitative) and 'When I am laid in earth' (aria) from *Dido and Aeneas* (Purcell)

Context

NAM 36 (page 356)   CD3 Track 14
Carolyn Watkinson (soprano)
with the English Baroque Soloists

Opera is drama set to music, sung on stage in costume and with scenery, accompanied by instruments and often including dance and spectacle. The very first operas started to appear in Italy at the end of the 16th century, just after the previous set work (NAM 14) was first published, at the time when Shakespeare was becoming famous as a playwright in Elizabethan England.

Opera spread from Italy to other European countries, although it was not until the second half of the 17th century that English composers tackled the genre, and even then in only a modest way. Purcell's *Dido and Aeneas* lasts for around an hour (although some portions are now lost) and the first known performance was at a girls' boarding school in Chelsea in spring 1689. It was probably written to celebrate the joint coronation of William and Mary which took place in Westminster Abbey that April.

The plot centres on the mythical story of the love of Dido, Queen of Carthage, and Aeneas, Prince of Troy. Evil forces plot their downfall, and Aeneas is tricked into leaving Dido to fulfill a duty to free his homeland. NAM 36 is taken from near the end of the opera, when Dido, overcome with grief at his departure, prepares for suicide. The extract consists of a continuous section of music in which a recitative leads into an aria, as explained *below*.

Recitative

The purpose of recitative is to move the story along clearly and rapidly with little or no repetition of the text, although it can also be very expressive. The melodic line tends to follow the natural inflections of speech and rhythms are often interpreted freely. Listen, for instance, to the dotted rendition of the even quavers in bar 1 and the lengthening of the last syllable of 'Belinda' on CD3.

The recitative in NAM 36 is short, but Purcell effectively portrays the mood of extreme despair by:

➢ A tonally ambiguous **melisma** to highlight the word 'darkness'

➢ Anguished chromaticism and unpredictable changes of key

➢ Short, detached phrases with silences to suggest sighs

➢ Grinding dissonances between the vocal solo and the bass

➢ Jagged rhythms and a melodic line which slowly descends a 7th to reach the key word, 'death'.

The accompaniment consists of a simple **continuo** part of the type we encountered in Corelli's trio sonata (which was published in the same year as the first performance of this opera). On CD3 the bass line is played on a bass viol (a bowed string instrument with frets, similar in range to a cello) while chords, improvised from the **figured bass** part, are played on an archlute (a large plucked-string instrument with frets).

Baroque composers frequently supplied minimal figuring, relying on performers to spot most harmonic progressions from the bass part alone. Modern editors sometimes add very full figuring (as in NAM 36), but performers are at liberty to disregard it. The example *below* shows what is actually played on CD3. This figuring represents the archlutenist's improvisation and takes no account of expressive dissonances between voice and bass (such as the minor 9th at the start of bar 4). The passing modulations and frequent cadences are typical of many kinds of recitative:

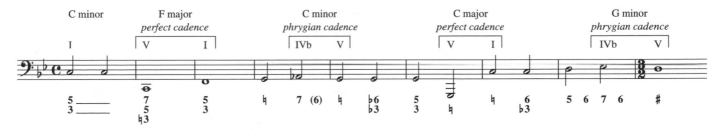

Aria

An air (or *aria* in Italian) is simply a song, and in opera it provides the opportunity for a character to reflect on the situation they are in. Rather like a soliloquy in a Shakespearean play, it allows the character to reveal their thoughts and emotions to the audience without the need to engage in dialogue with others.

The aria starts when the music moves to $\frac{3}{2}$ time and it begins with a five-bar bass part that is repeated throughout the song. This is known as a **ground bass** and is a compositional device particularly associated with Purcell, although it was also used by many other composers, particularly during the mid-Baroque period.

Purcell's ground bass implies a perfect cadence in G minor even when there is no harmony (bars 4^3–6). With the addition of the string parts the chords become clear in the perfect cadences that mark the end of the ground in bars 10–11, 15–16, 20–21 and so on. By remaining in one key and by emphasising it through so many perfect cadences, Purcell underlines the implacable fate that drives Dido to kill herself.

> Ground-bass arias are not always in the same key throughout. 'Ah, Belinda', from earlier in *Dido and Aeneas*, has 21 repetitions of a four-bar ground: 11 in the tonic, two in the dominant and eight back in the tonic.

This particular type of ground bass, falling chromatically from tonic to lower dominant in a minor key, was already associated with vocal works about sadness, weeping or cruel fate when *Dido and Aeneas* was written. Purcell's own skill is in avoiding any sense of mechanical repetition by using an unusual length of five bars for the bass, and by ensuring that many cadence points in the bass are overlapped by the vocal phrases or string harmonies (or both).

For example, the nine-bar vocal phrase starting at bar 16 runs straight through the perfect cadence in bars 20–21 and comes to rest half way through the ground-bass pattern at bar 24. In the same way, the three-bar vocal phrase starting at bar 29 runs across the join between the sixth and seventh statements of the ground bass in bar 31. At this point the strings move to dominant harmony two beats earlier than expected, thus forming expressive dissonances with the **ostinato** in the bass (A and F♯ sounding against G on the second beat of bar 31).

The melody of bars 6–14 expresses the doom-laden words through chromaticism (bar 7) and the drooping **tritone** in bar 12. This melody is repeated in bars 16–24, and repeated passages are often ornamented in Baroque vocal music, but Dido's only decoration on CD3 is a slide up to the third beat of bar 22. Can you spot added ornamentation in the first-violin part?

The melody of bars 25–36 (repeated in bars 36–46) is fragmented, giving the impression that Dido's despair is so deep that she can hardly continue. Yet it contains the climax of the whole song when she reaches her highest note in bar 33, after which it falls hopelessly through a flat 7th (F♮ in bar 34) back to the tonic (bar 36).

The pathos of the dramatic situation is underpinned by a rich harmonic vocabulary. The basic harmony of Dido's first phrase is essentially the progression I–V–IV–V but, as shown *below*, it is enriched with 7ths on dominant chords, poignant suspensions in both the vocal part and accompaniment, and a striking dissonance (marked ∗) in the melody. In addition, chromatic movement results in a juxtaposition of major and minor forms of the dominant chord (in bar 2) and subdominant chord (in bar 3), each decorated with melodic dissonances.

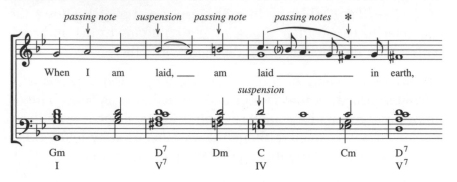

The result is a texture of deeply expressive dissonances (major and minor 9ths, 7ths, augmented 4ths, diminished 4ths and 2nds) between voice and accompaniment.

The aria ends with an orchestral passage marked *Ritornelle* (a ritornello or 'little return'). Here this simply signifies a passage in which the soloist is silent (she is busy with the dagger at this point in most productions). The ritornello is characterised by expressive clashes between the upper parts and the bass at the start of every bar except the last. It begins with a series of imitative entries above the ground bass, the last of which (in the first violin-part) develops into a long chromatic descent from upper tonic to lower tonic, reflecting the descending chromatic bass line with which the aria began and that has dominated the entire lament.

A new time signature appears in the last bar because in the opera (but not in NAM) the music leads without a break into the quadruple metre of a final chorus.

Exercise 9

1.   Explain the difference between recitative and aria.

2.   In the recitative the continuo instruments used on CD3 are an archlute and a bass viol. What two other instruments do you think might be appropriate to use for this continuo part?

3.   What is a melisma? Give one example of a melisma in the recitative and one example in the aria.

4.   What is a phrygian cadence? Where does one occur in the aria?

5.   What is the correct technical term for the dissonances that occur between second violin and bass on the first beats of bars 48–50, and between first violin and bass on the first beats of bars 51–54?

6.   How does Purcell achieve a sense of unity and continuity between the recitative and aria in NAM 36?

Pulcinella Suite: Sinfonia, Gavotta, Vivo (Stravinsky)

Drama expressed through staged dance – ballet – developed as an art form at the French court in the 17th century, but it was not until the great Russian ballets of the late 19th century, with scores by Tchaikovsky, that it became widely popular outside France.

In 1909 the impresario Serge Diaghilev formed the *Ballets Russes*, a Russian company that set new artistic standards by bringing together the most talented dancers, designers and composers of the day. Igor Stravinsky wrote large-scale ballets for the company in 1910, 1911 and 1913, but Diaghilev's work was interrupted by the outbreak of the First World War in 1914 and the Russian revolution of 1917. Lacking resources to continue commissioning substantial works, he asked the Italian composer Tommasini to produce some orchestrations of baroque keyboard sonatas by Domenico Scarlatti. The resulting ballet, with its characters dancing in Venetian masks, was a success and so Diaghilev decided to repeat the formula, handing his old collaborator Stravinsky a selection of 18th-century music that they both believed to have been written by Pergolesi.

Stravinsky adapted these pieces for a 32-piece chamber orchestra of 18th-century proportions: pairs of flutes, oboes (no clarinets), bassoons and horns, a trumpet, and strings divided into concertino (soloist) and ripieno (full) sections in the manner of a Baroque concerto grosso. Since most of the genuinely Pergolesi excerpts are vocal, there are also three singers (soprano, tenor and bass) who rather unusually perform from the orchestra pit. Even more novel was the inclusion of a trombone part in a style that would be more at home in a circus band than in any 18th-century orchestra.

Pulcinella was premiered by the *Ballet Russes* at the Paris Opéra on 15 May 1920. As usual, Diaghilev gathered together the finest talents of the age. In addition to music by Stravinsky, the sets were by Picasso, the choreography by Léonide Massine (who danced the title role) and the orchestra was conducted by Ernest Ansermet.

Despite some revivals in recent years, *Pulcinella* has never entered the mainstream ballet repertoire – its convoluted plot (see *right*) full of disguised characters and unlikely dramatic resolutions, together with a large cast and a disjointed succession of 21 tiny movements (most under two minutes in length), was not a formula for success.

Thus it is that the work is much better known in the concert hall than in the theatre, through the suite of eight movements that Stravinsky compiled in 1922. The three movements in NAM 7 relate to this suite (and the full ballet) as follows:

Sinfonia   Movement 1 of the suite
           Overture of the ballet
Gavotta   Movement 6 of the suite
           No.16 in the ballet (Scene VI)
Vivo   Movement 7 (*duetto*) of the suite
           No.17 in the ballet (Scene VII)

In art music, **Neoclassicism** was a 20th-century style popular between the two world wars. It was a reaction to the sometimes overblown and emotionally-charged romanticism of the previous

Context

NAM 7 (page 139)   CD1 Tracks 7–9
Academy of St Martin in the Fields
Conducted by Neville Marriner

In fact, of the 21 movements that Stravinsky selected for the ballet, only ten were really by Pergolesi (who died in 1736), the rest being by a variety of other 18th-century composers.

The story of *Pulcinella*

Pulcinella is a masked character from traditional Italian *Commedia dell'arte*. He is a rascal (the origin of Punch in Punch and Judy) who ignores his fiancée Pimpinella in order to flirt with the girls of Naples. Their own jealous fiancés plot to kill Pulcinella, but he outwits them by getting his friend Fourbo to dress as his double. The double pretends to die at the hands of a stranger (who is actually Pulcinella in disguise).

With their rival now apparently out of the way, the young men each disguise themselves as Pulcinella in the hope of becoming more attractive to their respective girlfriends. Pulcinella then returns, now disguised as a magician, and mysteriously revives the 'corpse' – who turns out to be neither dead nor actually Pulcinella. Finally, the magician throws off his disguise to reveal that he is the real Pulcinella. Magnanimously bearing nobody any malice, he arranges for the couples to marry and plans his own wedding to the long-suffering Pimpinella.

Neoclassicism

century. Composers sought to create a more detached and purer type of music by reinterpreting, in a modern idiom, some of the basic principles of 18th-century music.

However, the term 'Neoclassical' is confusing since composers usually found their inspiration in the Baroque music of the first half of the 18th century, rather than in the Classical style of the late 18th century – hence the Neoclassical slogan of 'back to Bach' and the preference of some writers to call the style 'Neobaroque'.

Pulcinella is unusual among Neoclassical works in being based on 18th-century music. More commonly, composers wrote entirely new material, as in Prokofiev's *Classical* symphony of 1917, one of the earliest Neoclassical works. However, *Pulcinella* is neither a pastiche (a stylistic imitation) nor merely a set of arrangements. Stravinsky described his technique as 're-composition'. Let's see what he meant.

Most of the sources for *Pulcinella* were pieces with two- or three-part textures. Stravinsky retained much of this original material, confining his changes to:

> Creating unusual timbres through innovative instrumention

> Adding precise details of articulation and vivid contrasts in dynamics

> Highlighting individual notes with accents and doublings, often in order to add (or emphasise) syncopation

> Realising ornaments and adding new melodic decoration

> Thickening musical textures by devising extra parts, additional doublings, pedal points and ostinati

> Eliding sections or inserting bars in order to produce unexpected phrase lengths

> Deliberately weakening bass-lines, destabilizing cadences and adding dissonances to create harmonic ambiguity.

Stravinsky becomes increasingly adventurous in his use of such techniques as the music unfolds. The inattentive listener might believe that the opening Sinfonia is genuinely 18th-century, but gradually the mask is lifted and by the time the Vivo is reached (some two-thirds of the way into the complete ballet score) there is no doubt that it is Stravinsky who is pulling the strings.

Sinfonia   The Sinfonia is in **rounded binary form**, its two sections being based on similar material. The first (bars 0^4–15^3) establishes the tonic key of G major and then modulates to the dominant (D major). The longer second section (bars 15^4– 44) begins in the dominant, wends its way back to the tonic via a range of related keys, and includes a varied restatement of the opening, starting at bar 33, thus 'rounding off' the binary structure.

Stravinsky's source for the Sinfonia was the first movement of a Trio Sonata by Domenico Gallo (born in Venice, c. 1730). He adds detailed performing directions (including bowing at some points) but retains Gallo's first violin and cello parts largely intact – usually, but not exclusively, in his own first-violin and cello parts. Gallo's second-violin part (often altered) is treated more freely, with phrases from it appearing in various orchestral parts.

As you know from our study of NAM 15, Baroque trio sonatas require a fourth performer to fill out the harmonies on an instrument such as the harpsichord, but this is not needed in *Pulcinella*, where the use of an orchestra offers ample resources for doubling parts and adding extra notes to chords. For example, Stravinsky blurs the harmonies in bar 3 by adding A to the G-major chord of beat 1 and G to the D-major chord of beat 2, seizing the opportunity to use bare 5ths on open strings (G–D–A) on both beats in the second violin parts. The second oboe repeats a low B throughout the bar, adding to the harmonic richness – so F♯, G, A and B all cluster on beat 2, while the B adds a major 7th to the C-major chord on beat 3.

In bars 7–9 Stravinsky adds new countermelodies to the texture (in the bassoon, second violin and solo cello parts) and then trips-up the metre by inserting an extra beat ($\frac{2}{4}$ + $\frac{3}{4}$ = five beats), allowing a crafty extra repetition of Gallo's little cadence figure:

There is only one other similar addition – this time of an entire bar (bar 18) – which is based on the same cadence figure. However, Stravinsky's enrichment of the texture with added-note chords and countermelodies continues throughout the movement. For example, in bars 24–26 the two original melodic parts are assigned to second violins and violas, so that the first violins can be given a newly-invented and gently dissonant descending scale that intertwines with Gallo's own suspensions and descending sequences. See if you can spot how Stravinsky gives this passage another new treatment when it returns in bar 37 (Gallo's material appears in the parts for solo violins and orchestral bass – all else is added).

As in most binary-form movements, the second section modulates more widely than the first, passing sequentially through G major (bar 21), A major (bar 22) and B minor (bar 23). A **circle of 5ths** progression in bars 24–27 ends with repeated perfect cadences in B minor (bars 26[4]–28) and then another modulating sequence quickly visits E minor (bar 29), D major (bar 30), A minor (bar 31) and finally the tonic, G major (bar 32).

The circle of 5ths progression in bars 24–27[1] is disguised by Stravinsky's added violin scale, mentioned in the paragraph above. The basic progression is Em–A–D–G–C♯dim–F♯–Bm.

The return of the opening material in bar 33 is done with typical Stravinskian whimsy. Shorn of its anacrusic start, it creeps back in on horns and bassoons, and it is only with the loud tutti entry in bar 35 that we realise that a recapitulation is already under way. Despite a chromatic passing note (C♯ in bar 36), the music remains in G major for the rest of the movement.

The Sinfonia has a largely **homophonic** texture with one main melody supported by subordinate parts. It varies in density from the three-part writing of bars 29–30, which comes straight from the original trio sonata (except that the bass has been transposed up two octaves) to passages such as bars 37–39. Here, Stravinsky's re-interpretation of the figured bass involves a dense accompaniment, with solo strings sustaining, and tutti strings repeating, harmonies that are smudged by the violas' insistence on sounding a double pedal (on E and B) through every one of the six different chords.

Gavotta

This was originally part of a keyboard suite by Carlo Ignazio Monza, published around 1735. The gavotte is a fairly fast duple-metre dance and Monza followed it with six *doubles* (that is, variations in shorter notes) of which Stravinsky used the first and fourth.

The gavotte is in simple **binary form** (like the movement by Corelli in NAM 15). The A section (which ends at the repeat sign in bar 10) first establishes the tonic key of D major and then modulates to the dominant (A major). The B section, as usual, modulates more widely. It starts with a four-bar phrase in G major (bars 11–14) that is repeated sequentially a tone higher in A major (bars 15–18). The first two bars of this phrase are then heard in a modified version, adapted to cadence in F♯ minor (bars 19–20), and are sequentially repeated in E minor (bars 21–22) and D major (bars 23–24). The final eight bars remain in the tonic and consist of a four-bar phrase (bars 25–28) that is repeated in decorated form in bars 29–32.

The variations follow the same pattern, each being in binary form, except that the shorter note values in the second variation allow it to be compressed into half of the number of bars.

Monza's original keyboard gavotte has a mainly two-part texture (one note in each hand) except for bars 19–26, where the left hand has chords. Stravinsky's principle contributions are the distinctive scoring for wind and the addition of numerous countermelodies and accompaniment figures. In the first ten bars, Monza's melody appears in the first oboe part and his walking bass (albeit with a few changes) in the second bassoon. Everything else has been added by Stravinsky.

Later additions include the sighing horn part (starting in bar 11) and the filling-in of Monza's bass with bassoon glissandi (starting in bar 15) – although the latter are unfortunately unconvincing on the NAM recording. Bar 19 sees a thickening of texture by the conventional device of doubling the tune in 3rds and 6ths.

In bars 25–28 Stravinsky veils the melody in sustained notes above and below, and adds an inverted tonic pedal, deliberately designed to weaken the effect of the perfect cadence, as seen in the example at the top of the next page. In total contrast, the final four-bar phrase is just as Monza wrote it, the original trill in bar 31 being notated in full.

Variation I is in the style of a gigue – a lively baroque dance in compound time. At the start, the first oboe plays Monza's melody, the second horn plays his bass part (with some simplifications), and Stravinsky adds a soaring countermelody for first horn. In bars 43–46, Monza's simple I and IV harmonies (outlined by woodwind) invite a tonic pedal – but Stravinsky supplies an entire tonic *chord*, reiterated by the brass and clashing gloriously with chord IV at the start of bar 44 – the first horn is still hanging onto an F♯ in bar 46. After the sequential repetition of this section, Stravinsky injects contrapuntal interest from bar 51 (oboe 2 and bassoon 1 are the added parts) as well as a brief inner pedal on F♯ in bars 57–58.

When reading the score in NAM, note that while horns in F sound a perfect 5th lower than written when in the treble clef, they sound a *perfect 4th higher* than written when in the bass clef. The brief trumpet part is in C, so its notes sound as printed.

The melody of Variation II is shared between flute and horn, while bubbling bassoons are allocated the Alberti-like accompaniment (which Stravinsky alters to make it less keyboard-like). Bar 69 reveals another way in which he weakened cadences. Monza harmonised this cadence with a conventional Ic–V–I progression in A major; Stravinsky undermines this modulation by retaining G♮ in the first bassoon part. At the start of the second section Stravinsky uses **octave displacement** to change the shape of the original melody:

The **Alberti bass** is named after Monza's contemporary Alberti, who was particularly fond of these busy accompaniment patterns. Its most typical form can be seen on page 255 of NAM, in the left hand of bars 71–80.

Stravinsky adds some exuberant ornamentation in the form of upward rushing scales in bars 73, 76 and 78. The second flute and first oboe parts in this section are countermelodies that have been added by Stravinsky, often in a clearly unbaroque style, such as the chain of unprepared dissonances generated by the second flute in bar 77 and the barely disguised consecutive 5ths of bar 79. Both reveal that this is a work of re-composition, not pastiche.

These scales are like a type of 18th-century ornament called the *tirade*, in which two notes of a melody would be joined by a rapid scale, but Stravinsky's versions are rather more flamboyant.

Vivo

Stravinsky's source for the Vivo is the last movement from a work for solo cello by Pergolesi. Typical of such Baroque music, it also includes a bass part, from which the player of an instrument such as a harpischord or lute could improvise an accompaniment.

The movement is another **rounded binary** structure, with a first section ending at bar 21. It is in F major and doesn't modulate to the dominant (C major) until the very last moment, in bars 20–21.

The second section begins with the 'false start' described *below*, and then at bar 25 the opening of the first section is heard in the key of C major. Bars 38–45 are a re-scored repeat of bars 6–13, back in F major. At bar 46 the music plunges into the **tonic minor** key (F minor) for four bars (the sudden switch from major to parallel minor key being a fingerprint of Pergolesi's style).

Finally, to round off the binary form, a re-scored and abbreviated version of the first section returns at bar 53. It omits bars 5–13 of the opening section, and concludes with a cadence figure (bar 65) that inverts the motif first heard in bar 2. The texture throughout most of the movement is melody-dominated **homophony**.

Stravinsky assigns Pergolesi's cello line to solo double bass until bar 52. After bar 52 the melody is shared with the trombone – that most unbaroque of solo timbres.

The original bass part is allocated to the orchestral double basses (except in bars 30–37, where it is taken by the trombone) but, as we shall see, it is often much altered. Following Baroque practice, Stravinsky supplies accompanying harmonies, but often in a way that no 18th-century musician would recognise!

> Melody-dominated homophony can also be described as 'melody and accompaniment'.

Pergolesi:

Stravinsky:

Stravinsky's doubling of the first phrase with trombone glissandi immediately sets the slap-stick tone of this movement. Rather more subtle is the way that the bass is changed to weaken the perfect cadence by omitting the dominant (C) in the second half of bar 4 – see *left*. Stravinsky then knocks the cadence into shape with a clout from a syncopated accent on the second quaver of bar 5. The detailed performing directions underline Stravinsky's humourous intentions – sudden changes in dynamics, exaggerated accents and special effects such as the trombone glissandi and the instruction for lower strings to play 'du talon' (at the heel of the bow) in order to produce a rough and rasping quality.

Another technique employed by Stravinsky could be described as 'melodic smudging'. Sometimes rather crudely referred to as 'Neo-classical wrong notes', the brassy effect in the following passage is actually one of extreme brilliance. Upward swoops in the second horn part (shown by diagonal lines) and plummeting octaves in the lower strings enliven the semiquaver slides of the melody:

Pergolesi

Stravinsky

Pergolesi ended the A section of his rounded binary form in a rather perfunctory fashion by repeating bars 14–17 to form bars 18–21. This is far too predictable for Stravinsky, who abandons the expected sequential repetition in bars 20–21 in favour of a tumbling glissando followed by an accented semiquaver ascent.

What happens after the repeat is a musical joke worthy of Haydn. The rushing strings have withered away to a solo double bass, whose solitary ascending scale of F major leads us back to the opening theme in the tonic for a *third* time (bars 22–23)! The bass, realising its ghastly mistake, then projects the scale up to the dominant (C) in its most stratospheric register, allowing Stravinsky to pick up the threads of Pergolesi's B section at bar 25. (In other words, to achieve this bit of fun, he has interpolated three extra bars, 22–24, into his source material.) But even though the solo bass is now in C major, the orchestral basses have been so won over by the idea of returning to the tonic, that they subvert the implied C-major cadence of the tune by sticking on F (see *right*).

Stravinsky's treatment of bars 30–37 can only be described as re-composition. Here is Pergolesi's original phrase for the first four of these bars – it ends in G minor and is then repeated sequentially a tone lower to end in F major:

Now look at these bars in NAM 7 and you will see that Stravinsky:

➢ Overlays bars 30–32 with repetitions of a C-major chord

➢ Cadences in G major, not G minor, in bar 33

➢ Employs a total silence on the first quaver of bar 33 to create a cheeky syncopated cadence on the next two quavers

➢ Smudges both chords of that cadence by including the tonic (G) in the D^7 chord, and then leaving the second oboe stuck on F♯ while everyone else is playing G major for the second chord.

The result is as topsy-turvy as the plot of the ballet. The rhythmic equivalent of 'melodic smudging' occurs in bars 38–45. The flutes double the bass melody three octaves higher, but in rhythmically different versions, producing a **heterophonic texture** (which is easier to see in the score than to hear on CD1). The weak-beat tonic pedal accompanying this section is also pure Stravinsky – at this point Pergolesi's bass replicates that starting in bar 6 (shown in the lower example *opposite*).

In the brief excursion to F minor in bars 46–49, Stravinsky's very high **tessitura** for the double bass has the effect of de-focusing the intonation, making the flat 3rd sound very blue. And, while the orchestral basses faithfully outline the original F–F–E–E bass line, the solo cello stays put on a tonic F, adding yet more to the bleary-eyed quality of this tantalisingly short interlude.

Cadences mark out the territory in tonal music and, as we have seen, Stravinsky ruthlessly undermines many of them in this movement. In bars 54–55 he omits both V and I in the bass and then even removes the key note from the tune in bar 55, leaving the ear to imagine the missing notes of the now non-existant cadence.

By changing Pergolesi's sequential bass in bar 59 (marked * *below*) Stravinsky anticipates the tonic and so weakens the effect of the cadence in bars 60–61; he also removes the dominant from that cadence, and rewrites the bass of bar 61 to make it less tonic-centred, thus de-stabilising the entire cadential progression:

The final cadence is singled-out for special treatment. By changing the penultimate bass note from C to A, Stravinsky transforms a standard baroque perfect cadence into a much weaker (and very skeletal) III–I progression. The Vivo simply stops, rather than coming to a convincing tonal conclusion.

Exercise 10

1. Which aspects of Stravinsky's instrumentation reflect 18th-century practice, and which do not?

2. Explain octave displacement and heterophonic texture, and give an example of each from NAM 7.

3. In bars 33–34 of the Sinfonia, show how Stravinsky divides the melody between two different soloists.

4. Compare bars 29–32 of the Gavotta with bars 25–28.

5. What is the **sounding pitch** of the first bass note in Variation I (bar 33, beat 1)?

6. Briefly list the features of NAM 7 which reveal that it is a work of the early 20th century.

Planet of the Apes: The Hunt (opening) (Goldsmith)

Context

The American composer Jerry Goldsmith (1929–2004) studied film music before working in radio and television. He wrote the music for a popular 1960s' television series called *Dr Kildare*, but he is chiefly remembered for some 200 film scores, including *Alien* and *Star Trek: The Motion Picture* (both 1979).

> NAM 44 (page 388)   CD4 Track 3
> Conducted by Jerry Goldsmith

Planet of the Apes (1968) centres on a group of American astronauts who become stranded on a remote planet. When they eventually stumble on life-supporting vegetation they also come face to face with a population of gorillas on horseback who, in this spectacular chase scene, succeed in capturing the humans.

> *Planet of the Apes* was remade in 2001 with a different cast, and a rather more conventional and, some have felt, less memorable score by Danny Elfman.

The harsh images and alien landscapes of the film are reflected in the modernist style of Goldsmith's music, some parts of which are very sparse. He reserves the full forces of his large orchestra for only the most dramatic scenes, of which 'The Hunt' is one of the most memorable. NAM 44 consists of just the first part of the complete cue, which in total consists of more than five minutes' worth of continuous music in the film.

> In film music, a cue is a more or less continuous passage of music designed for a particular point in the film.

The score is written for a large symphony orchestra, to which is added a number of unusual instruments. The electric harp and electric bass clarinet that Goldsmith specified are normal acoustic instruments equipped with pick-ups. These allow the low notes of the harp to be processed with reverberation and a special 'buzz' effect, and the squeaks from the bass clarinet reed to be amplified, simulating the excited chatter of the apes at bar 52. They are joined in this bar by the ram's horn (a Jewish religious instrument) and the fearsome sound of the ten-foot long Tibetan horn. Both are used to give musical expression to the frightening image of horse-riding gorillas in pursuit of humans.

Percussion instruments play an important role in developing and sustaining the drama of the chase, starting with the solo timpani notes on each downbeat of bars 1–8 and culminating in the climax at bar 52, where four percussionists are required.

As well as standard percussion (timpani, side drum, bass drum and xylophone) Goldsmith uses boo bams, timbales and friction drums (see *right*), plus a bass resin drum (a large drum with a shell made from a resin compound), a conga drum and a vibra-slap (a device that produces a chattering sound, like a rattlesnake). Notably absent are metallic percussion instruments such as the cymbals, triangle or glockenspiel, the composer preferring his wide range of drum colours plus the dry wooden sound of the xylophone to portray the fearful chase.

Although not a standard orchestral instrument, a piano introduces the main motif of the cue in octaves in bar 4, but when this is later developed into ostinato patterns (bars 11–22, 45–51 and 59–73) the piano is used mainly to articulate driving semiquaver rhythms. This percussive treatment of the piano is most evident in bars 84–91, where its syncopated and doubled major 7ths cut through a variety of other simultaneous riffs.

Throughout the score Goldsmith is very specific in the effects he requires – for example, wooden horn mutes in bar 10, felt mallets for the conga drum in bar 16 and **harmonics** for the violins in bars 68–73. Starting at bar 55, the trumpets are required to use plunger mutes – rubber suction cups that result in a very thin tone when held directly in front of the bell of a brass instrument. At the same time, second and third trombones have to combine this effect with flutter-tonguing (which involves rolling an 'r' while producing the notes).

Instruments are sometimes used at the extremes of their range, particularly to add to the tension of bars 55–58, where bassoon, double bassoon, first trombone, cellos and double basses are all very low, horns swoop to the top of their range, and violins, flutes and piccolo rush upwards to their own highest registers.

Another important aspect of Goldsmith's vivid orchestration is his tendency to score much of the more prominent material for wind or piano. He uses the strings for chordal accompaniments (as in bars 1–7), short links (bar 10), special effects (such as the inverted pedals above the riff in bars 11–21) and punctuating rhythmic patterns (bars 26, 30–31 and 42–44).

Instrumentation

The boo bam, or tamboo bamboo, comes from Trinidad. Tamboo is a corruption of *tambour* (French for a small drum). The instrument consists of a hollowed-out and tuned bamboo stem, sounding like a small tuned bongo drum. Timbales are cylindrical drums with metal shells that produce a powerful sound with very clear attack. Notes on a friction drum are produced by vibrating the skin with a dampened cloth or fingers, or by means of a cord that passes through the drum skin.

The orchestra on CD4 is not identified. Film soundtracks are often recorded by 'session musicians', who may include members of well-known orchestras as well as other professional musicians, who come together specifically to record the soundtrack.

When reading the score, note that:

➤ Parts marked E.H. are for English horn (cor anglais) and sound a perfect 5th lower than written

➤ Clarinets in B♭ sound a tone lower than written; the bass clarinet sounds an octave plus a tone (a major 9th) lower than written

➤ Horns in F sound a perfect 5th lower than written

➤ Trumpets in B♭ sound a tone lower than written

➤ Double basses and double bassoons sound an octave lower than written; piccolos sound an octave higher than written.

Listening guide

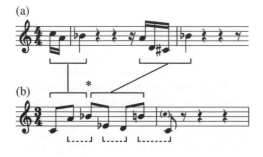

Structure in film music is usually dictated by the visual image. This can lead to a treatment that may seem 'bitty' and unconnected, but Goldsmith guards against this by manipulating and developing short **motifs** that permeate and unify the entire film score. Most notable is the piano figure in bar 4, transposed to the treble clef in example (b), *left*. It derives from the start of the twitchy main theme of the film, shown in (a), which is heard before the extract in NAM begins. The transformation is achieved through:

➤ Changes of metre and rhythm, so that two separate ideas in (a) become a continuous quaver motif in (b)

➤ Melodically inverting the first interval of (a) – a falling minor 3rd – so that it becomes a rising major 6th in (b)

➤ Transposing the second idea in (a) by a semitone to start on B♭

➤ Linking both ideas in (a) by making the second start on the last note of the first (the B♭ marked ✳ in (b)).

This transformation results in six different pitches of the 12-note chromatic scale being used in bar 4. Goldsmith repeats this motif in bar 8, but this time extends it to all 12 pitches of the chromatic scale, ending at the F♮ in bar 9. Just as (b) finished by returning to its starting note (C) in bar 5, so this extended version returns to its starting note by a further small extension (D♭–C). This final semitone is not padding – it reflects the semitones heard or suggested at the start of the motif, shown by dashed brackets in (b) and it also looks back to the **parallel-** and **contrary-motion** semitones heard in the wind and string parts of bars 1–7. The prominent use of semitones will prove to be another a unifying idea in NAM 44.

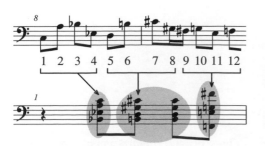

The 12 different pitches in bars 9–10 may remind you of a note row in **serial music**. They form the chords in bars 1–3 and 5–7 (see *left*) – a serial technique known as verticalisation. Fragments from the row are manipulated to form the woodwind motifs in bars 13–22, and material derived from the row appears in many other places. However, Goldsmith doesn't use such processes in the systematic way found in most serial music – he is selective in their application. In fact, while NAM 44 is chromatic and dissonant, it is not **atonal**. We can see this in the way that the note C is heard as an anchor at the start of each of the first eight bars. The piano motifs in bars 4–5 and 8–10 begin on (and return to) C and are transposed to start on G (left hand) from bar 11 onwards – much more like the tonic and dominant of tonal music than the atonality of most serial music.

Goldmith uses a bar of $\frac{5}{4}$ time (bar 10) to mark the end of the first section. The piano motif from bar 4 is then transposed to start on G and turned into a bass riff, above which the right hand's offbeat semiquavers increase the rhythmic drive. These form a double pedal on G and E. If you have any doubt that 'The Hunt' is tonal at heart, despite its dissonance, notice that it is now the note G that is heard as an anchor on every down-beat in bars 11–22.

Above the riff, a high sustained violin note crescendos into an offbeat semitone at the end of bar 13. This transformation of the semitone motif from a melodic to a harmonic idea is anticipated by lower strings and harp on the second beat of bar 13 (F–E). The violin crescendo is heard three times at different pitches, but the F–E anticipation remains constant each time. Now look at the tiny figure played by flutes, piccolo and xylophone in bars 13–14. Can you see how this is related? If not, look back at (a) *opposite*. Before we move on, take note of the conga part that enters in bar 16. This increases the rhythmic tension by introducing **cross-rhythms** of two main notes per bar (effectively ♩. ♩.) against the predominant three-beat pulse (♩ ♩ ♩) of triple time.

At bar 22, a bar of $\frac{5}{4}$ time again marks the end of the section. In the next bar the tonal centre moves to E♭ (there is no modulation), the piano motif transfers to electric harp and woodwind, and the trombones take over the crescendo on a sustained note (now lengthened by one beat) previously played by the violins. Notice how Goldsmith winds up the tension by adding a diminished 5th to the concluding semitone in bar 26 (G♭ in trombone 1 against C in trombone 3, while the second trombone's D♭ simultaneously supplies the semitone against C). Meanwhile, the strings play fragments of the wind parts from the start of the movement (bars 26, 30–31 and 35–37). You might also spot that the conga's cross-rhythm appears sporadically in double bass and side drum parts.

In bar 40 the idea of a long note leading to a semitonal dissonance is turned on its head – the opening note is reduced to a quaver and the offbeat semitone becomes the part of the motif that is sustained – with powerfully dissonant results. This idea forms the impetus for the repeated semitonal dissonances in the next four bars. Notice the melodic use of falling semitones in the trumpet figures and the strident cross-rhythms between strings and wind.

After this first climactic section (marked out again by changes in metre) the tonal centre returns to C at bar 45. The piano riff returns, transposed to provide its articulated pedal on C, and the crescendo motif returns in abbreviated form in the horns, also on C.

This brief respite leads to a second climax at bar 52, in which the array of ethnic and electric instruments enters as the full horror of the apes on horseback becomes clear. At the bottom of the texture the lowest instruments repeatedly rise from E♭ to E♮ against a sustained E♭, creating the most earth-shaking semitonal dissonance of all. In bar 54 four horns in unison join the bellowing ram's horn, swooping to their highest register. And then in bar 55 Goldsmith unleashes his full orchestral resources. Adding to the elements already noted, trumpets repeatedly climb to a piercingly high

Although Goldsmith doesn't employ such tonal devices as modulation or cadences, the use of third-related tonal centres (here C, G and E♭) is not a particularly modern aspect of NAM 44. Such 'tertiary relationships' were common in 19th-century music.

dissonance (it is a semitone, of course) on which they open their plunger mutes, the third trombone growls its flutter-tongued melodic semitones, and the upper woodwind and strings pile on scales and cross-rhythms, increasing the cacophony by decorating their repeated Gs with semitones above and below.

After this brilliantly scored climax the piano riff returns (bar 59) in almost its original version, based on G. However, there are some significant changes. Bars 11–21 were in triple metre, while now we are in quadruple metre. This results in two more quavers being added to the riff (G♯ and D♯ at the end of each bar). Why these two pitches? Because they both create semitonal dissonances against the G♮–E ostinato in the pianist's right hand.

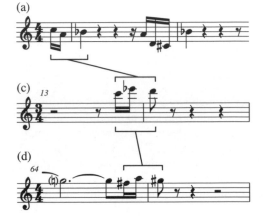

(a)

(c) 13

(d) 64

There are also changes in scoring. The violas double the pianist's right-hand ostinato, but in a rhythm of their own, and the cellos and basses also have a three-note ostinato figure. Can you see how it relates to the first three-note motif in the film's main theme, shown again in example (a), *left*?

In bars 63–64 Goldsmith transfers the crescendo on a sustained note to muted trumpets, but instead of terminating in a semitonal scrunch, it ends with an inversion of the three-note figure we noticed in bars 13–15, shown in example (c) – notice that this is doubled by the highly unusual combination of three piccolos in unison, as well as xylophone. This three-note figure was originally derived from the start of example (a), and in this new transformation we can see that it has morphed into yet another variant of the semitonal idea that has dominated this work – F♯ below the long G♮, ending with G♯ above it, as shown in example (d). Even when this in turn starts changing (bars 68–69) the omnipresent semitone is heard high above in violin harmonics (which sound two octaves above the printed black notes).

A very condensed version of the long-note-plus-semitone appears in the horn parts at bar 75, but now the urgent rhythms cease and for the first time Goldsmith uses predominately minim movement and mainly strings. They double the horns in bar 75, but sustain the terminating minor 2nd (the semitone between G and A♭). The following passage of two-part counterpoint for strings provides a brief relaxation in tension (although no respite from dissonance), designed to throw into relief the final section of the extract, which starts at bar 84. It is based on three simultaneous **ostinati**:

➤ A much more rhythmic variant of the semitone pattern, heard high in the flutes and piccolo.

➤ Repeated clashes of a minor 2nd and its inversion (a major 7th) between the B♭s and As heard high in the piano and violin parts. First violins play on the beat, against which second violins and piano have a syncopated cross-rhythm. The latter looks more complicated than it sounds – the pattern is shown without barring by the upper notes *left*. It is the rhythm first introduced on the conga drum in bar 16, but now in $\frac{4}{4}$ instead of $\frac{3}{4}$ time.

➤ A repeated quaver-based figure in the lower strings that begins and ends with falling semitones from B♭ to A.

Piano

Violin 2

Violin 1

From the end of bar 88, the string parts in this third ostinato are shadowed by bassoons in crotchets, and the violas start moving in contrary motion (shadowed in crotchets by the English horn).

The repetitive rhythms of the ostinati, the expansion of the third ostinato by contrary motion, the addition of more instruments and the accompanying side-drum rolls all increase the tension as the music moves towards the next section, signalled by a change of time signature in bar 91. There the score in NAM 44 comes to an end, but 'The Hunt' continues.

Exercise 11

1. What is the relationship between the parts for bass clarinet, first bassoon and horns in the first three notes of bar 10? Remember to take account of the transposing instruments.

2. What is the *sounding* pitch of the trumpet note in bar 63?

3. What term describes the relationship between all of the string and horn notes in bar 75 beat 1?

4. What special effect do the trumpets use in bars 71–73?

5. Compare the piano part in bars 11 and 59.

6. Explain the terms riff and cross-rhythm, giving examples of each from NAM 44.

7. What helps establish a sense of tonality in bars 1–22 of this work, and what helps to destabilise that sense of tonality?

Baris Melampahan (traditional Balinese)

NAM 59 is an extract of traditional music from Bali, one of the thousands of islands that form Indonesia. Although it is small (less than the size of the county of Devon), Bali has become famous as the most popular tourist destination in the region because of its tropical climate, coral reefs and rich cultural heritage in the visual and performing arts.

Baris is a traditional ritual dance performed by the young men of Bali to demonstrate their military skill. In its most ceremonial form it involves dressing in costumes that imitate armour, wearing distinctive conical hats and other adornments, and carrying weapons such as lances or shields. The movements of the dance emphasise firmness of step and skill in handling weapons.

In *Baris Melampahan* the participants use the *baris* style to enact a dramatic scene from an ancient epic poem. This usually leads up to the start of a stylised battle which signals the end of the dance. *Baris Melampahan* is a long and complex dance, and although NAM 59 is only a short excerpt (the complete piece lasts over 12 minutes) it is long enough to convey the regular pulse and rather warlike quality of this dance.

Although the dance is very ancient, the music in NAM 59 is in the relatively modern *gong kebyar* style, noted for sudden outbursts, vivid contrasts and brilliant sounds, all of which suit the stylised aggression of the dance-drama particularly well. On CD4 it is

Context

NAM 59 (page 522)   CD4 Track 17
Gong Kebyar de Sebatu

Baris Melampahan became almost extinct in the 20th century. It is only due to recent investment in Bali's heritage that traditional dances of this kind are starting to be learned once again, and presented at arts festivals and similar cutural events.

played by a *gong kebyar* ensemble from Sebatu, a village in the centre of Bali, famed for maintaining important local traditions in craftwork and music.

Gamelan   NAM 59 is played on a gamelan – an ensemble of instruments consisting mainly of tuned gongs and metallophones. They are made, tuned and kept together as a set, and are not separately owned by each musician as happens in most western ensembles. Gamelan players don't regard themselves as individuals when performing, but as musicians playing one common instrument.

Every gamelan is tuned in a slightly different way, using pitches that are not directly related to western scales. NAM 59 is **pentatonic**, using five notes (1, 2, 3, 5 and 6) from the seven-note pelog scale. This set of pitches is known as the *pelog selisir* mode, and is particularly associated with the instruments used in *gong kebyar*. The five pitches are shown at the head of the score but they can only be approximated in western notation – notes 1 and 5 are flatter than indicated, the others are slightly sharper by varying amounts.

In addition, a tradition in *gong kebyar* is to tune each pair of metallophones slightly differently, causing a beating effect called *ombak* when they play the same note. *Ombak* can clearly be heard in NAM 59, and helps give the music its shimmering quality.

Texture   The basis of the music is a 'core melody' called the *balungan*. The entire piece develops from this melodic outline, with instruments simultaneously performing different versions of the same melody. This type of texture is called **heterophony**.

The piece is punctuated by gong strokes to mark its main divisions. Between these the music is organised into four-beat groups, each called a *keteg* (rather like a bar). The whole rhythm cycle is known as a *gongan*.

Instruments   The various instruments are explained in the score, but it can be helpful to think of them as four groups, each with its own function that stays the same throughout:

➤ *Balungan* instruments play the main theme; they include one-octave metallophones and the *suling* (a quiet bamboo flute)

➤ Gongs divide the *gongan* into sections. The largest, which hangs from a frame and is called the *gong ageng*, marks the end of the *gongan*. Smaller gongs mark the fourth or eighth *keteg*, and the smallest ones, which are mounted horizontally over resonator boxes, outline the pulse

➤ *Panususan* instruments (larger metallophones that have bamboo resonators) decorate and embellish the theme

➤ Drums and cymbals, which add contrast, particularly in the loud *angsel* sections.

Structure   The excerpt consists of an introduction in free time performed on the *kendhang*. The player has a role similar to that of the master drummer in African music – he sets the tempo and cues features such as repeats and the starts of new sections.

The *ugal* then introduces the core melody, which is simultaneously outlined by the other *balungan* instruments. Drums, cymbals and *panususan* instruments enter for the loud *angsel* section, after which the music contines with alternations of (and variations on) these two patterns, between which the shorter sections marked 'kendhang accents' offer contrast by featuring mainly drums and the simpler versions of the core melody.

The musicians memorise the piece and don't play from scores, but the system of notation used in NAM 59 was developed around 1900 for study purposes. However, it is not easy to read without practice and you may find it easier to follow the music by listening for the main gong strokes. The rhythmic cycle of the *gongan* is particularly clear in this piece, since the four-beat groups in the *ketag* tend to dominate the texture and give a firm sense of pulse to the dance.

Nevertheless, the score reveals several important points about the music. Unlike western stave notation, accents occur at the end of each metrical group rather than on the first note. This can be seen most clearly at the end of each full system, where most instruments come together on note 6. It can also be seen in the position of the main notes of the core melody (1, 2, 5 and 6) which are all played at the *end* of a *keteg* by the *calung* (doubled by the *suling*).

Illustrations of *gong kebyar*, including pictures and sound files, can be found at http://hkusua.hku.hk/~gamelano/content.htm

Exercise 12

1. What is a metallophone?

2. Explain the term heterophony. Where do you first hear a heterophonic texture in NAM 59?

3. Explain how the function of the gongs differs from the function of *panususan* instruments such as the small metallophones.

4. What two features are heard at the end of every *gongan* in *Baris Melampahan*?

Sample questions

In Section B of the Unit 6 paper you will have to answer two questions (from a choice of three) on pieces from the Applied Music area of study. Here are three to use for practice.

You can write in continuous prose or short note form. You will be allowed to refer to an unmarked copy of NAM, and you should give the location of each specific feature that you mention. Aim to complete each question in 20 minutes.

(a) The aria from *Dido and Aeneas* (NAM 36, pages 356–358) is often described as 'Dido's Lament'. Identify the features of Purcell's music that help to create an intense sense of grief in this aria.

(b) Jerry Goldsmith was famous for the modern style of his music for *Planet of the Apes*. Identify features of NAM 44 (pages 388–408) that reveal a novel approach to tonality and orchestration.

(c) *Baris Melampahan*, as performed by the Gong Kebyar de Sebatu, is music to accompany a war-like dance. Identify the features in NAM 59 (pages 522–528) that make it suitable for this purpose.

Set works for 2011

If you are taking A2 Music in summer 2011, you have to study the seven pieces of instrumental music *below*, plus the five pieces of applied music in the section starting on page 103.

Instrumental music

The pieces for this area of study span musical periods from the end of the Renaissance to the middle of the last century:

1550		1600		1650		1700		1750		1800		1850		1900		1950		2000

Renaissance	Baroque	Classical	Romantic	Modern

Holborne
NAM 13
1599

Bach
NAM 21
1728

Haydn
NAM 2
1767

Brahms
NAM 18
1865

Ellington
NAM 49
1927

Shostakovich
NAM 25
1951

Davis
NAM 50
1954

Pavane 'The image of melancholy' and Galliard 'Ecce quam bonum' (Anthony Holborne)

Context and forces

NAM 13 (page 191)   CD2 Tracks 1–2
Rose Consort of Viols

One of the best ways to get to know NAM 13 is to play or sing it with a group of friends. It will suit various different combinations of performers, as the original publication indicates.

These two movements were first published in London in 1599, during the reign of Queen Elizabeth I, as part of a large collection of similar pieces by this composer. Little is known about Anthony Holborne, who died in 1602, but he was highly regarded as a writer of instrumental music by his contemporaries.

They are written for five soloists and were probably intended for performance in the home, either for the enjoyment of the players or for a small, educated audience. **Chamber music** of this type was known as consort music in Elizabethan England and was usually played on whatever instruments were available (as indicated in the note printed above the score). Music printing was still relatively new (and expensive) in the late Renaissance and so publishers frequently indicated that pieces could be played on a variety of instruments in order to maximise sales. The parts are not typical of any one particular instrument and are fairly limited in range.

On CD2 Holborne's pieces are played by a consort of viols of different sizes. These were bowed and fretted string instruments, held on the lap or between the knees. A consort of five viols was the most popular medium for the performance of chamber music at this time, but wind instruments (such as a consort of recorders) were also used.

The pavane was a moderately slow courtly dance in duple time, performed by couples in a stately, processional style. In contrast, the galliard was much more energetic and in triple time. The two dances were often paired in Renaissance music. However, while the pavane and galliard in NAM 13 were printed next to each other in the original publication, it is unlikely that they were intended as a matching pair – their keys, instrumental ranges, themes and descriptive titles are all different.

Although Holborne used dance forms for both movements, the dense **counterpoint**, which provides independent melodic interest for all five players, indicates that this is music for the ear rather than the feet.

Holborne added descriptive titles to a number of his dances, often of a seemingly private nature that is now sometimes unclear. Many of these, such as 'The image of melancholy', express sorrow and may reflect the grief of his patron, the Countess of Pembroke, who had lost three close family members in a single year. 'Ecce quam bonum' ('Behold how good a thing it is') is the Latin title of one of the Biblical psalms that she had famously adapted into English rhyming verse and presented to Queen Elizabeth in 1599.

'Ecce quam bonum' is also a quotation used by the poet Dante, to whose works Holborne refers in several other of his descriptive titles.

Structure

Like much dance music of the period, both movements consist of three independent sections (at the time known as 'strains'), each of which is repeated. We could summarise this as AA BB CC form. The symmetry of the galliard, in which each strain is eight bars long, with cadences every four bars in sections A and B, reflects the dance style of the movement. But the sections in the pavane are 16 + 17 + 26 bars, such irregularity being another indication that this is not music for dancing to.

Tonality

The pavane is in D major, with perfect cadences in the tonic at the end of the first and third strains, and in the dominant (A major) at the end of the middle strain. The tonal system of related major and minor keys was only just beginning to emerge in the late Renaissance, but here it is reinforced by a tonic **pedal** in bars 34–39 and a dominant pedal in bars 54–57. However, traces of older modality are evident in **false relations**, such as the G(♮) followed by G♯ in the outer parts of bar 13.

Today D minor is written with a key signature of one flat, but at this time it was usual to flatten the 6th degree of the minor scale (B♭ in this key) only where needed.

The galliard is in the key of D minor (see *right*). The first and last strains end with perfect cadences in D minor (both including a **tierce de Picardie**), while the second strain ends with a **phrygian cadence** (IVb–V) in the same key.

Melody and rhythm

The pavane starts with a dotted figure in the top part that descends by step from tonic to dominant. Holborne's contemporaries would easily have recognised this as a gesture frequently associated with grief in Elizabethan music – compare it with the start of the vocal melody in 'Flow my tears' (NAM 33).

The melodic writing is much like that found in vocal music of the period – mainly **conjunct**, with occasional small leaps. Wider leaps are generally followed by balancing stepwise movement in the opposite direction, as in the top part of the pavane, bars 34–37. The lowest part has more leaps than the others, because it is often providing the bass of chords whose roots are a 4th or a 5th apart.

Holborne captures the elegant style of a pavane through the use of simple minim- and crotchet-based rhythms, enlivened with a little discreet **syncopation** (as in the top part of bar 19).

The lively style of a galliard is conveyed in its first section through the use of dotted rhythms and two different types of syncopation. The first is caused by the off-beat entry of the dotted figure in the fourth voice down and occurs every time this rising figure enters (the second crotchet of bars 2, 5 and 6). The second is caused by temporarily switching from triple to duple metre, although without changing the time signature. There are clearly three minim beats ($\frac{3}{2}$ time) in each of the first two bars, but in bars 3 and 7 the metre changes to two dotted-minim beats, as found in $\frac{6}{4}$ time, emphasised by the change of chord halfway through these bars.

The rhythms in the second and third strains of the galliard are less busy, but are enlivened by the use of **hemiola** in bars 10–11 and 14–15, where the triple pulse becomes, without change of time signature, a count of 1–2, 1–2, 1–2, in each pair of bars. Hemiola is yet another type of syncopation and is characteristic of many triple-time dances written in the Renaissance and Baroque periods.

Texture   The pavane is written in five-part imitative counterpoint. A lack of rests means that the imitation is not always obvious. For example, the opening notes of the top part are imitated one minim later by the fourth part down. At the start of the second section this figure is adapted to make a longer motif, imitated by the second part down in bars 18–19. The third section begins with a scalic figure in the middle part that is an **inversion** of the initial 'melancholy' motif and that is imitated by all parts except the bass.

Despite an even greater scarcity of rests, the texture of the galliard is more varied, with pervasive imitation in sections A and C, and a largely **homophonic** central section.

Harmony   The majority of chords are root-position or first-inversion triads. Cadences at the end of strains are perfect, except in section B of the galliard, which is imperfect (or, more precisely, phrygian). The only on-the-beat discords are **suspensions**, often decorated as they resolve and sometimes overlapped with suspensions in other parts. In the example *left* you can see how the dissonant 7th between the outer parts at bar 4^1 is prepared (P), suspended (S), decorated (D) and resolved (R). As it resolves to C♯ the second part down starts a similar process with a note that is to form a 4th above the bass (regarded as a dissonant interval in Holborne's day) in bar 5.

Be aware that not all tied notes are suspensions: for example, those in bars 1 and 2 of the pavane do not form discords. There are only three suspensions in the galliard: can you find them?

The score   Notice that the third part down has an alto C clef, in which the middle line of the stave represents middle C. The first note of the pavane in this part is therefore A. Also be aware that the parts frequently cross each other: so, for example, the highest notes in bar 41 of the pavane are played by the middle part.

Upper three parts (bars 9–10)

Second part (bars 13–15)

In common with most music of the period, there are no performance directions, not even tempo or dynamic markings. However the performers on CD2 introduce variety by adding ornamentation when each of the sections is repeated, some of which is shown *left*. Decoration of this sort was an important performing convention at the time this music was written. Can you identify other places where the music is ornamented in the repeats?

Exercise 1

1. What is a false relation? Identify the location of a false relation in bars 17–33 of the pavane.

2. Name the harmonic device used in bars 54–57 of the pavane.

3. In bar 1 of the galliard, how does the music played by the fourth part down relate to the music played by the top part?

4. How does the top part in bar 22 of the galliard relate to the same part in the previous bar?

5. What are the main similarities and differences between the pavane and the galliard?

6. Which features of NAM 13 suggest that this was not music intended for actual dancing?

7. Which features of NAM 13 indicate that it dates from the late Renaissance?

Sarabande and Gigue from Partita in D (Bach)

Context

One of the most popular types of keyboard composition in the late Baroque period was a set of dance movements known as a suite. Like NAM 13, these works were not intended for actual dancing, but to be played at home, usually on the harpsichord (the most common keyboard instrument of the time).

> NAM 21 (page 249) CD2 Tracks 10–11
> András Schiff (piano)

The two dances in NAM 21 are the fifth and seventh movements of such a suite, published by Bach in 1728 under the Italian title of *partita*. On CD2 they are played on the piano rather than the harpsichord. Bach had a reputation as a great keyboard player and teacher in his day, but his compositions received little attention until scholars rediscovered his surviving works during the course of the 19th century. Now he is appreciated as one of the greatest composers of the late Baroque era.

The score

Performance directions are rare in music of the Baroque period and earlier, as we saw in the previous set work. There are no tempo markings because Bach could assume that musicians would know from experience that sarabandes are slow and gigues are fast.

The ∿ sign above the last beat of bars 1, 13 and 29 in the sarabande is an upper mordent and implies the rapid alternation of the printed note with the note above. The small C♯ on the first beat of bar 20 is an appoggiatura, played on the beat and then resolving to B. Baroque performers would frequently add their own ornaments, in accordance with the conventions of the time, especially when a passage was repeated. See how many ornaments you can hear in András Schiff's repeats on CD2, track 10.

Structure

As in most Baroque suites, the stylised dances in NAM 21 are in the same key (D major) and each is in **binary form**. This consists of two repeated sections, the first (in both movements) ending in the dominant (A major), and the second passing through other related keys before ending in the tonic. It is convenient to think of the structure as ‖:A:‖:B:‖, but note that the letters A and B don't represent contrasting themes: the initial musical ideas and mood are maintained throughout each movement, as they are in much Baroque music.

Sarabande

The history of the sarabande goes back nearly two centuries before Bach wrote this movement. By 1728 it had long ceased to be used for dancing and had become a stately, if not solemn, movement in triple time, often with a stress or long note on the second beat of the bar. Bach only fleetingly refers to this rhythmic feature (the minims in bars 1–2) before embarking on a series of complex rhythms that sound as free as an improvisation.

The first section consists of three four-bar phrases, the first ending with a perfect cadence in D, the second with an imperfect cadence in A major (the dominant), and the third with a perfect cadence in A major. Apart from G♯, accidentals indicate chromatic notes.

> If your copy of NAM has a tie between the first and second beats of bar 13, it is a misprint. The rhythm should be the same as in bars 1 and 29, and this is how it is played on CD2.

The longer second section begins with a reworking of material from the first section modulating through the relative minor (B minor, bars 19–20) and E minor (bars 21–24) before returning to the tonic key for the last ten bars (see *left*). In these final bars Bach recapitulates most of the first section: bars 29–30 are the same as bars 1–2 and bars 31–32 and 36–38 are slightly modified and transposed versions of bars 6–7 and 9–12 respectively. Movements like this that are rounded off with material from the opening section are appropriately described as being in **rounded binary form**.

$$\| {:}\ \underset{\text{I}}{\text{D}} - \underset{\text{V}}{\text{A}}\ {:} \| {:}\ \underset{\text{vi}}{\text{Bm}} - \underset{\text{ii}}{\text{Em}} - \underset{\text{I}}{\text{D}}\ {:} \|$$

The texture is mainly two-part, with melodic interest in the right hand and a supportive bass in the left, but is thicker at important structural moments (the beginning and ending of the two main sections plus the return of the first section at bar 29). Bach creates an extraordinary sense of unity by constructing almost the entire movement from motifs heard in its opening few bars.

Gigue

As was customary in Baroque suites Bach ends with a rollicking binary-form gigue in compound time. The unusual time signature of $\frac{9}{16}$ indicates nine semiquavers per bar, grouped into three very fast dotted-quaver beats.

> The French word gigue is related to the English word jig and is pronounced with a soft initial 'g': *zheeg*. For more about the jig, see page 114.

As in many Baroque gigues, the first 21 bars are in a **fugal** texture. The opening melody is known as the fugal subject and is followed by a fugal answer (the same tune as the subject, but transposed down a 4th) in the left hand of bars 7–12, above which the right-hand part is known as the countersubject. After a passage of free **counterpoint** the subject is stated again (left hand, bars 16–21). However, Bach does not intend this to be a full-blown, serious fugue. As early as bar 20 counterpoint gives way to a whirling semiquaver melody accompanied by two-part chords.

Bach introduces what sounds like another entry of the subject in bar 27, but it evaporates after only four beats. A version of the subject reappears in bars 36–41, but the opening arpeggio is turned upside down. The end of this version of the subject guides the music to the expected key of A major and the perfect cadence that marks the end of the first section.

The second section begins with a new fugal subject (bars 49–54). It is answered a 4th higher by the right hand in bars 55–60, beneath which Bach ingeniously fits a complete restatement of the first fugal subject from the start of the gigue. After this the second fugal subject is heard in modified form in bars 64–69 and 74–77 (the latter without its ending) and the final entry of the first fugal subject (without its first two bars) appears in the left hand of bars 86–89.

Unlike the sarabande, the two sections of the gigue are of equal length, but the tonal plan is similar – the first section ends in the dominant and the second passes through a variety of related keys before ending in the tonic.

Exercise 2

1. What form did Baroque composers most often use for each of the dances in a suite?

2. Name another feature that is normally common to all the dances in a Baroque suite.

3. On what instrument might Bach have played this music?

4. What sort of dance is (a) a sarabande, and (b) a gigue?

5. Look at the motif on beat 1 of bar 17 in the sarabande. How is this motif treated in beats 2 and 3 of that bar? Where was this motif *first* heard in the sarabande?

6. What happens at bar 29 in the sarabande?

7. What melodic feature is common to bar 2 of both dances in NAM 21?

8. Look at bar 3 of the gigue. How is this melody treated in bar 4? In which bars of the countersubject does Bach use the same technique?

9. Describe what is meant by a fugal texture.

Symphony No. 26, movement 1 (Haydn)

The type of music that most people associate with the orchestra is the three- or four-movement symphony. It first became popular in the Classical period and central to its development were the 104 (or more) symphonies of Joseph Haydn.

For much of his life Haydn was director of music to the Hungarian Prince Esterházy at a magnificent palace 50 kilometres south-east of Vienna. Here he had a small orchestra and every facility to perfect his craft. He said to his friend and biographer, Georg Griesinger,

> I could experiment, observe what created an impression and what weakened it, thus improving, adding, cutting away, and running risks. I was cut off from the world … and so I had to become original.

The title of Haydn's *Lamentatione* Symphony comes from an inscription on a manuscript of ancient plainsong melodies which reads *Passio et Lamentatio* (Passion and Lamentation). This is a reference to the passion of Christ, the story of which is told in the plainsong. Here is its opening:

Context and forces

NAM 2 (page 31)   CD1 Track 2
Academy of Ancient Music
Directed by Christopher Hogwood

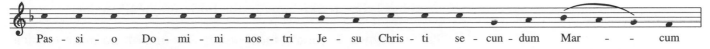

Pas - si - o   Do - mi - ni   nos - tri   Je - su   Chris - ti   se - cun - dum   Mar – – cum

Translation: The passion of our Lord
Jesus Christ according to Saint Mark

This chant was well known in Austria at the time when Haydn composed the *Lamentatione* Symphony since it was sung, with congregational participation, on the Tuesday of Holy Week (the week before Easter Sunday). It is therefore almost certain that the Esterházy household would instantly have recognised it when they heard it played on oboe and second violins in bars 17–38. The pitches shown in the example on the previous page exactly correspond with those in bars 17–21. The various words above the score refer to the plainsong passion. The *Evangelist* is the narrator of the story while the passages labelled *Christ* (bar 26) and *Jews* (bar 35) are direct speech in the original plainsong. When the Jews call for Jesus to be crucified, the semiquaver run (bar 37) and the following wild leaps (bars 40–41) suggest the excited cries of the crowd.

> Haydn used a wide range of material in his many symphonies; the idea of basing a movement on plainsong, as happens here, is highly unusual.

It is likely that the first performance took place on the Tuesday of Holy Week 1768, in the lavish concert hall of Prince Esterházy's new palace, where regular concerts were given on Tuesdays and Saturdays. These were primarily for the pleasure of the prince and his court, and to demonstrate his wealth and culture to his guests, but rather unusually they were also free for others to attend.

Haydn's orchestra at this time consisted of only about 13 players (although it was soon to grow in size). Usually there were two first violins, two second violins, and one player to each of the other parts. Although not shown in the score, a double bass would have joined the cello on the lowest part, sounding an octave lower than written. The Italian word 'cembalo' in bar 1 indicates that this part would also have been used by a harpsichordist as the basis for improvising chords to bolster the rather thin textures. This had been an almost universal practice in Baroque music, but it was to become unnecessary as orchestras grew larger during the Classical period.

The score The viola part is written with a C clef, but it is easy to follow since it doubles the cello part in unison or an octave higher for much of the movement. The horn parts are marked 'in D' – they sound a minor 7th lower than printed. These parts would have been played on natural horns, which have no valves and so can play only a limited selection of pitches.

Unlike the earlier set works we have studied, the score includes dynamics and articulation (slurs and staccato). The direction 'a 2' in the wind parts tells the two players to play the same notes.

Structure and tonality As you listen to the music see if you can follow its structure:

➢ An opening idea (called the first subject) in D minor followed by a contrasing second subject in F major (the plainsong theme starting in bar 17). These 44 bars are then repeated

➢ A middle section (bars 45–79) in a variety of keys

➢ A return of the opening section at bar 80. The first subject is extended by four bars and is again in D minor, but the second subject (bar 100) is now in the **tonic major** (D major).

This is known as **sonata form** and it was one of the main musical structures of the Classical period. The first section is called the exposition and introduces the idea of two contrasting keys. Most (but not all) sonata-form movements also use, as Haydn does here, contrasting melodies for the first and second subjects.

Can you hear how the music of the middle section sounds different and yet seems to fit into the whole? This is because it develops ideas from the exposition and is thus called the development. For instance, bars 45–52 are based on a variant of the syncopated idea from the first subject, transposed to F major and treated in sequence. The more extended sequences of bars 57–64 are based on a **circle of 5ths** (B♭–E–A–D–G–C♯–F♮–B♮ in the bass part on the first beat of each bar) that carry the music to the key of A minor. Above a dominant **pedal** in this key (bars 65–68) the oboes play a variant of Christ's plainsong (first heard at bar 26).

The final section recaps (with changes) the exposition and is therefore called the recapitulation. Compare bars 92–99 with bars 13–16 to see how Haydn modifies and extends the end of the first subject to allow the second subject to return in the tonic major (D major). The movement ends with a **coda** (bars 126–133) which is an expansion of bars 43–44 from the end of the exposition.

We can summarise this structure in the following diagram:

Bar numbers: 1	17	45	80	100	126
Exposition :‖		**Development**	**Recapitulation**		
1st subject 2nd subject			1st subject	2nd subject	Coda
Main keys: **D minor** **F major**		**Various**	**D minor**	**D major**	

Understanding how structure and tonality are closely linked in Classical music can help you to identify the location of an excerpt used in the exam. For instance, if you spot the start of Haydn's second subject in an excerpt, the key will tell you if it is from the exposition (F major) or the recapitulation (D major).

Other points

Haydn uses mainly root-position and first-inversion chords and, as in almost all music from the Classical period, chords I and $V^{(7)}$ play an important role in defining the main keys of the movement. However, listen for the dramatic use of **diminished-7th chords**, for example in bar 13 and (marked f) in bar 69.

While most of the chords are fairly simple, Haydn creates tension with the **syncopation** and **suspensions** that dominate the first subject. **Appoggiaturas** also play an important role in the melodic writing. Some are long and diatonic, such as the E in the melody of bar 16 against D in the bass, while others are short and chromatic, such as the F♯ in bars 40 and 42.

While the score may look complex, your ears should tell you that the textures are often thin (there are effectively only two parts in the first eight bars, for instance). This is because:

➤ The violas mostly double the bass part

➤ The two violin parts are sometimes in unison

➤ The two oboes and bassoon mainly double the string parts

➤ The horns are used sparingly until bar 99 because of the limited pitches available on natural horns – when the music moves into D major at bar 100 a greater number of notes can be used.

Haydn uses one of his favourite techniques at the start of the second subject (bar 26) – the theme in the oboes and second violins is simultaneously decorated by the first violins, creating a **heterophonic** texture between the two parts. In general, though, the texture is mainly one of melody-dominated **homophony**.

The dramatic style of this music, and of other Haydn symphonies of the same period, later became known as *Sturm und Drang* (Storm and Stress), a term borrowed from German literature of the time. It is characterised by many of the features present in this movement – minor keys, syncopation, sudden contrasts, wide leaps and bold diminished-7th chords.

Exercise 3

1. What is the pitch of the first note sounded by the horns? (Remember that they are transposing instruments.)

2. Describe the rhythm of the bass part in the first seven bars.

3. Name the cadence heard in bar 12.

4. Identify the chord in bar 71, and name the key and the type of cadence in bars 73^3–74^1.

5. Of which bars in the exposition are bars 74–79 a development?

6. Compare bars 100–104 with bars 17–21.

7. Why was Haydn able to make a significant contribution to the development of the symphony?

Piano Quintet in F minor, movement 3 (Brahms)

Context and forces

A piano quintet is a work for five solo instruments – often, as here, two violins, viola, cello and piano. It is therefore a type of chamber music, like NAM 13, but there the similarity ends. This is just one of four movements in a substantial work with a total length of around 45 minutes, not a short pair of dances.

> NAM 18 (page 231)   CD2 Track 7
> Guarneri Quartet with
> Peter Serkin (piano)

Brahms clearly intended this work for highly skilled performers: the movement in NAM is fast and technically demanding, and all of the instrumentalists are required to use a wide range, which is particularly evident in bars 146–157. Compare the string writing throughout with that in NAM 13.

Brahms was a Romantic composer with a great respect for earlier music. He studied Baroque counterpoint, helped to edit the music of Handel, and wrote variations on themes by Handel and Haydn. He was also strongly influenced by Beethoven's music, especially its intensive use of short motifs and its use of tonality to define the structure of large movements. These influences led some of his contemporaries unfairly to dismiss Brahms' music as conservative, but in other respects, such as lyrical melody and rich harmonies, he was as Romantic as most late 19th-century composers.

Brahms often revised his music many times before he was satisfied; this work was first composed as a string quintet in 1862 then rewritten for piano duet in 1864. NAM 18 is from the third version, composed in 1865 for piano quintet. It was first performed, probably privately, the following year, but its scale and difficulty suggest that Brahms intended the work for professional performance in small concert halls, for audiences who enjoy chamber music.

NAM 18 consists of a scherzo followed by a trio, after which the scherzo is repeated. This gives the overall movement a **ternary** (ABA) structure. A scherzo (meaning a joke) was a fast triple-time movement in the Classical period, but Brahms uses both $\frac{6}{8}$ and $\frac{2}{4}$ metres, and his style is much more serious than that found in the light and witty of scherzos of earlier times. A trio is a section which contrasts with the outer parts of a movement – such sections were once written for just three instruments, hence the name trio.

Structure

First, listen for the three themes of the scherzo:

Scherzo (bars 1–193[1])

The first is a rising melody in C minor and compound time. It is characterised by frequent syncopations and is *pianissimo*. Brahms' interest in counterpoint is evident at bar 9 where the theme played in octaves by violin and viola is imitated by the piano.

A (bars 1–12)

The second is a jerky melody (staccato notes separated by tiny rests) also in C minor but in simple time. It revolves obsessively around the dominant and is also played *pianissimo*.

B (bars 13–21)

The third is a very loud march-like theme in C major with strong second-beat accents (marked *forzando*). It is immediately repeated at bar 30, where Brahms adds variety by using the piano to imitate the strings two beats later (starting at the *ff* in bar 31).

C (bars 22–37)

> Notice how the motif in bars 22–24 is an **augmentation** of the semiquaver figure in bar 14, but now in the major.

There are then varied repeats of A (bars 38–56) and B (bars 57–67), modulating rapidly in the process. This leads to the distant key of Eb minor and the central section of the scherzo, in which counterpoint becomes the most important element.

Brahms uses a **fugal** texture in which the viola treats the first four bars of theme B as a fugue subject (bar 67). This is answered by the piano (right hand, bar 71). There are further entries of the subject starting in bars 76 (violin) and 84 (viola). These are combined with no fewer than three countersubjects, introduced as follows:

Fugato (bars 67–100)

1. Piano left hand, bar 67 (next heard in viola, bar 71)
2. Piano left hand, bar 71 (next heard in viola, bar 76)
3. Viola, bar 80 (next heard modified by violin 2, bar 84).

In bars 88–100 all of these melodies are fragmented into tiny cells in a complex five-part contrapuntal texture. The example *below* shows how, in the first-violin part, ten notes of the subject are detached (*a*), then just five notes (*b*), then three notes (*c*). Notice how the pitches rise sequentially until the climax at bar 100.

Can you spot similar processes at work in the cello and piano parts in the same passage? These fragments (and those of the viola from bar 92) are heard in a type of close imitation known as **stretto**.

The fragment marked *x* in the example on the previous page is a motif that will recur in various transformations, imparting a sense of unity to the structure.

After this central section Brahms repeats the themes of the first part in the following order:

B   (bars 100–109): E♭ minor
C   (bars 109–124): E♭ major (the relative major of C minor)
A   (bars 125–157): E♭ minor modulating to C minor
B   (bars 158–193): C minor (greatly extended to form a coda and with a **tierce de Picardie** in the C major chord at the end).

Violin 2 (bars 105–108)

Violin 1 (bars 109–112)

Shown *left* are just two of Brahms' transformations of motif *x*. The first is an **augmentation** of *x* (every note is four times longer than before). The second is in E♭ major instead of E♭ minor and an ornament has been added to its fifth beat (at *y*).

The entire work is unified by devices of this sort. The falling semitone that constantly appears in the final bars of the example on the previous page is heard prominently throughout the scherzo. Even the contrasting trio is linked with the scherzo by several common motifs, the most obvious being motif *y* (*left*) which becomes an integral part of its main melody (bars 197 and 199).

Trio (bars 193²–261)   The trio is in ternary form:

A   Bars 193–225: This section begins with a broad 16-bar melody in C major that modulates to B major in the last five bars. It is introduced by piano and then repeated by strings, and strongly contrasts with the episodic nature and contrapuntal textures of the scherzo.

B   Bars 225–241: Legato melody with staccato bass; in bars 233–241 these parts are then reversed – melody in the bass with staccato accompaniment above. The harmony is chromatic but anchored to C major by a dominant pedal (on G) whose triplets form **cross-rhythms** against the quavers in the other parts.

A   Bars 242–261: The first 11 bars of the melody from the first section return, in a dark texture in which all instruments are in a low **tessitura**. This leads to a plagal cadence in C (bars 253–254) and a tonic pedal (bars 254–261).

The performers are then instructed to repeat the scherzo – *Scherzo da Capo sin al Fine*, meaning repeat the scherzo as far as the word *Fine* (the end).

Other points   Apart from the bold, rising theme at the start, Brahms' melodic material is based mainly on motifs of a narrow range which are manipulated in many different ways, as we have seen. His textures are equally varied, ranging from the **monophonic** opening to the fugal texture starting in bar 67. Question 4 in the next exercise invites you to identify some other textures for yourself.

One of the hallmarks of the Romantic style is the use of chromatic harmony. Even in the first phrase Brahms gradually builds up the notes of an **augmented-6th** chord (Ab–C–Eb–F♯) that resolves to chord V in the second half of bar 6 over a continuing tonic pedal in the cello part. Pedal points also play an important role in the trio, which begins and ends over a tonic pedal on C (bars 194–201 and 249^2–261). The chromatic writing of its entire central section (bars 226–241) is underpinned by a dominant pedal on G, which starts in the piano and then transfers to the cello in bar 233.

But occasionally, Brahms' interest in early music seems to surface. For example, the root-position triads in bars 18–21 are given a modal colour by the minor version of chord V (bar 19^2), and the cadence in bar 21 features chord V without a 3rd, a feature often found in Renaissance music.

Brahms' preference for the dark sound of Eb minor as a secondary key, rather than the simple relative major of C minor (Eb major) introduces a more complex type of tonal relationship than we saw in the *Lamentatione* symphony, although Brahms slips from the tonic minor to tonic major (C major in bars 22–29), just as Haydn did at bar 100 in NAM 2.

Brahms establishes each key in the movement with clear cadences, and the pedal points also help to reinforce the tonal structure. However, notice that most sections end with an imperfect cadence to project the music forward, rather than with a decisive perfect cadence to punctuate the onward flow.

Exercise 4

1. What in the music suggests that this movement was written to be played by professional performers in the concert hall rather than by amateurs at home?

2. Describe some of the ways in which the main themes of the scherzo (up to bar 193) are contrasted.

3. In bars 18^2–20^1 the first violinist is required to use **double-stopping**. What does this mean?

4. Look at the texture in bars 15–17, 57–59 and 88–90. Use an appropriate word or phrase to describe each of these textures.

5. Name the harmonic device used in the bass part of bars 53–56.

6. How is the trio contrasted with the scherzo?

Black and Tan Fantasy
(Duke Ellington and Bubber Miley)

Duke Ellington is one of the few major figures in jazz whose reputation rests more on his compositions and arrangements than his work as a performer. In 1924 he took over the leadership of a small jazz band in New York which he expanded in size and which in 1927 was awarded a contract to play at the Cotton Club, one of the city's leading nightclubs and a venue for frequent radio broadcasts. Although located in the heart of the black community of Harlem it catered for an entirely white audience, who came to see

Context

NAM 49 (page 465)   CD4 Track 8
Duke Ellington and his orchestra

floorshows based on highly stereotyped ideas of African culture. To accompany these, Ellington developed what is known as his jungle style, featuring heavy drums, dark saxophone textures and rough, growling brass sounds, all evident in the *Black and Tan Fantasy*, first recorded in 1927.

Listen to the recording and make sure you can identify the three main sections of the orchestra: reeds (saxophones and clarinet), brass (trumpets and trombone) and a rhythm section of piano, banjo, drums and bass. Collective improvisation is difficult to achieve in a band of ten players and so written arrangements became increasingly common as jazz groups grew larger. Ellington worked closely with his band, adapting his arrangements to the individual talents of its members and leaving space for their individual solos. He often involved members of the band in the arrangement, as in the *Black and Tan Fantasy*, which was a collaboration between Ellington and his lead trumpeter, Bubber Miley.

Black and Tan

NAM 49 has a title that is unusually full of meaning. 'Black and Tan' refers to the venues in Harlem, such as the Cotton Club where Ellington worked, in which black and white people came together, although in a very segregated way (audiences were white, staff were black). A fantasy is a work in which the composer follows his own fancy, rather than a set form, but here Ellington is using the word in its everyday sense to express his own fantasy that racial integration might one day be possible. This duality of meaning is reflected in two unusual aspects of the work, both of which refer to the social commentary implied by the title:

Bars		
1–12	*Tutti*	12-bar blues (B♭ minor)
13–28	Sax	16 bars (B♭ major)
29–52	Trumpet	12-bar blues (B♭ major)
		12-bar blues (B♭ major)
53–64	Piano	12-bar blues (B♭ major)
65–75	Trombone	12-bar blues (B♭ major)
76–86	Trumpet	start of a 12-bar blues (B♭ major), interrupted after seven bars by a modulation to …
87–90	*Tutti*	Coda (B♭ minor)

➢ The opening 12-bar blues (suggesting black-American music) in B♭ minor is immediately followed by a contrasting section of 16 bars in B♭ major (see *left*) that features chromatic harmony – a phrase structure and harmonic style more associated with European music

➢ The first blues chorus is an adaptation of a popular ballad that was familiar to both black and white audiences of the day, and the last chorus is interrupted by a coda that offers a pessimistic final comment by quoting from Chopin's *Funeral March*.

The last of these two quotations is as familiar to audiences today as it was in Ellington's time, but the first requires explanation. The opening 12 bars of NAM 49 are an adaptation of the chorus of *The Holy City*, an immensely popular song by the white composer Stephen Adams. Ellington's lead trumpeter, Bubber Miley, recalled it as a 'spiritual' sung by his mother – which in a sense it was, because black Americans identified with the song's dream of a new Jerusalem, where there would be no more oppression. The following example shows the relationship between the two melodies:

The last three bars of Adams' tune (not shown in the example) are more freely adapted but remain recognisable in outline. To expand the eight-bar melody to a 12-bar blues structure, the first four bars are spread over eight bars, but Adams' simple harmony needs few changes except – significantly – it has been darkened by being played in the minor mode in *Black and Tan*. Perhaps this is a bleak realisation that the new Jerusalem is just a mirage? As a result of this transformation, the bright major 3rd of B♭ major (D) becomes a much more blues-like minor 3rd (D♭). Its 'blue' quality is heightened with **pitch bends** in bars 3 and 7, and in both cases the D♭ falls to B♭, producing the falling minor 3rd that is one of the most characteristic features of a blues melody.

Ellington uses one of the common structures in jazz, known as a head arrangement. This is based on a harmonised theme known as the head because it is provides the pattern of chords (known as the changes) that the players must keep in their heads as the basis for improvisation. The changes are then repeated by the rhythm section, while a series of soloists improvise new melodies to fit the harmonies. Each repeat of the chord pattern is known as a **chorus**. At the end there is a section for everyone (*tutti*) which may be a repeat of the theme and/or a coda.

The arrangement

In NAM 49 Ellington adopts the most common of all changes, the 12-bar blues, and he uses the type of head arrangement we have described, apart from the two exceptions noted in the bullet points *opposite*. The 12-bar blues progression is the common element in the choruses, but the trombonist makes occasional references to the theme, such as the fall from tonic to dominant in bar 65, and the cadential pattern in bar 75, while Ellington seems more attracted to the chromatic style of the second section in his own solo.

The muted trumpet melody is accompanied mainly in parallel 6ths by clarinet and trombone, while the rhythm section provides four accented beats a bar, sometimes in-filled by the piano. The bass outlines the root and 5th of each chord in steady crotchets. The head is **diatonic** (apart from a passing D♮) and its minor-key mood is severe, with narrow instrumental ranges, mournful **pitch bends** and no display of virtuosity. The firmly-accented pulse negates the legato style of the ballad on which the music is based.

The head (*tutti*)
Bars 1–12

A complete change of mood is achieved with a transition to the major mode, 'western' chromatic harmonies that complement the 'western' 16-bar structure, and the mellifluous tone of the saxophone. The wide **vibrato** and almost constant use of portamento (gliding between notes) in this solo are characteristic of saxophone playing in the early 20th century.

16-bar alto sax solo
Bars 13–28

The difference in harmonic style is just as significant, including a chromatic **substitution chord** ($G♭^7$ instead of F^7 in bars 13–14 and 21–22) and a rapid **cycle of 5ths** in bars 19–20. The solo is also rhythmically more complex than the head, particularly in its use of cross-phrasing (the patterns of three quavers that cross the usual divisions of beats and bar-lines in bars 17–18 and 25–26). The first eight bars of this section are given a varied repeat in bars 21–28, still with an accompaniment of chords on low reeds.

The style of writing in the previous two sections would have required notated parts rather than improvisation. But from bar 29 until bar 84 Ellington makes provision for improvised solos that each act as a showcase for the talents of his principal players.

Double chorus: trumpet solo
Bars 29–52

> A plunger mute looks like the rubber suction cup at the end of a plumber's plunger. It results in a very thin tone when held directly in front of the bell of a brass instrument.

At bar 29 the blues changes return and Ellington's co-writer, lead trumpeter Bubber Miley, takes two consecutive choruses (24 bars). Virtuosity immediately comes to the fore with his slide up to a top Bb, held for four bars. Much of the rest of the solo features Miley's rhythmic freedom as an improviser, which is thrown into relief by the stark accompaniment from the rhythm section. His melodic style is characterised by frequent blue notes and slides, as well as by his use of a plunger mute and the growling effects that are such a feature of Ellington's jungle style.

The growl (also used later in the trombone solo) involved using a small straight mute inserted into the bell of the instrument. The sound was then produced by shaping the mouth cavity to amplify a gargling from the throat while producing the required pitch with the lips and valves in the usual way. A plunger mute was also used to modify the sound. It can be held close to the bell to suppress the sound, as in bars 29–32, or moved further away for a more open sound, as in bar 33. Listen carefully for the frequent transitions between different positions of the mute. The reference to straight quavers in bar 45 means that these notes are not swung.

The backing remains mainly simple and triadic, harmonic interest arising from the interaction of the improvisation against the chords of the 12-bar blues. However, 7ths are sometimes added (bars 32 and 33) and chord substitutions start to appear – for instance, ii^7 (Cm^7) instead of V in bars 37 and 49.

Piano solo
Bars 52–64

Ellington enters during the last note of the trumpet solo in bar 52, starting his piano solo with a long **anacrusis** (know as a 'pick-up' in jazz) to avoid losing momentum. This section forms a **break** (an unaccompanied solo) and the absence of other instruments allows Ellington much greater freedom with the blues harmony. Chord subsitutions can thus become much more adventurous, including:

➢ **Secondary dominant chords** (C^7–F^7–Bb^7 in bars 54–55, leading to Eb in bar 56 and thus forming a short **circle of 5ths**)

➢ A **diminished-7th** chord in bar 58

➢ A longer circle-of-5ths progression in bars 59^3–63.

Ellington plays in a style known as stride bass because of the wide leaps between bass notes and chords in the left hand (seen also in in NAM 48, page 463). The right hand is equally athletic, with more wide leaps and rapid decoration (bar 61). Between them, both hands cover a very wide range of the keyboard.

Trombone solo
Bars 65–76

The rhythm section and jungle style return for Joe Nanton's solo (the band nicknamed him 'Tricky Sam' because of his dexterity in juggling both the trombone slide and plunger mute). Like Bubber Miley he uses two mutes, a small trumpet mute placed in the bell of the trombone and a plunger mute held in the hand. He plays in the trombone's highest range and, with the plunger held close to the bell, produces an almost trumpet-like tone at the start. The plunger is moved away from the bell for the growl in bar 67, and this is followed by the characterstic 'wah-wah' sound as the mute is then moved in front of the bell and away again.

One of Nanton's most famous effects occurs in bars 72–73. Known popularly as a 'horse whinny', it begins with an upward *glissando* produced by increasing lip pressure without moving the slide. It is followed by a long downward *glissando* produced by jagged movements of the slide to introduce ripples as the pitch descends.

In many head arrangements, each soloist seems to try to outdo the previous one in virtuoso technique. In this, his second solo, Miley focuses on fast lip trills and the brilliant articulation of rapidly repeated pitches. However, this chorus is brought to a premature end by the unexpected entry of the reeds in bar 84. A series of secondary dominants ($G^{7(\flat9)}$, C^7 and F^7) leads to a return of B♭ minor and the quotation from Chopin's funereal march in the last four bars. The gloom of this unhappy little coda is enhanced by a type of ending rarely heard in jazz – a massive *rallentando* over repeated plagal cadences.

Trumpet solo and coda
Bars 76–90

Exercise 5

1. Name three features of Ellington's 'jungle style'.

2. What is meant by the term 'the changes' in jazz? What forms the changes in this work?

3. Compare the melodic ranges used in the first chorus and coda with the melodic ranges used in the other choruses.

4. Explain the terms 'subsitution chord' and 'pick-up'.

5. What is the meaning of 'straight ♪s' in bar 45?

6. Give one example of each of the following type of blue note in bars 29–52: (i) a flat 3rd, (ii) a flat 5th, and (iii) a flat 7th.

7. Where is a circle of 5ths used after bar 64?

8. Comment on the role played by the rhythm section in NAM 49.

Prelude and Fugue in A (Shostakovich)

Dmitri Shostakovich was a Russian who periodically suffered harsh criticism from the Soviet state for the modernist style of his compositions. While it is true that *some* of his music, like that of many of his contemporaries, is dissonant, his works are actually very diverse in style. They reveal such influences as Russian folk music, jazz and (in the case of NAM 25) the Baroque traditions of Bach. Indeed, his music for *The Gadfly* (1955) includes one of the most popular and romantic melodies ever written for film.

In 1950 Shostakovich visited Leipzig in East Germany to serve on the jury of an international piano competition held to commemorate the 200th anniversary of Bach's death. The winner was the pianist

Context

NAM 25 (page 262) CD2 Tracks 17–18
Tatiana Nikolayeva (piano)

who performs NAM 25 on CD2. She so impressed Shostakovich with her playing of Bach's 48 Preludes and Fugues (some of which had been composed in Leipzig) that Shostakovich set to work on his own preludes and fugues for keyboard, completing a set of 24 (one prelude and one fugue in each of the 12 major and minor keys) the following year.

The idea of modelling new music on 18th-century styles had been popular since the early years of the 20th century, especially among Russian composers. Such works are described as **Neoclassical**, although it was often Baroque ideas rather than Classical ones that were recycled.

> Stravinsky's *Pulcinella* (NAM 7) is also Neoclassical, although it consists of *arrangements* of Baroque pieces in a 20th-century style rather than new music that evokes the techniques and spirit of the Baroque, as in NAM 25.

Prelude

The prelude (the word simply means an introductory movement) reflects the style of the Prelude in A major in Book 2 of Bach's '48'. Both are in $\frac{12}{8}$, largely **diatonic** and make extensive use of **pedal** points. Shostakovich uses these pedals to define his very slowly changing chords: I in bars 1–3, VI in bars 4–5, and V in bars 8–9.

However Shostakovich also makes use of some very un-Bachian techniques. Gently dissonant notes are freely introduced without preparation and, while the chords in bars 6–8 remind us of a series of Baroque suspensions, their layout does not.

In bar 10 the mainly diatonic tonality is suddenly disturbed by the appearance of a chord of C major over the continuing dominant pedal. It is related to A major only by the common note E (the pedal note itself).

Equally un-Baroque is the style of the chromatic writing starting in bar 13 and even more remote from A major is the plunge into A♭ major in bars 19–22. However, while the chromatic and tonally ambiguous style of bars 13–22 form a contrasting section, like most Baroque movements the melodic material is mainly derived from the opening bars.

> The ternary form of the prelude arises from Shostakovich's tonal scheme:
>
> A   Bars 1–12 Mainly diatonic in the key of A major
> B   Bars 13–22 Tonally ambiguous chromatic harmony
> A¹ Bars 23–28 Entirely diatonic in the key of A major

To complete the **ternary form** (ABA) of the prelude, Shostakovich slips back into A major with no fuss at bar 23 and ends with an innocent version of a plagal cadence in the upper range of the piano.

Fugue (first section)
Bars 1–40

We have already seen that Bach's gigue in NAM 21 opens with a fugal texture. This movement, which is a complete three-voice fugue, begins in a similar way:

➤ The subject is heard in bars 1–4

➤ The answer (which is always a transposition of the subject in a fugue) is heard in the left hand of bars 5–8, while at the same time the right hand plays the countersubject.

What is totally unlike Bach, though, is the triadic nature of these melodies. The subject is entirely constructed from the notes of chord I. When transposed down a 4th to form the answer, all of the notes come from chord V, as do the notes of the countersubject which fits with it. These ideas are extended into bars 9–10 (each containing a IV–Ib progression), after which the subject returns in the tonic (bar 11, lowest part), accompanied by the countersubject (middle part) and a second countersubject (top part).

These first 14 bars form the exposition of the fugue and establish a serene pattern in which the **harmonic rhythm** is generally very slow – chords last for four bars whenever the subject or answer is stated – and dissonance is totally avoided.

Bars 15–20 form the first of several episodes derived from motifs in the exposition but in which the harmonic rhythm is faster – here there are mainly two chords per bar and new chords (IIIb and IIb) are added to the diet of three primary triads heard so far.

This episode is followed at bar 21 by the first of several middle entries of the subject and countersubjects in which the parts are contrapuntally inverted – the subject is now in the middle part, the first countersubject (slightly varied) in the top part, and the second countersubject in the bass. This is followed by the answer, which starts in the middle part of bar 25 (accompanied by the countersubject in the bass) and then transfers to the top part after three crotchet beats.

> The only modifications to the main countersubject are those needed to keep the notes within the span of the pianist's hand, as in bars 21–24, or where the subject and countersubject swap hands (shown by the dashed line in the middle of bar 47).

The first section of the fugue ends with another episode (bars 29–32) followed by a further set of fugal entries (bars 33–40), entirely in two-part counterpoint (a texture that Shostakovich maintains right through to bar 50). The whole of the first section is entirely diatonic and never leaves the key of A major.

Fugue (second section)
Bars 41–61

The second section, starting in bar 41, follows a similar pattern, with episodes in bars 41–46 and 55–57 between the sets of fugal entries in bars 47–54 and 58–61. The last of these are called 'false entries' because each consists of an incomplete statement of the subject, coming in at one-bar intervals in the two lowest parts.

The tonal centres are much more fluid in this section, moving from A to F major, and then Bb major, before a series of unrelated chords in bars 58–61 leads back towards A major. In a movement that contains no dissonance, this side-stepping to unrelated chords or keys is Shostakovich's main way of creating tension.

Fugue (closing section)
Bars 62–99

The final section begins with a complete restatement of the subject and main countersubject (bars 62–65) above a dominant pedal that continues into a final episode (bars 66–69). In bar 70 Shostakovich begins a **stretto** – a fugal passage in which entries of the subject are telescoped together so that they come closer together than before. These are incomplete entries, but the full subject appears again in the top part of bars 79–82, after which frequent references to its opening notes are supported by long bass notes that refer back to the pitches that were pedal notes in the prelude (A, F♯, E and C♯), all asserting the A-major tonality. The last four bars consist of a final statement of the fugue subject over sustained tonic harmony.

Exercise 6

1. What do you understand is meant by the term Neoclassical?

2. List some of the features in NAM 25 that you would *not* find in a prelude and fugue by Bach.

3. What is the form of the prelude?

4. Explain the difference between the subject and the answer in a fugue.

5. Explain the following features of a fugue: (i) an episode, (ii) a false entry and (iii) a stretto.

6. In the fugue, give the bar numbers of (i) a section that uses an entirely two-part texture, and (ii) a passage of two-part counterpoint heard over an eight-bar dominant pedal.

Four (performed by Miles Davis)

Context

NAM 50 (page 468)   CD4 Track 9
The Miles Davis Quintet

On page 92 we noted that the increasing size of jazz bands in the 1920s led to composed arrangements replacing improvisation in the *tutti* sections of a piece. This trend continued in the age of the big swing bands of the 1930s, but by the early 1940s some jazz musicians were finding swing too limiting, and developed a new style called bebop or simply bop. Played by a small combination of musicians (known in jazz as a 'combo'), bebop was music for listening rather than dancing. Its main features can all be heard in *Four* (which dates from 1954):

➢ Fast, driving rhythms

➢ Fragmented melodies with phrases of irregular lengths

➢ Complex, dissonant harmonies

➢ Much solo improvisation, accompanied by a rhythm section of piano, bass and drums.

Gramophone records were limited to just a few minutes of continuous music until the invention of the LP (long-playing) vinyl record in 1948. The LP, offering some 20 minutes of playing time per side, enabled jazz musicians from the 1950s onwards to record the much longer structures they were used to improvising in live performances.

Four was composed for Miles Davis by the jazz saxophonist Eddie Vinson, and was first recorded by the Miles Davis Quartet in 1954. This version for four players (hence the title) lacked the saxophone doubling heard in NAM 50, which consists of the first two minutes of a recording from a live concert given in New York in 1964, at which the complete performance lasted over six minutes. On other occasions Davis recorded extended versions of the work that could last as long as 15 minutes. So NAM 50 doesn't represent a definitive version of *Four* – it is simply the way in which Davis felt moved to interpret the piece on the evening of 12 February 1964.

Instrumentation and texture

The tenor saxophone has no independent material and plays only in the head, where it simply doubles the trumpet an octave lower. This is because the work was originally a quartet (and essentially remains so here), although it also indicates that the head was a composed element, even though the choruses are improvised.

The type of piano playing in the extract is known as **comping** – a jazz term derived from 'accompanying' and indicating a chordal, non-melodic style of accompaniment. The part is rhythmically varied – often syncopated and staccato – but it doesn't have a solo role in this excerpt, which is essentially a showcase for the talents of Miles Davis. If you compare the piano chords in the head with the basic harmonies printed over the trumpet stave, you will see how musicians in cool jazz freely add 'upper extensions' (9ths, 11ths and 13ths) to triads and 7th chords, as well as embroidering basic progressions with chromatic notes and additional chords.

The △ symbol in some of the chord labels above the piano part indicates that the chord includes a *major* 7th above the root.

The bass part is played **pizzicato** on a double bass. After the composed head it maintains a **walking bass** pattern that elaborates the harmonies of the changes. Occasionally the bassist explicitly outlines the harmony with a simple broken-chord pattern, such as the G-minor triad in bars 1.9–1.10^2, but more commonly harmony notes are filled in with passing notes and other forms of melodic decoration to produce a more conjunct line. Like Miles Davis, the bassist focuses on higher chord extensions rather than the chord itself, as in bar 1.8, where E♭ is the 9th, and B♭ the minor 13th, of D♭^{7} – he entirely avoids the root and 3rd of the chord in this bar. He also occasionally plays entirely 'away from the chord', as in bar 1.4 where the notes are a semitone below, and a tone and semitone above, the root of the chord – the root itself is avoided.

The drummer sets the tempo in his introductory solo, after which he plays a supportive role, maintaining a steady beat (played with sticks on a ride cymbal), and punctuating melodic phrases with short fills and rim shots on the snare drum.

Miles Davis uses a range of extended instrumental techniques in his playing, including:

> A rim shot is an accented note produced by striking the rim and the head of the snare drum simultaneously with the same stick, or by positioning one stick with its tip on the drum head and its shaft on the rim, and then striking it with the other stick.

➤ A deliberately split note (the second note in bar H31, two bars before the start of the first chorus)

➤ A short downward slide called a fall-off (shown by the wavy line in bar 1.15)

➤ **Pitch bend** (bars 1.19–1.20)

➤ A ghost note (the bracketed note in bar 2.1) – a deliberately weak, almost inaudible note

➤ A quarter tone (half of a semitone, indicated by the arrow on the ♮ sign in bar 2.31)

➤ Half-valving (partially opening a valve to produce a note of thin tone and uncertain pitch, indicated by '½v.' and the diamond-shaped notes in bar 3.32, and in this case having the effect of ornamenting the main note).

The texture of *Four* is melody-dominated homophony, with a tune in the trumpet part and an accompaniment provided by a walking bass part and piano chords. Variety is provided by the doubling of the melody at the lower octave by tenor saxophone during the head, and by occasional changes in the **tessitura** of the parts, such as the high bass part (indicated by an ottava sign) starting in bar 1.21 and the very high trumpet part at the start of the third chorus.

Structure

Four is, like the *Black and Tan Fantasy*, a head arrangement – essentially a type of variation form. After the drum introduction the theme is announced by the trumpet. The chords of the theme (the changes) are then repeated in each 32-bar chorus, while Davis improvises new material to fit the harmonies. The head is notated as a 16-bar repeated section (with different first- and second-time endings) but all 32 bars are notated in full in the choruses, since there are too many variations in the repeated sections for repeat signs to be used.

Harmony and tonality

Four is in E♭ major throughout and its underlying chord sequence, which is more clearly seen in the choruses than in the head, is actually fairly simple. In the following table the shaded row shows the basic chord progression, with added notes and chromaticisms omitted. The other rows show the actual chords used in the three choruses:

Bar numbers	1 / 17	2 / 18	3 / 19	4 / 20	5 / 21	6 / 22	7 / 23	8 / 24	9 / 25	10 / 26	11 / 27	12 / 28	13 / 29	14 / 30	15 / 31	16 / 32
E♭ major	I			IV	ii		IV	♭vii	iii		ii	V	iii		ii	V
Chorus 1	E♭		E♭m^7	A♭^{7}	Fm^7		A♭m^7	D♭^{7}	Gm^7		Fm^7	B♭^{7}	Gm^7		Fm^7	B♭^{7}
	E♭		E♭m^7	A♭^{7}	Fm^7		A♭m^7	D♭^{7}	E♭	C^7	Fm^7	B♭^{7}	E♭	B♭^{7}	E♭	B♭^{7}
Chorus 2	E♭		E♭m^7		Fm^7		A♭m^7		Gm^7		Fm^7	B♭^{7}	Gm^7		Fm^7	B♭^{7}
	E♭		E♭m^7		Fm^7		A♭m^7		E♭	C^7	Fm^7	B♭^{7}	E♭	B♭^{7}	E♭	B♭^{7}
Chorus 3	E♭		E♭m^7	A♭^{7}	Fm^7				E♭		Fm^7	B♭^{7}	E♭		Fm^7	B♭^{7}
	E♭		E♭m^7		Fm^7		A♭m^7	D♭^{7}	E♭		Fm^7	B♭^{7}	E♭		Fm^7	B♭^{7}

We can see from this table that every 16-bar section:

➢ Begins with two bars of chord I and then moves to the minor form of chord I (with added 7th) in the third bar

➢ Uses chord ii^7 in the first half of its second four-bar phrase (bars 5–6 and 21–22 of each chorus)

➢ Contains the progression ii^7–V^7 at the end of its third four-bar phrase (bars 11–12 and 27–28 of each chorus)

➢ Concludes with either ii^7–V^7 (bars 15–16) or I–V^7 (bars 31–32). This is known in jazz as a **turnaround** – a chord progression, usually ending on chord V^7, which is designed to lead back to the next repeat of the changes.

But as well as similarities there are differences:

➢ Instead of a change of harmony the previous chord may continue (for example, bars 4, 8, 20 and 24 in chorus 2)

➢ Sometimes an extra chord is inserted, as in bar 26 of choruses 1 and 2. This chord (C^7) is a **secondary dominant** of chord ii (Fm) in the key of E♭ major and it launches a route back to E♭ by way of a **circle-of-5ths** progression (C^7–Fm^7–B♭^{7}–E♭ in bars 26–29)

> Chords have a similar tonal function if one can replace the other in a progression. For example, viib might be used instead of V^7 in a perfect cadence, or ii might be used instead of IV as a cadence approach chord.

➢ A chord is sometimes changed to one that has a similar tonal function. This is known as a **substitution chord** in jazz. For example, bars 25 and 29 in the first two choruses both contain chord I (E♭) instead of iii^7 (Gm^7). In chorus 3, E♭ totally replaces Gm^7, being used in bars 9 and 13 as well as in bars 25 and 29.

Now look at the chord symbols printed above the trumpet stave in the head. They are summarised in the next table:

Bar numbers	1 / 17	2 / 18	3 / 19	4 / 20	5 / 21	6 / 22	7 / 23	8 / 24	9 / 25	10 / 26	11 / 27	12 / 28	13 / 29	14 / 30	15 / 31	16 / 32
E♭ major	I			IV	ii		IV	♭vii	iii		ii	V	iii		ii	V
Head	E♭		E♭m^7	A♭^{7}	Fm^7		A♭m^7	D♭^{7}	Gm^7	F♯m^7 B^7	Fm^7	B♭^{7}	Gm^7	F♯m^7 B^7	Fm^7	B♭^{7}
	E♭		E♭m^7	A♭^{7}	Fm^7		A♭m^7	D♭^{7}	Gm^7	F♯m^7 B^7	Fm^7	B♭^{7}	Gm^7 F♯m^7 B^7	Fm^7 B♭^{7}	E♭	

If you compare these chords with those in the table at the top of this page you can see that this is the chord sequence on which the choruses are based, but there are two important differences:

> ➤ Bars 10, 14 and 26 each contain two chords which form the progression F#m^7–B^7. Although unexpected in E♭ major, in each case F#m^7 occurs between Gm^7 in the previous bar and Fm^7 in the next bar, forming a chromatic descent to which B^7 adds the type of additional colour typical of modern jazz

> ➤ The entire chord progression in bars 13–16 (the four 'first time' bars) is condensed into just two bars on the repeat (bars 29–30). This allows tonic harmony (E♭) to replace the turnaround for the short solo break in bars 31–32.

Both of these features are omitted in the choruses, leaving a slightly simpler harmonic framework as the basis for the improvisation, but this framework is itself subjected to much embellishment, since harmonic complexity is at the heart of bebop.

Much of the dissonance typical of bebop arises from the technique of playing away from the chord – in other words, playing non-chord notes. We have already noted how the bassist plays notes either side of the root (but not the root itself) in bar 1.4. A more extreme example occurs in bars 3.9–3.10, where the majority of pitches clash with the underlying chord of E♭ major. In bebop, dissonances of this sort are rarely resolved onto chord notes.

The first eight bars of the head reveal how the basic harmonies of *Four* are elaborately varied from the outset. The chord pattern of the first four bars is | E♭ | E♭ | E♭m^7 | A♭^{7} |. The pianist begins by adding a major 7th and a major 9th to the tonic chord (E♭$^{\Delta 9}$) and then piano and bass rise through the chromatic progression Fm^7–F#$^{\dim 7}$ to a first inversion of E♭$^{\Delta 9}$ (G in the bass) in bar H2. All four chords are very short and are 'pushed' (played just before the beat). All of this results in the E♭ tonality of the music emerging only gradually, rather than being clearly established from the start.

When the opening four bars are repeated sequentially in bars H4–H8, the melodic sequence in the solo part is a perfect 5th lower. However, the free harmonic sequence in the accompaniment begins a major 2nd higher, (chords based on F, G, A♭ and F, rather than on E♭, F, F# and E♭) thus adding to the harmonic complexity.

The melody in bars H5–H6 outlines an E♭-major triad (ending on a blue 3rd), so might seem to bear little relation to the underlying F-minor harmony. However, E♭, G and B♭ are the 7th, 9th and 11th respectively above the root (F). This concentration on the dissonant upper extensions of chords is another characteristic of bebop.

Melody and rhythm

The theme is based on the three-note figure heard at the start and has a modest compass of a 10th, in the middle range of the trumpet. The fragmentary, scalic nature of this material is the trigger for an exploration of scalic figures over a much greater melodic range in the first two and a half choruses. Many of these involve chromatic patterns, although Davis has a preference for a gapped chromatic descent that avoids the flattened 7th (D♭), as in bars 1.1, 1.14, 1.29, 2.2–2.3 and 2.22. He makes almost no reference to the melody of the theme in these improvised choruses, only to its chords. Instead, Davis substitutes a series of short motifs, each of which he briefly develops before moving on to the next idea.

The predominantly quaver-based rhythm gives way to longer note values when Davis needs time to use the extended techniques mentioned earlier. Towards the end of NAM 50 longer note lengths are used again for the first significant exploration of wide leaps in bars 3.19–3.24. As the extract fades out, quavers return, but in a new pattern of repeated notes on single pitches.

The pulse is as elusive as the tonality at the start, with few of the chords on downbeats and phrases that neither start nor end on a strong beat. A clearer sense of the beat arrives with the tentative introduction of the walking bass in bar H9, although it is not until the choruses that this becomes continuous. From there on, bass and drums combine to provide a firm rhythmic backing against which Miles Davis can develop his own syncopations.

Exercise 7

1. What are the main stylistic features of bebop?

2. What is meant in jazz by (i) playing away from the chord, (ii) a head arrangement, and (iii) upper extensions of chords?

3. How do the changes in *Four* differ from the changes in the *Black and Tan Fantasy*?

4. What type of chord is played by the pianist on the last quaver of bar H1?

5. Which notes are blue notes in the first eight bars of the trumpet solo?

6. What do you understand is meant by a substitution chord in jazz? Give an example of one in *Four*.

Sample questions

In Section C of the Unit 6 paper you will have to answer one of two questions about the instrumental works you have studied. Your response is expected to be an essay, written in continuous prose, and your clarity of expression, spelling and grammar will be taken into account in the marking.

Remember that it is important to give locations of each specific feature that you mention, but there should not normally be any need to write out music examples. You will be allowed to refer to an unmarked copy of NAM as you write.

Here are two essay topics to use for practice. Aim to complete each essay in 50 minutes.

(a) Compare and contrast the structures and use of instruments in the three following works:

Holborne's Pavane 'The image of melancholy' (*only*) (NAM 13, pages 191–192)
Haydn's Symphony No. 26 in D minor: movement I (NAM 2, pages 31–41)
Ellington's *Black and Tan Fantasy* (NAM 49, pages 465–468).

(b) Compare and contrast the use of tonality and fugal textures in the three following works:

Bach's Gigue (*only*) from Partita No. 4 in D (NAM 48, pages 251–252)
Brahms' Piano Quintet in F minor: movement III, bars 67–100 *only* (NAM 18, pages 233–235)
Shostakovich's Fugue (*only*) (NAM 25, pages 263–265).

Applied music

Cantata 48, movements 1–4 (Bach)

A cantata is a work for one or more voices with accompaniment. NAM 48 consists of the first four (of seven) movements from a sacred cantata by J. S. Bach. Cantatas of this sort were performed during the main service on Sundays and religious festivals in the principal Lutheran churches of major cities in Protestant Germany during the late Baroque period.

In 1723 Bach was appointed to direct the music at St Thomas in Leipzig, a position that he held until his death in 1750. His duties included providing weekly cantatas for performance by the choir and small orchestra, most of whose members came from the boys' school attached to the church where Bach taught.

The texts of Bach's cantatas were related to the bible readings for the day concerned and consisted of German verse, biblical quotations and one or more hymns (known in Germany as chorales). In his early years in Leipzig, it is believed that Bach wrote at least 300 church cantatas. Only one was published in his lifetime and, while some 200 have survived in manuscripts, it is thought that at least 100 were lost after the composer's death.

Bach's cantatas include a huge variety of music, from works for solo voice with orchestra (probably sung by one of Bach's many unfortunate sons when the rest of the choir was on holiday) to large-scale cantatas for festive occasions that would have required extra musicians from the town and its university. The cantatas also encompass almost every type of music known to Bach, from the most serious counterpoint to the jolliest of dance styles.

Scholars have been able to establish that the first performance of Cantata 48 was almost certainly given on Sunday 3 October 1723, so it dates from Bach's first few months in Leipzig. It follows the pattern of most of his cantatas by including:

➢ Elaborate pieces for choir and orchestra (movement 1)

➢ Harmonised chorale tunes with melodies that the congregation would have known and might possibly have joined in singing (movement 3)

➢ Music based on the operatic forms of recitative (movement 2) and aria (movement 4).

Listen to the first movement and then state where the opening 12 bars are repeated exactly. Did you notice that these bars also appear in abbreviated versions in other places? This is known as **ritornello form**. Ritornello means 'a little return' and reflects the use of shortened repetitions (between contrasting episodes) as a structural device. It is a form that was widely used in the late Baroque period, especially in concertos such as NAM 1. The ritornello here is characterised by minor keys, sequences and discords (on the first beats of bars 1, 2, 6 and 8) that underline the rather grim text.

Context

NAM 28 (page 288)   CD3 Tracks 3–6
Yorkshire Bach Choir
Fitzwilliam Ensemble
Clare Mathias (alto)
Conducted by Peter Seymour

A translation of the text of these four movements from Cantata 48 is given on page 538 of NAM.

The three final movements, not in NAM, are a recitative and an aria for tenor soloist and then the chorale on which the first movement is based.

Movement 1
Chorus

1st movement

Final chorale

Rhythmic outline of bars 42–43

(i) Hemiola as notated:

(ii) Aural effect of hemiola:

An adaptation of the chorale melody with which the complete cantata ends is played in **canon** by the trumpet and oboes (see *left*). A pre-existing melody (such as this) against which other tunes are set in counterpoint is known as a cantus firmus. Around the cantus firmus the choir declaims the text in a succession of imitative entries (often canonic in style, but not strictly in canon), and below both sets of parts the ritornello emerges frequently in the type of contrapuntal complexity for which Bach is famous.

Because of the incorporation of the chorale melody, the music is mainly in G minor with modulations to related minor keys (again reflecting the solemn text). Most of the main sections end with a rhythmic device called a **hemiola**. This has the effect of highlighting the cadences by making two bars of $\frac{3}{4}$ time sound like three bars of $\frac{2}{4}$ (see *left*) and is found in much triple-time Baroque music. Notice the calming effect of the long tonic pedal at the end of this movement, and the **tierce de Picardie** in the final cadence.

The string parts in NAM 28 are printed on two staves, the lowest notes of which are played by the **continuo**. The continuo always includes a chordal instrument which, in church music like this, would be an organ. The figures and other symbols below this part form a **figured bass** to indicate the chords to play. For example, '7' in bar 1 indicates a 7th above the bass note C, which in this context the organist would play as a Cm^7 chord. Most of the figures have been added by modern editors – Bach himself wrote very few.

Movement 2
Recitative

Listen to the word-setting in this movement. Do you notice that it is entirely different from the first movement? The text flows past at a much faster rate, the word setting is almost entirely **syllabic** and the rhythms seem to reflect those of natural speech. The accompaniment is purely supportive and it modulates very rapidly through a number of keys. This type of music is called recitative.

Recitative is often accompanied by only continuo instruments, as in the opening of NAM 36. When parts for other instruments are included, such as the sustained parts for strings used here, the music is described as accompanied recitative (despite the fact that recitative supported only by continuo instruments is not literally unaccompanied!).

The somewhat lurid text is of a type very popular among some German Protestants at the time and is expressed through:

➢ Detached melodic fragments to highlight the sighs and dramatic expressions of self-contempt ('O the pain, O the misery')

➢ Angular melodic lines with tortured leaps such as the diminished 7th on *Elend!* (misery) in bar 2

➢ Extreme dissonance such as the minor 9th between the singer and the bass on the first beat of bar 2

➢ Modulation to a foreign key at bar 10, where the music suddenly moves to E major at the words *stärkste Gift* (strongest poison).

Listen to the recording and try to spot how the singer embellishes the repeated quavers at the start of bars 7, 11 and 14. Such decoration is typical of the performing practices of Bach's day.

This chorale tune was already at least 100 years old when Bach included it in Cantata 48. The melody is purely **diatonic**, but it is totally transformed by Bach's **chromatic** harmonisation. The use of chords such as the diminished 7th allows some unexpected modulations to G minor (bar 2) and Ab major (bar 6). Instead of the expected perfect cadence in Bb major at the end of the melody, Bach introduces an Ab which sparks off a series of anguished **suspensions** (for instance, the alto Gb against the tenor F in bar 9).

Movement 3
Chorale

If you are working on chorales for the technical study in Unit 5, this is a valuable opportunity to hear one performed – notice that it is played by instruments as well as sung by four-part choir, and that the double bass sounds an octave below the printed bass. However, the chromatic style adopted by Bach to portray the text of this particular chorale is considerably more complex than the style of harmonisation expected in exam submissions.

The fourth movement is an obbligato **aria** – a song with an equally important (obligatory) instrumental solo. When you listen to it try to note where and how the opening music returns. Did you spot that sometimes only little fragments of it come back? For instance, the singer starts with the opening four bars of oboe music, and in bars 23–24 the oboe itself plays a fragment from bars 5–6. Do you recognise this musical form?

Movement 4
Aria

Supporting the duet between singer and oboe is a bass that moves almost entirely in quavers. This is a much earlier example of the type of 'walking bass' that we saw in Miles Davis' *Four*.

The aria is in Eb major and falls into two main sections. The first ends in the dominant key of Bb major at bar 38 while the second moves straight into C minor and then passes through a number of closely related keys before returning to Eb major in the perfect cadence of bars 78–79. The performance direction *D.C. al Fine* – repeat from the beginning as far as the word *Fine* (finish) – means that the opening ritornello (bars 1–16) should then be repeated to conclude the aria.

Exercise 8

1. Which of the four movements in NAM 28 are homophonic and which are contrapuntal?

2. What is a cantus firmus? How is one used in the first movement?

3. What similarity do you notice between the final chord of the first movement and the final chord of Holborne's Galliard on page 193 of NAM?

4. Is the word-setting in the recitative melismatic or syllabic?

5. What are the main differences between the recitative and aria?

6. What is a chorale? Name two ways in which Bach uses chorales in NAM 28.

7. What is the obbligato instrument in the aria and which other instruments play in this movement?

8. For what type of musical texture is Bach famous?

'Der kranke Mond' from *Pierrot Lunaire* (Schoenberg)

Context

NAM 40 (page 364)   CD3 Track 18
Yvonne Minton (reciter)
Michael Debost (flute)
Directed by Pierre Boulez

In the early decades of the 20th century a style to become known as Expressionism developed in art, literature, drama and music, particularly in Germany and Austria. A common aim was to give expression to inner fears and obsessions through such means as distorted images in painting or heightened speech and scenes of extreme violence in plays.

In parallel with the artists who used exaggerated forms and non-naturalistic colours and textures to express their emotions, Arnold Schoenberg abandoned the late Romantic style of his early works in favour of a musical language that deliberately avoided any suggestion of tonal melody or harmony, and that used extreme chromaticism and dissonance as the primary means of expression.

While *Pierrot Lunaire* is atonal, it is not a serial work. Serialism developed some years later as a way to structure atonal music in the absence of keys.

All of this is immediately apparent in NAM 40, an **atonal** song from Schoenberg's most famous Expressionist work, *Pierrot Lunaire* (the moon-struck clown) of 1912. In the first three bars he uses all 12 notes of the chromatic scale and nowhere in the song is there anything that sounds like a tonal chord progression or a key note.

The grotesque images of the poem are expressed through:

A translation of the text of this song is printed on page 540 of NAM.

The title *Pierrot Lunaire* is perhaps best expressed in English as the moon-struck clown: a sad clown who is obsessed with the moon – although it isn't clear if he is really a lunatic or merely deluded by its lunar magic.

Schoenberg described *Pierrot Lunaire* as a melodrama – a dramatic work with spoken words that are recited to music. Today it is often described as a music theatre piece.

➤ Enormous melodic leaps (flute, bars 9–10 and reciter, bar 15)

➤ Fragmented melody (bars 14–15)

➤ Extreme range (voice bar 15)

➤ Extreme dynamics (flute, bar 14)

➤ *Sprechgesang* ('speech-song' – the half-sung, half-spoken notes of the reciter indicated by crosses through note stems).

The text that Schoenberg used is a German adaptation of a cycle of 50 poems, called *Pierrot Lunaire*, written by the Belgian poet Albert Giraud in 1884. Schoenberg chose 21 of these poems for his work, which was commissioned by the German actress Albertine Zehme. She was the vocalist at the first performance in Berlin, which was presented in a clown's costume, with the instrumentalists hidden behind a screen. Although some of the audience were perplexed by the work, others demanded an encore. *Pierrot Lunaire* has been performed and recorded many times ever since, including by artists as diverse as the jazz singer Cleo Laine and the pop star Björk.

The complete work requires an ensemble of five players in addition to the reciter. In *Der kranke Mond* (the sick moon) Schoenberg uses only flute and voice. In such a thin texture he is able to exploit the flute's very quiet lowest notes without fear of their being masked by other instruments.

Sprechgesang

Try to compare the recording on CD3 with one in which the reciter adopts more of a speaking tone, and compare Minton's tremolo on each of the last five notes with other interpretations of the mordent signs on these notes.

In the score of the complete work, Schoenberg explained that the rhythms of the vocal part should be strictly observed but that the pitch of notes with crosses through their stem should be immediately quitted in a downward or upward direction. There are many ways to interpret this. Most singers give an approximation of the written pitches with *portamenti* (slides) between them. But on CD3 Yvonne Minton chooses to sing sustained pitches with *portamenti* mainly reserved for slurred notes, such as those in bar 4.

Although this song includes fragments that link it with other songs in the cycle, there is no formal musical structure. The text consists of three stanzas, with lines of eight alternately weak and strong syllables, but for Schoenberg this is far too structured to express madness. He therefore avoids using the same music for each of the three verses, although he does separate them with passages for flute alone, and he even writes phrases of very irregular lengths (9, 13, 8½ and 9 beats in the first stanza, for instance) to avoid any sense of musical symmetry.

Instead of repetition, Schoenberg's music reacts to the imagery of the moment, using a very wide vocal range (nearly two octaves) and an unpredictable variety of semitonal movement (bars 1–2), angular leaps (bar 14), and abrupt changes of direction (e.g. bar 23), all to express the wanderings of the mad clown's thoughts.

There are, though, a few small-scale repetitions in the song. In bars 14–15 the notes of 'an Sehnsucht' are repeated for 'tief erstickt' and the flute part in bars 22–24 consists of a long descending sequence. The most obvious use of repetition occurs at the end of the vocal part where three highly contrasting lines of text are perversely set to the same pattern of pitches. The eight-note phrase in bar 23 is immediately repeated to new words although, by starting a beat earlier than before, the pattern of accents is different. Nevertheless, in bar 24 Schoenberg instructs the reciter to make no difference by writing 'use the same tone as in the previous bar'. The phrase is then heard once more in **augmentation** (notes of twice their previous length), above which Schoenberg writes in bar 25 'this bar differently, but not tragically'.

The thin two-part texture, in which flute and voice are equal partners, allows every word to be heard. Indeed it often sounds as though the flute is trying to speak. But this is not a rational conversation since they share no common melodic material. Each is absorbed in its own form of madness (for instance, compare the manic raging of the flute in bars 5–6 with the introspective ruminations of *Pierrot* in the same passage). Nor is there any traditional harmonic logic in the intervals formed between them. In the first six bars every interval from a semitone to a perfect octave is heard, but Schoenberg studiously avoids any suggestion of conventional resolution when discords occur.

Structure and style

Notice that Schoenberg doesn't even reuse the opening phrase when the same words return in bars 15⁵–17 and again at the end.

Schoenberg, along with his pupils Berg and Webern, came from Vienna. They are collectively known as the Second Viennese School (the first Viennese School being composers who worked in and around Vienna in the Classical period, such as Haydn and Mozart). The word 'school' in this context refers to similarities in style and not to any sort of educational establishment!

The German instructions in these bars are translated on page 537 of NAM in case you need to refer to them in the exam.

Texture

Exercise 9

1. Define the terms atonality, Expressionism and *Sprechgesang*.

2. Concisely describe the texture of NAM 40.

3. How does the flautist respond to the words *fremde Melodie* (strange melody) that occur in bars 7–8?

4. Comment on the dynamics in the flute part of bars 13–15.

5. Compare Schoenberg's use of performing instructions in NAM 40 with Bach's in NAM 28.

6. What musical techniques does Schoenberg use to convey the emotions of Pierrot, the tormented clown, in this song?

On the Waterfront: Symphonic Suite (Bernstein)

Context

NAM 43 (page 374)   CD4 Track 2
New York Philharmonic
Conducted by Leonard Bernstein

The 1954 film *On the Waterfront* tells a story, based on reality, of crime and extortion in New York's dockland, and of the struggle of a young dock worker (played by Marlon Brando) who fought against the corrupt practices exposed in the film. It was in stark contrast to the romantic comedies and Hollywood epics usually seen in the cinema and its harsh social realism made a great impact.

Bernstein's most famous musical, *West Side Story*, was completed in 1957 and reflects the musical style of *On the Waterfront* in some of its numbers.

Leonard Bernstein had achieved success in writing musicals for the theatre before being asked to compose the music for this film. Some of these musicals had been filmed, but *On the Waterfront* was the only actual film score that he ever wrote. The social realism of the film does not entirely extend to its music, which uses the large symphony orchestra that was the norm for big-budget American movies. However the exhilarating percussion rhythms and fearsome brass writing (both characteristic of Bernstein's style) give the music a hard edge which echoes the intensity and violence of the film. In 1955 Bernstein arranged some of the music from the film into a symphonic suite for performance in concert halls, and it is from the opening of this version that NAM 43 is taken.

Instrumentation

When reading the score note that:

➤ The clarinet in E♭ sounds a minor 3rd *higher* than written while the alto saxophone in E♭ sounds a major 6th *lower* than written

➤ Clarinets and trumpets in B♭ sound a tone lower, and the bass clarinet in B♭ sounds a major 9th lower, than written

➤ Horns in F sound a perfect 5th lower than written

➤ The piccolo sounds an octave higher, while the double bassoon and double basses sound an octave lower, than written.

Bernstein's orchestration is dominated by wind and percussion, while strings have little independent material before bar 88 and mainly double other parts – Bernstein treats the orchestra like a huge jazz band. Only in the last four pages are the strings given a role of their own, and even then it is more in the nature of a special effect, sustaining single pitches or icy dissonances against the forceful interjections of wind and percussion.

Slow introduction

The very high notes in the horn and trumpet solos are technically very demanding, especially since there is little or no accompaniment and the dynamics are mainly quiet. Notice that Bernstein cues them into other parts (shown by small notes) in case alternatives are needed.

The work opens with a long **monophonic** melody for solo horn. Its notes are taken from a blues scale on F (sounding pitches) whose blue notes (the flattened 3rd, 5th and 7th, marked ✻ *left*) help to establish a desolate, mournful mood at this slow speed.

Starting in bar 7, the opening theme is repeated in two-part **canon** between the unusual combination of flutes (in octaves) and muted trombone. The blues is again evident at the start of bar 11, where the flat 5th (C♭) in the flutes clashes against B♭ in the trombone.

The second part of this theme then appears on muted trumpets (bar 13), a 5th higher than in bar 4, sounding *lontano* (distant). The simple two-part harmonisation is underpinned by a pedal on F, sustained by clarinets and articulated by the harp.

When the clarinets move off this pedal at the end of bar 17 they play fragments of the first part of the theme in 'subtone' (very quiet and breathy) – Bernstein has returned to the monophonic texture of the opening, but now heard in bare octaves. Finally, in bar 19 the ascending minor 3rd of this motif is transformed into a major 3rd in preparation for the next section.

The sparse scoring of this introduction for wind and harp reflects the film's theme of a lonely individual faced with a regime of corrupt practices. It contrasts strongly with the percussive *Presto* that follows, with its depiction of the seething, dangerous atmosphere of the New York docks in the 1950s.

Presto barbaro means fast and barbaric, and its two time signatures indicate that bars of ¢ and ¾ alternate. It begins with a six-bar syncopated idea for piano and timpani (played with hard sticks) that features the rising minor 3rds from the opening theme of the work, joined by its major-3rd variant in bar 24.

Presto barbaro

'Una corda' in bar 20 of the piano part is an instruction to use the left-hand ('soft') pedal.

A second timpanist enters in bar 26, playing the rhythm of bars 20–21 on C♯ and F♯, forming dissonances of a tritone and a major 7th respectively above the continuing pedal on G. In bar 32 three drums of different pitch levels join in with an outline of the same idea. The effect is like the start of a very dissonant fugue for percussion.

The three percussion parts come together in bar 40 to form a **riff** which then accompanies a loud jazz-like solo for alto saxophone. Bernstein marks this 'crudely', leaving little doubt about the brash atmosphere he wishes to create. The sax melody consists of three four-bar phrases, the first two of which are similar. This is the melodic structure of a 12-bar blues, but there is no sign of a blues-based chord pattern. The sax and lowest timpani notes focus on notes from a blues scale on G, but the high level of dissonance leaves the music sounding essentially atonal.

In bar 53 the side drummer plays a rim shot (explained in the margin note on page 99). This type of accented off-beat ending is another Bernstein fingerprint.

In bar 54 high wind instruments enter with a compressed version of the sax melody in which the long notes have been shortened. This melody is a 3rd higher than before, although the timpani riff (now joined by lower strings) remains on the original pitches.

The dynamic level drops dramatically and the texture thins in bars 62–63, but the drum rhythm continues and almost immediately Bernstein begins another build-up as he develops the cadential saxophone motif from bar 52. Starting in bar 64, this is played by first violins and oboes, combined with its own inversion in the second-violin and clarinet parts. Two bars later, low strings and bassoons add variants of the falling 4th idea from bar 44.

Tremolo upper strings and timpani rolls add to a crescendo which culminates in a powerful *tutti* at bar 78, where the whole orchestra stamps out the percussion patterns in dissonant block chords. Notice how Bernstein increases the impact of this section by adding further dissonances above the already discordant riff. The texture is not just homophonic but **homorhythmic** (all parts having exactly the same rhythm for ten bars).

The rhythm of the percussion riff is maintained by a solitary side drum from bar 88, while high sustained strings (punctuated by upper woodwind) remind us of figures from the sax solo that started in bar 42. Rising and falling semitones converge on a unison in the violins, the latter replaced by the falling 4th in bar 94. The pattern is reversed in bar 98: a unison D♭ expands outwards to form a major 2nd on C and D♮, sustained by high woodwind, trumpets and violins, below which the timpani return. To support the increasing dynamic, more instruments are added, the violins re-energise their major second with tremolo, the E♭ clarinet trills between C and D (notated as a tremolo), the flutes, oboes and trumpets are instructed to use flutter-tonguing (*flutt.* in bar 105, produced by rolling an 'r' with the tongue while blowing), a roll on a suspended cymbal brings the crescendo to its climax and at last the rhythmic ostinato (heard constantly since bar 20) ceases on the pause chord in bar 105.

Coda (Adagio)   Starting in bar 106, the eight-bar **coda** begins with a slow and very loud restatement of the motif from bar 52. Beneath it Bernstein reaffirms the importance of the tritone in this music by slowly superimposing two triads a tritone apart (F major and B major – the 3rd of the latter enharmonically notated as E♭ rather than D♯).

This colossal dissonance is hammered out by wind and percussion in bars 108–109. In the rests, the strings can be heard very quietly sustaining the same dissonance using the thin, icy tone produced by playing *sul ponticello* (with the bow close to the bridge).

In the last four bars Bernstein uses a similar pattern but ratchets up the dissonance still further. This time a triad of E major (the 3rd again enharmonically notated as A♭) is overlaid by the note B♭ (a tritone above E) plus a further tritone formed by C and F♯.

Because the bass in the coda moves down a semitone from F to E while the upper part moves up from A to B, there is sense that the music has reached a stopping point. But this is no cadence – the atonality of these bars is even more forceful than the dissonances of bebop jazz that had so influenced Bernstein in the early 1950s.

Leonard Bernstein described the work from which NAM 43 is taken as a 'symphonic suite'. He wrote it for a symphony orchestra, but he used its resources more like a huge jazz band. Perhaps what he really meant by 'symphonic' is the way in which he develops and exploits his motifs with much greater rigour than can be found in most earlier film scores.

Exercise 10

1. In which bars does Bernstein use each of the following textures? (i) homophonic, (ii) monophonic, (iii) two-part counterpoint.

2. What are the *sounding* pitches of the first two horn notes in bar 1?

3. Explain the meaning of 'con sord.' in the trombone part of bar 7.

4. What *two* features do bars 20 and 78 have in common?

5. Explain how the trumpet and alto saxophone parts are related in bars 52–53.

6. Describe the two different types of tremolo on page 385 of NAM.

7. The film *On the Waterfront* sometimes depicts an atmosphere of bleak despair, but at other times a mood of anger. Show how Bernstein's music reflects both of these moods

ET: Flying theme (Williams)

The American composer John Williams (born in 1932) has become one of the best known film composers of the last 40 years, writing scores for such box-office successes as *Jaws*, *Star Wars*, *Superman*, *Raiders of the Lost Ark*, *Schindler's List*, *Saving Private Ryan* and the first three *Harry Potter* films.

ET: The Extra-Terrestrial (1982) is a children's fantasy in which the scary alien of traditional science fiction is transformed into a cute animatronic who is befriended by an American schoolboy. As the sun sets on halloween, the ten year-old takes ET for a ride in the front basket of his bicycle. ET uses his telekinetic powers to take control of the bike, which flies through the night sky silhouetted against the moon to the stirring music of NAM 45.

Although the 'Flying Theme' from *ET* sounds conservative in style, especially compared with Bernstein's music for *On the Waterfront* composed nearly 30 years earlier, this is one of the reasons for Williams' popular appeal. He has a gift for memorable melodies, constructed, harmonised and orchestrated in traditional, familiar ways. The result is a score that sounds romantic in style, intended to capture the chilhood innocence of the film, and with none of the gritty dissonance, jazzy syncopation and motivic complexity that characterise Bernstein's music in NAM 43.

The essence of the 'Flying Theme' is an eight-bar melody that is heard five times in the extract, accounting for almost half of its 87 bars. The third of these repetitions is in the dominant key and is separated from the others by transitional passages on either side, creating a **rondo**-like structure. The movement starts with an eight-bar introduction, and ends with a lengthy coda that makes further references to the main theme (see *right*).

John Williams' essentially conservative style is reflected in his use of a traditional symphony orchestra – smaller than that used by Bernstein, with no unusual instruments and with only very modest use of percussion. Notice, for instance, how the orchestral (crash) cymbals are reserved for only two notes in the entire extract – one at bar 55, for the most triumphant appearance of the flying theme, and the other for its repeat eight bars later.

ET was orchestrated by Herbert W. Spencer, who worked on many of Williams' scores of the period. The use of a specialist orchestrator is not unusual in film music, especially by someone as busy as John Williams, but the composer would have been involved in the main decisions about timbres, textures and instrumental effects.

Unlike *On the Waterfront*, the warm sound of strings dominates. The orchestration gives prominence to the principal melody which, on its main appearances, is presented in octaves by woodwind and most of the strings, the accompaniment for brass and piano being supportive and chordal.

Textures are thus mainly **homophonic** – homorhythmic in the eight-bar introduction, and melody-dominated homophony ('tune and accompaniment') in most of the remainder.

Context

NAM 45 (page 409)   CD4 Track 4
City of Prague Philharmonic
Conducted by Paul Bateman

Like NAM 43, this extract is not taken directly from the film score, but from a concert suite based on music from the film.

Structure, instrumentation and texture

Bars	Structure	
1–8	Introduction	8 bars
9–16	A (theme)	8 bars
17–24	A (repeated)	8 bars
25–33	B (transition)	9 bars
34–41	A (in dominant)	8 bars
42–54	B (transition)	13 bars
55–62	A (in tonic)	8 bars
63–68	A (repeated)	6 bars
69–87	Coda	19 bars

When reading the score, remember that clarinets and trumpets in B♭ sound a tone lower than written, while horns in F sound a perfect 5th lower than written.

Introduction

The entirely **diatonic** introduction consists of a four-note staccato figure for flutes, clarinets and violins, repeated as an **ostinato** over chords I and V^7 of C major. If you look at the piano part you will see that the tonic chord includes an added 2nd (D) while the dominant 7th chord has a suspended 4th (C instead of B). The notes C, D and G are common to both chords, so there is little sense of harmonic movement. A repeat of the first four bars leads straight into the main theme, which begins with the two chords heard in the introduction and has an accompaniment that maintains the same chugging rhythm of repeated quavers, but now in $\frac{3}{2}$ time.

Theme (in the tonic)
Bars 9–24

The eight-bar theme is first heard in bars 9–16. Despite some chromaticism it is essentially in C major. It is worth considering what makes this tune so memorable.

It begins with a two-bar phrase based on one of the main building blocks of tonal music, the tonic triad, decorated with a turn on the third beat (see *left*). The confident sound of the opening rising 5th from tonic to dominant is balanced by a descent to the lower dominant in bar 2.

Williams then repeats this two-bar pattern in a free sequence. The rising 5th becomes an octave in bar 11 (and the end of the motif rises instead of falls) and a 7th in bar 13 (where the end of the motif introduces some chromatic colour with an E♭).

The repetitions of the basic pattern help fix it in the memory, but the varied sequence prevents it sounding too predictable. For the last two bars of the eight-bar theme Williams avoids a fourth appearance of the motif; bar 15 repeats the E♭–C of the previous bar and bar 16 provides an unusual cadence point with the theme on the leading-note (B) but harmonised by a chord of C.

The complete theme is then given a varied repeat in bars 17–24. Low strings are now pizzicato and second violins have semiquavers (indicated by the strokes through the stems). Flutes and bells introduce a **countermelody** in bar 18. It is heard in each alternate bar and will appear more prominently in the next section.

First transition
Bars 25–33

If the main theme captures the exhilaration of the bicycle flying through the air, the transition in bars 25–33 seems to reflect the magic of the star-lit scene. It develops the countermelody of the previous section, although the continuous quaver accompaniment is still present. Tonality is more fluid due to the use of triads in root position and first inversion whose roots are a 3rd apart: B major and G major alternate in bars 25–28, then E♭ major in bar 29, followed by F♯ minor, D minor and B♭ major. The imminent return of the theme in the dominant (G major) is signalled by rolls on timpani and a suspended cymbal plus, in bar 33, a diminished 7th chord on the leading note of G (F♯–A–C–E♭, with E♭ in the bass).

Theme (in the dominant)
Bars 34–41

This is the most fully-scored version of the theme so far, and includes the three trumpets which were silent at the start. There are also small changes to the harmonisation. For instance, the first chord in bars 34–35 is I$^{\text{maj}7}$ in G major, rather than I$^{\text{add}2}$, and the last note in bar 41 is now supported by clear dominant harmony.

The second transition begins with a brief development of bar 25 from the start of the first transition. This is joined in bar 47 by the double-dotted figure from bar 26, now forcefully articulated by most of the brass and woodwind, with contrasts of pizzicato and tremolo from the strings. The harmony is again based on a succession of unrelated chords. Bars 50–54 are based on the music from bars 29–33, transposed up a 4th to prepare the way for the main theme to return in the tonic.

Second transition
Bars 42–54

A crash of cymbals announces the fourth appearance of the theme, scored in double octaves with a mainly thickly-spaced and low accompaniment. A turn-like figure in semiquavers leads into a fifth statement at bar 63, followed by unison horns entering a bar later in **imitation**, but this time the theme is interrupted by quavers descending in whole tones (bar 68) that run straight into the **coda**.

Theme (in the tonic)
Bars 55–68

Ascending scales from the brass and piano form successions of parallel triads that rise over a dominant pedal, leading to a colossal discord – the C-major chord in bar 74 is underpinned by a loud E♭ anticipated on the previous beat. The woodwind combine the openings of the themes from sections A and B in bars 75–76. This pattern is repeated and then the bass at last moves down to C. Four bars of pure tonic harmony, supporting a triadic ascent into the night sky from the weirdly-tuned bells, conclude the extract.

Coda
Bars 69–87

Exercise 11

1. What word best describes the texture of bars 1–8?

2. How does the orchestration help make the main theme in bars 9–16 sound heroic?

3. What are the two main differences between bars 34–41 and bars 17–24?

4. Identify the chord in bar 54 (its pitches are all present in the piano part).

5. What is the difference between the two types of cymbal in the percussion part of bars 62–63?

6. What are the *sounding* pitches of the first two horn notes in bar 64?

7. Explain what is meant by a coda.

8. List the features of NAM 45 that help to make this music immediately appealing.

Tom McElvogue's (jig) and New Irish Barndance

Although this pair of folk dances seems well matched, the jig was written in the early 1980s by Tom McElvogue while the New Irish Barndance is of uncertain origin but from a much earlier period. This is a reminder that while folk music has a very long heritage, it is also a living tradition, enjoyed daily in pubs and folk clubs.

Context

NAM 61 (page 530)   CD4 Track 19
Niall Keegan (Irish flute)

Part of this tradition is that melodies are usually learned by ear, and are then ornamented and improvised upon in performance, so there is seldom any definitive version of a folk tune. The score in NAM is a transcription, made by writing down what is heard on the recording. Both pieces could sound very different when played on other occasions or by other folk musicians.

The Irish traditional flute

For more about the Irish flute see the website of the flute maker, Terry McGee: www.mcgee-flutes.com

The dances are played on an Irish traditional flute, a wooden instrument based on the design of the flute as it was in the early 19th century, before the complex keywork of the modern flute was invented. In fact, it became popular in Irish folk music as a result of these older instruments becoming readily available after flautists switched to the modern style of instrument. Some players of Irish folk music use a flute with only fingerholes and no keys, while others prefer instruments that include a small number of keys to facilitate the production of notes such as F, G♯, B♭ and E♭.

The Irish flute has a conical bore (unlike the cylindrical bore of the modern flute), large fingerholes and a range of about two octaves. If you play the flute or recorder, you will know of the importance of tonguing to articulate the notes in classical music. In folk music tonguing is often very light and is sometimes reserved to mark the starts of phrases. As you can hear on CD 4, the music is articulated primarily through ornamentation. Some of these ornaments are printed in NAM 61, including the slide (bar 9), mordent (bar 34), acciaccatura (bar 60) and trill (bar 81). A less familiar type of decoration, although common in Celtic folk music, is the treble – a division of a note into three repetitions of the same pitch, as shown by the triplet semiquavers in bars 66, 71 and later.

Other characteristics of Irish flute playing include an absence of breath vibrato (finger vibrato is sometimes used as an ornament), strong attack on lower notes, little dynamic variation and no hard staccato. Styles and repertoire vary in different parts of Ireland.

The recording on CD4 illustrates a typical style of performance for folk dance, in which a basic idea is repeated with increasingly exciting elaboration. The texture is entirely **monophonic** and you can hear that audible foot-tapping and shouts of encouragement from the audience are all part of the performance.

Tom McElvogue's (jig)

The origins of the jig date back to at least the 15th century. By the time that late-Baroque composers such as Bach concluded their suites of stylised dance music with a jig (or *gigue* in French), it had become well established as a fast movement in compound time, as we saw in our study of NAM 21.

The jig in NAM 61, though, is much more recent. It was written in 1984/5 by Tom McElvogue, a player of the Irish traditional flute who comes from Newcastle upon Tyne. It was apparently his first composition, and its original form can be seen on his website at: www.tommcelvogue.com/music/Compositions/jig_08.jpg – if you compare this with the version in NAM you will see how even recent folk music can rapidly develop and mutate.

The music is in the style of a double jig. This is the most common type of Irish jig, and is characterised by six quavers a bar in $\frac{6}{8}$ time (the single jig, in contrast, is built on ♩ ♪ patterns). McElvogue's jig is also traditional in its phrase structure, consisting of eight-bar sections in the order AABB (bars 1–32). This 32-bar structure is itself repeated in NAM 61, to make a 64-bar dance.

The repetitions are invariably decorated in different ways, but you should be able to spot that the A section always starts with a bar containing an upward leap of a 5th from low G to D (bars 1, 9, 33 and 41), while the B section always starts on a high G (bars 17, 25, 49 and 57). However to follow this you need to develop a feel for the eight-bar phrase lengths (or note the sections shown *right* on the score) since the ear can be deceived by the many repetitions and variations of small motifs that occur within these phrases. For instance, the motif of bar 1 is heard again in bar 3, while the whole of bars 1–2 are given a varied repeat to form bars 5–6). Such small-scale internal repetition also binds together the material of the two main sections, so the third and fourth bars of each B section are actually variants of the first two bars of the A section (compare bars 19–20 with bars 1–2, for example).

The jig is in G major, the most natural key for the traditional flute as it avoids complicated fingerings. Each eight-bar phrase ends with a cadential pattern in that key (the notes outlining V–I in the A sections and VII–I in the B sections). Between the cadences the leading note (F♯) is often altered to F♮ in the style of much Irish traditional music. This gives the dance a modal tinge, but the cadences clearly indicate that this is not modal music. The A♭ in bar 57 is neither modal nor a feature of traditional Irish music. This chromatic passing note is a reminder that the flautist on CD4, Niall Keegan, is famed for the way in which he has introduced ideas from jazz and other styles to Irish folk music.

The final note of the jig is also the first note of this traditional barndance – a word that is often used to describe any sort of social country dancing but that here refers to a specific type of dance.

In NAM, this piece is described as a reel, which is incorrect, although the two dances are musically similar. The barndance is characterised by accents on the first and third beats of $\frac{4}{4}$ time, here represented by the dotted crotchets in the first bar of the melody. The origins of this particular melody are unclear, but it was recorded in 1930 by folk musicians in America in a rather simpler version than the one performed by Niall Keegan.

The most common structure for the dance is the same AABB form that we saw in the jig. Bars 65–68 are the A section (repeated in bars 69–72) while bars 73–76 are the B section (repeated in bars 77–80). This entire AABB structure is then repeated with ever more elaborate decoration in bars 81–96.

As in the jig, there are many internal repetitions of motifs within these sections – for example, compare bar 67 with bar 65, shown *right*. Another similarity with the jig is a lack of distinction between the A and B sections, resulting from the use of common material. The first bar of B enshrines the bracketed figure from the first bar of A (see *right*) – the similarity is even more obvious in bar 77, which begins on a low G. The easiest way to distinguish the two main tunes is to spot that melody A always continues with an alternation of the notes B and C, while melody B continues with an upward scale that starts on a low D.

A similar structure of repeated and decorated four-bar sections underpins the second half of the dance, but as the speed increases, and the elaboration and recycling of similar ideas (now often based

Jig	*(all repetitions are varied)*	
1–8	A	8 bars
9–16	A	8 bars
17–24	B	8 bars
25–32	B	8 bars
33–40	A	8 bars
41–48	A	8 bars
49–56	B	8 bars
57–65	B	8 bars *(the last note*
forms the first note of the Barndance)		

New Irish Barndance

Barndance	(first half)	
65–68	A	4 bars
69–72	A	4 bars
73–76	B	4 bars
77–80	B	4 bars
81–84	A	4 bars
85–88	A	4 bars
89–92	B	4 bars
93–96	B	4 bars

on the octave G–G) becomes more intense, the dance structure is overtaken by a whirl of virtuoso ornamentation.

The key of the barndance is G major, the same as that of the jig, and most of its motifs are based on chords I, IV and V of that key. Every alternate bar begins on G in the first half of the dance while, in the second half, every single bar (except bar 117) starts on this pitch, which acts almost like a pedal note, tying the tonality to G major. Again, there are indications of Niall Keegan's modern approach to traditional music in the occasional chromatic decoration (e.g. bars 66, 75, 114 and 124–125).

Exercise 12

1. Explain to a listener without specialist knowledge how to recognise the distinctive sound of the Irish traditional flute and its music.

2. Outline the differences and similarities between a jig and a barndance.

3. In what way is the purpose of the score of NAM 61 significantly different from the purpose of notation in western art music?

4. The structure of Bach's gigue in NAM 21 is defined by modulations to related keys. How does the structure of Tom McElvogue's (jig) differ?

5. Why does the barndance create such a hypnotically exciting effect?

6. Comment on the rhythm of the barndance in (a) bars 96–98 and (b) bar 121.

7. What single word defines the texture of both of the dances in NAM 61?

Sample questions

In Section B of the Unit 6 paper you will have to answer two questions (from a choice of three) on pieces from the Applied Music area of study. Here are three to use for practice.

You can write in continuous prose or short note form. You will be allowed to refer to an unmarked copy of NAM, and you should give the location of each specific feature that you mention. Aim to complete each question in 20 minutes.

(a) Bach's Cantata No. 48 (NAM 28, pages 288–299) was composed to be performed as part of a church service. Identify features of the texture, style and word-setting that make it particularly suitable for this purpose.

(b) Comment on the aspects of 'Der kranke Mond' (NAM 40, pages 364–365) that audiences would have found revolutionary at the first performance of *Pierrot Lunaire* in 1912.

(c) *On the Waterfront* is a film that depicts the struggle of an individual against corruption and violence. Discuss the way in which this theme is reflected in the music of NAM 43 (pages 374–387).

Set works for 2012

If you are taking A2 Music in summer 2012, you have to study the seven pieces of instrumental music *below*, plus the five pieces of applied music in the section starting on page 131.

Instrumental music

The pieces for this area of study span musical periods from the early Baroque to the late 20th century:

1550	1600	1650	1700	1750	1800	1850	1900	1950	2000
Renaissance		Baroque			Classical		Romantic		Modern

Sweelinck	Corelli	Mozart	Berlioz	Cage	Shostakovich	Narayan
NAM 20	*NAM 15*	*NAM 22*	*NAM 3*	*NAM 10*	*NAM 9*	*NAM 58*
1615	1689	1783	1834	1948	1960	1980

Pavana Lachrimae (Sweelinck)

Among the most popular types of instrumental music in Elizabethan England were sets of variations on dance tunes or songs. Of the many new songs composed around 1600, Dowland's *Flow my tears* (NAM 33) was perhaps the most famous. Dowland himself wrote variations on it, as did his fellow Englishmen Byrd and Farnaby. All three entitled these works *Pavana Lachrimae* for two reasons. Firstly the song is in the style of a slow processional dance of the late Renaissance known as a pavane. Secondly *Lachrimae* (meaning tears) refers to the image of falling tears with which the words of Dowland's song begins.

A number of English composers, including Dowland, travelled and worked in northern Europe at this time. John Bull, who had earlier been organist of the Chapel Royal in London, was appointed to Antwerp Cathedral and while in the Netherlands became a friend of Sweelinck (organist at the Old Church in Amsterdam for over 40 years). There can be little doubt that Bull introduced Sweelinck to Dowland's lute songs and the variations written on them by English composers.

Sweelinck's *Pavana Lachrimae* was composed in about 1615 and was not published in the composer's lifetime. The manuscript was probably used as teaching material to be played on the harpsichord (or possibly the organ) by Sweelinck's many pupils.

The work follows the structure of Dowland's song but instead of a repeat of each of its three sections there is a variation. The printed note values of *Flow my tears* are doubled in the *Pavana*, which means that:

➤ Bars 1–8 of the song = bars 1–16 of the pavane

➤ Bars 9–16 of the song = bars 33–48 of the pavane

➤ Bars 17–24 of the song = bars 65–81 of the pavane.

Context

NAM 20 (page 245)	CD2 Track 9
Peter Seymour (harpsichord)	

Structure

Bars	1–16	A	Dowland bars 1–8
	17–32	A¹	Variation on A
	33–48	B	Dowland bars 9–16
	49–64	B¹	Variation on B
	65–81	C	Dowland bars 17–24
	82–98	C¹	Variation on C

The example *below* shows the first phrase of Dowland's melody in its original note values and Sweelinck's free transcription of it:

Sweelinck leaves Dowland's harmonies mainly unchanged in these bars, including the **false relation** between G (bass) and G♯ (treble) in bar 10, but he embellishes the cadences in bars 8 and 14–15.

You won't be asked questions about Dowland's song in the exam, but comparing NAM 20 with NAM 33 is a good way to understand Sweelinck's variation technique.

Figural variations

At bar 17, instead of repeating the first part of the song to new words, as Dowland did, Sweelinck writes a variation on it, in which mainly **stepwise** semiquavers replace the longer notes of the vocal melody, bass and sometimes an inner part. The constant use of elaborate rhythmic figures to decorate the original has led to this technique being called 'figural variation'. Here we can see how, in bars 17–20, Sweelinck retains all of the pitches of the melody of bars 1–4 within his figural variation:

Sweelinck's variation technique is not only confined to the tune. In bar 18, for instance, the bass is allowed a share in the melody by repeating the treble of the previous bar (with one slight change). The same technique is used in bar 24 where the middle 'voice' is allowed a moment of glory.

The remainder of the pavane follows a similar pattern: first a free transcription of eight bars of the song (forming 16 bars in NAM 20 due to the longer note values) and then a variation on it in a more keyboard-like style, forming the structure $AA^1BB^1CC^1$.

Tonality and harmony

Sweelinck's harmony follows that of Dowland and shows the lingering influence of Renaissance modality. While there are cadences in A minor at the end of each four-bar phrase in the first 16-bar section, the first three are modal-sounding **phrygian cadences** (IVb–V) and the fourth is a perfect cadence with the characteristic **tierce de Picardie** of the late Renaissance style.

Even the brief visit to G major in bars 9–10 sounds quite modal compared with the modulations to closely-related keys that are a feature of later tonal styles (as we shall see in the next work that we study). And in the G-major chord at the start of bar 10, the G♮s in the bass and alto parts are immediately contradicted in the second half of the bar by the G♯s in the melody – such **false relations** are another feature of Renaissance modality. The most pungent example of this device is the simultaneous false relation in bar 96 where the treble G♮ (the highest note in the pavane) sounds against the sustained G♯ on the bass stave.

The majority of chords in NAM 20 are root-position triads and most of the rest are triads in first inversion. The only dissonances that occur on minim beats are **suspensions**, such as those on the second of each pair of tied notes in bars 89–92. Both of these features are typical of late Renaissance styles.

Texture

The sections transcribed from Dowland's song (A, B and C) are mainly in four parts, each of which is like a vocal part – the ranges correspond to those of soprano, alto, tenor and bass voices, and the melodic lines move largely by step or small intervals. Most of these passages are in free **counterpoint**, with occasional **imitative** entries – for example, compare the soprano part in bars 3–4 with the alto part that started two crotchets earlier. More concentrated imitation occurs in bars 42–45, where the initial four-note figure in the soprano is imitated by bass (with a longer first note), tenor, then by the soprano followed by the bass again, and finally by the alto.

The actual variations (A^1, B^1 and C^1) are in a much more idiomatic keyboard style. For instance, the semiquaver figuration that starts in the bass of bar 28 rises through almost two and a half octaves to a top D in the right hand of bar 30, and Sweelinck often alternates between three- and four-part textures in these sections.

Passages such as the one in bars 17–19, where almost identical melodies are heard in the soprano, then the bass, and then the soprano again are not contrapuntal because the other parts merely provide accompaniment. However, Sweelinck introduces a short **canon** towards the end, where the soprano part starting in bar 91^3 is imitated exactly by the bass a compound 4th lower in bar 92 (with the first note split into two crotchets an octave apart).

Exercise 1

1. What sort of dance is a pavane?

2. Why was English music so well known in northern Europe at this time?

3. Explain what is meant by idiomatic keyboard writing and give an example of it from NAM 20.

4. On the first beat of bar 73 the tenor B clashes with the bass C a major 7th below. What is this type of dissonance called?

5. Using the correct terminology, describe as precisely as you can the cadences in (a) bars 62^3–64 and (b) bars 96–98.

6. Listen to the recording and describe how Peter Seymour plays the opening chord. Can you spot any other types of ornamentation he uses in the performance?

Trio sonata in D, movement 4 (Corelli)

| NAM 15 (page 200)   CD2 Track 4 |
| Fitzwilliam Ensemble |

This was a set work in 2010, so you will find a discussion of it on pages 35–37 of this guide. Remember to complete the exercise on page 37 before continuing.

Piano Sonata in B♭, movement 1 (Mozart)

Context

| NAM 22 (page 253)   CD2 Track 12 |
| Alfred Brendel (piano) |

K. 333 is the number of this work in the catalogue of Mozart's compositions compiled in the 19th century by an Austrian scholar named Köchel.

By 1783, when Mozart wrote his Sonata in B♭, K. 333, the Baroque style of Corelli had given way to the elegance of the Classical style, and the piano had started to replace the harpsichord as the keyboard instrument of choice in both concert hall and home. Although the 18th-century piano was lighter in tone than a modern instrument, it was sufficiently powerful for Mozart to be able to show off his virtuosity in the piano concertos he wrote for the purpose and it was also capable of delicate dynamic effects, making it ideal for domestic performances of the series of piano sonatas that he wrote for himself and his amateur pupils. This work was first published in Vienna in 1784, as one of three sonatas (two for piano, and one for violin and piano), all by Mozart.

Structure

Like many Classical sonatas, this work has three movements in the order fast–slow–fast, of which we are to study the first. This is in **sonata form**, the most important musical structure of the Classical style, and has three main sections, each defined by key:

In minor-key sonata-form movements the second subject is usually in the relative major rather than the dominant: see the diagram on page 87.

The **exposition** begins by establishing the home key of B♭ major with a theme called the first subject (1–10). The next 12 bars move towards the contrasting key of the dominant (F major). Starting in bar 23 Mozart presents the first of several ideas in this key (the second subject group). The exposition ends with a **codetta** (bars 50–63) in which F major is affirmed by a succession of perfect cadences (bars 53–54, 57–59 and 62–63).

Bars
1–63   An **exposition** of the main themes, grouped into two contrasting tonal centres (tonic and dominant: B♭ and F)
63–93   A **development** of these themes passing through several related keys (including C minor and G minor)
93–165   A **recapitulation** of the principal themes in the tonic

The **development** (bars 63^4–93^3) is characterised by a wider range of keys. It begins with the first subject in F major but soon veers off to pass through the keys of F minor, C minor, B♭ major and G minor until Mozart signals the imminent return of the home key with seven bars of **dominant preparation** starting in bar 87.

The **recapitulation** (bar 93^4 to the end) sees the material of the exposition return, but now centred on the home key of B♭ major. The conflict of keys has been resolved in a perfectly balanced sonata-form structure (summarised *left*).

Style

The Classical style of this movement is markedly different to the styles of the two earlier works we have studied. Some of its key features are:

Periodic phrasing – pairs of equal-length phrases sounding like questions and answers. For example, the eight-bar phrase starting at bar 23 ends with an imperfect cadence in F major, and the eight-bar answer starting at bar 31 ends with a perfect cadence in the same key. However, Mozart is often ingenious in avoiding the predictability of periodic phrasing. The work opens with a four-bar phrase, but it is answered by a phrase that is extended to six bars in length, ending on the third beat of bar 10.

Melody-dominated **homophony**. The chief focus of the music is the ornate right-hand melody supported by the broken chords of the left-hand accompaniment. The melodies include frequent use of non-chord notes, especially **appoggiaturas** – both **diatonic** (such as the first B♭ in bar 88 which clashes with the dominant-7th chord beneath it) and **chromatic** (C♯ in bar 110).

Thin, crystal-clear textures. The first 22 bars are almost entirely in a two-part texture. When full chords are used they draw attention to the beginnings or endings of important sections (as in bar 23).

Broken-chord accompaniments. These are evident in the first four bars where Mozart achieves a delicate effect by beginning each left-hand pattern after the first beat of the bar. Elsewhere (notably bars 71–80) he uses an **Alberti bass** accompaniment.

Clear harmonic progressions with regular cadences to define keys. Mozart starts with the chords shown *right* and reaches a perfect cadence in B♭ major in bar 10. The modulation to the dominant (F major) in bars 11–22 is equally clear – notice how E♮ occurs with increasing frequency in these bars.

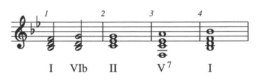

Much of the harmony is based on simple triads, especially tonic and dominant in various keys, but chromatic harmony appears in the development: **diminished-7th** chords in bars 67 and 69, the minor version of chord IV (E♭ minor) in bar 76, and **augmented-6th** chords on the last beats of bars 80 and 82. The augmented 6th in these is the interval E♭–C♯; the E♭ leans down to D in the next bar and the C♯ leans up to D, in a section that sounds for all the world like dominant preparation for a recapitulation in G minor. After six bars Mozart cheekily moves up a 3rd and begins proper dominant preparation for the return of B♭ major, as expected.

The movement includes two of the most characteristic harmonic features of the Classical style:

➤ The **cadential** $\frac{6}{4}$ – chord Ic used as the approach to a perfect cadence, forming the progression Ic–V$^{(7)}$–I. The example in bars 57–59 is preceded by a spectacular scalic descent from top F, the highest note on Mozart's piano.

➤ Accented dissonances on the final chord of a perfect cadence, as in bars 63 and 165, where the upper notes in the right hand are appoggiaturas and the lower ones are suspensions.

Exercise 2

1. In bars 1–10 which are the only bars that do *not* start with appoggiaturas or accented passing notes?

2. Where does Mozart use an Alberti bass in the exposition?

3. What do you understand is meant by dominant preparation?

4. State the key of the second subject in (i) the exposition, and (ii) the recapitulation.

5. Identify the harmonic progression in bars 159–161[1].

6. Unlike NAM 15, the mood of this music seems to change rapidly. Choose a section of about 24 bars and explain the techniques Mozart uses to create variety without the music sounding disjointed.

Harold in Italy, movement 3 (Berlioz)

Context

NAM 3 (page 42)   CD1 Track 3
London Symphony Orchestra
Conducted by Colin Davies

Hector Berlioz was one of the most original creative talents of the early Romantic period. His *Symphonie fantastique* of 1830 was a new type of work which illustrates a highly personal 'episode in the life of an artist' (the artist being Berlioz himself) using the medium of the symphony. The composer's beloved is represented by a melody that appears in different guises in every one of its five movements, called an *idée fixe* (a fixed idea, but used in French to mean an obsession). Berlioz wrote detailed notes for publication in concert programmes explaining how this 'programme music' expresses his hopeless fixation with a woman, her rejection of him, and the drug-induced nightmare in which he imagines he has killed her and then witnesses his own execution for the crime.

Harold in Italy arose from a commission by the famous **virtuoso** Paganini for a viola concerto. Berlioz actually wrote a symphony, containing only a modest part for solo viola, intended to represent Harold, the hero of a long poem by Lord Byron. In fact, none of the scenes depicted in the symphony's four movements bear much resemblance to the poem and it is obvious that the hero is, once again, Berlioz himself. Paganini was disappointed at the lack of virtuoso display in the viola part and the first performance was given in 1834 at the Paris Conservatoire of Music without him.

The idée fixe

Although this work is far less programmatic than the *Symphonie fantastique*, it too has an *idée fixe* – here it is as it appears near the beginning of the symphony's first movement:

This *idée fixe* makes an appearance in every movement, but it is not obsessive like its counterpart in the *Symphonie fantastique* – it simply turns up to represent Harold, the vagabond dreamer, as an onlooker in picturesque Italian locations. The next example shows Harold's theme as it appears in bars 65–80 of NAM 3 (the viola player needs to use **double-stopping** to produce the octaves):

Finally, this example shows how Berlioz derives the theme (which first starts in bar 34) from from reordered motifs of Harold's theme:

Cor anglais (sounding a 5th lower)

Orchestration

Berlioz is renowned for superb orchestration. Natural horns were still common in 1834 and, because these valveless instruments could play only a limited set of pitches, he uses four of them, and in three different keys (C, F and E) to cover as many notes as possible. The score also includes three instruments that were still uncommon in the symphony orchestra: the harp, the piccolo (which sounds an octave higher than written) and the cor anglais (a low oboe which sounds a perfect 5th lower than written). Notice the orchestral colours Berlioz obtains by, for instance, doubling the opening oboe solo an octave higher on the piccolo, and accompanying it with divided violas.

Commentary

At the start, attention is focused on an impression of Italian bagpipes represented by a double **pedal** on notes I and V of C major. Above this, the melody played by the oboe and piccolo uses the rhythm of the *saltarello*, an ancient Italian folk dance.

At bar 32 Berlioz carefully notes that the speed should halve and the cor anglais introduces the main theme of the movement (notice the syncopation in bars 37 and 38). The sequel to this melody introduces an oboe playing in octaves with the cor anglais and this double-reed tone becomes even more biting when the bassoon joins in an octave lower at bar 53. Horns in C (sounding an octave lower than printed) take over the first phrase of the cor anglais theme in bar 59. At bar 65 Harold's *idée fixe* enters (shown in the second example *opposite*) and is combined with earlier material.

The music becomes more chromatic and the textures become more complex (although the harp chords that enter at bar 72 helpfully show the basic harmonies). Passages in G major (bars 89–96) and D minor (bars 97–115) provide tonal variety, but are unrelated to the **ternary** (ABA) structure of the whole movement.

Berlioz frames the central section (bars 32–135) by returning to the folk dance style of the start (bars 136–165 repeat bars 1–30). But at bar 166 a final section begins – so vanishingly quiet that it must surely be Harold dozing off into another daydream in the hot Italian sunshine. Berlioz combines solo viola phrases from the main theme of the Allegretto with Harold's *idée fixe* (flute, pinpointed with harp harmonics), the folk-dance rhythm (on divided violas) and the bagpipe drone (also violas). Gradually instruments drop out to leave isolated fragments of the saltarello melody (bars 194–198) and the bagpipe drone (violas ***ppp*** at bar 201). Finally everything winds down to the lowest note of the muted solo viola (C, the tonic) and the movement ends with repeated C major triads played almost inaudibly on muted strings.

Exercise 3

1. What is an *idée fixe*? How does the term relate to this movement?

2. What type of instrument is a cor anglais? What is special about the notation of music for this instrument?

3. Name the chord played by the violas on the first beat of bar 1. How does this chord relate to the key of the movement?

4. Identify the type of chord used at the start of bar 97 (all of its notes are present in the harp part).

5. Summarise the structure of this entire movement in a single short sentence.

6. State **two** reasons why Paganini might have found this work unsatisfactory to reflect his talents as a virtuoso string player.

Sonatas and Interludes: Sonatas I–III (Cage)

> NAM 10   CD1 Tracks 12–14
> (page 166)
> Joanna MacGregor (piano)

This was a set work in 2010, so you will find a discussion of it on pages 54–59 of this guide. Remember to complete the exercise on page 59 before continuing.

String Quartet No. 8, movement 1 (Shostakovich)

Context

> NAM 9 (page 163)   CD1 Track 11
> Coull Quartet

Dmitri Shostakovich lived all his life in Russia, where he was one of several prominent composers who periodically suffered harsh criticism from the Soviet state. His opera *Lady Macbeth of Mtsensk* was denounced in 1936 as 'chaos instead of music' and banned for its decadent western modernism. Shostakovich then responded by supplying suitably heroic and wholesome music to glorify the state – only to be denounced again in the cultural purges of 1948.

In 1960 Shostakovich was deeply humiliated by being forced to join the Communist Party – the price the composer had to pay for the removal of the ban on some of his earlier works. In July of that year Shostakovich visited Germany where he saw the remains of the beautiful and historic city of Dresden after its intensive bombing in the Second World War. It is said that this experience inspired his eighth string quartet, completed in just three days and dedicated to the 'memory of the victims of fascism and war'.

This dedication may not be as clear-cut as it seems – the words have the potential double meaning that many Russian dissidents used under the Soviet regime in Russia. They had long referred to the Communists as 'fascists' and they would have understood that 'victims of fascism' did not necessarily refer exclusively to those persecuted by the Nazis. It is likely that Shostakovich saw himself as one of those victims, and intended the eighth quartet to be his final work and his own memorial. However, this was not to be, for Shostakovich went on to write a number of other works before his death in 1975.

The string quartet (for two violins, viola and cello) has been the most popular type of **chamber music** since the late 18th century, and Shostakovich contributed 15 such works to the **genre**. This quartet is in five interconnected movements, of which we are to study the first. It was given its first performance in Leningrad (now known by its original name of St Petersburg) on 2 October 1960.

The cipher and the quotations

> Russian is written in the Cyrillic alphabet and this can result in inconsistency when names are transliterated. You may find books that refer to 'Dimitri' and German scores that call the composer Schostakowitsch.

The personal nature of this work is evident in Shostakovich's use of quotations from earlier works, almost as if he is looking back on his life, and in his use of a cipher – in this case, a group of letters with a hidden meaning. It is first heard in the opening cello notes: D–E♭–C–B♮. In German these pitches are known as D–Es–C–H and, since Es is pronounced like the letter 'S', they transliterate to D Sch(ostakovich), a musical encryption of the German version of part of the composer's name. He used this motto in other works, but in the eighth quartet it permeates the music, giving the work a powerful sense of unity.

Structure

The first movement of the quartet is in **arch form**, which we can represent as $ABCB^1A^1$. In other words, the last two sections are modified repeats of the first two sections, with their order reversed, as shown *right*. When using bar numbers, notice that the movement begins with an anacrusis (an up-beat), so bar number 1 starts with the second note of the opening cello solo (E♭). Although the time signature is $\frac{4}{4}$, Shostakovich's metronome mark ($\downharpoonright$=63) suggests a slow minim beat. So, when we have added superscript figures to bar numbers in the following account, they refer to the first or second *minim* beat in the bar.

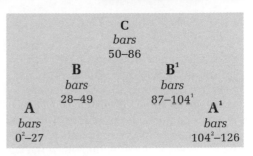

Commentary

The movement opens with **imitative** treatment of the DSCH motif, heard first in the cello (C minor), answered by the viola (G minor), restated by the second violin (C minor) and answered by the first violin (F minor). Although the harmony is dissonant, this choice of keys (I, IV and V in C minor) reveals how Shostakovich's style is often essentially tonal, although there are no simple cadences to define this tonality. The low **tessitura** of all the parts establishes the sombre tone of the movement from the outset.

DSCH returns to the viola (marked 'solo') in bars 8–10 and then a clearer sense of C minor briefly emerges as the viola sustains G as a dominant pedal, above and below which the three other parts play DSCH in octaves. However, the last note is harmonised with a totally unexpected triad of E minor (bar 13), signifying the start of the first violin's quotation (in greatly expanded note-lengths) of the opening theme from the composer's first symphony, the work that had established his reputation some 34 years earlier.

While the first violin sustains B♮ as an inverted pedal, the lower strings add to the tonal ambiguity by shifting chromatically from the chord of E minor at the start of bar 13 through triads of E major, E♭ major, D major and back to E♭ major in bar 16. Meanwhile, the second violin returns to DSCH in bar 15 (marked 'solo'). The decoration of the third note of the cipher by a quaver D in bar 17 is the point at which the quotation from the symphony moves down to the second-violin part. It is restored to the first-violin part at bar 19^2 and comes to an end in bar 23^1. DSCH then returns, this time in a **homophonic** texture and terminating in a perfect cadence (bars 25–27) that now seems to make the C minor tonality totally clear, even though the tonic chord lacks a 3rd.

From here on, the tonality remains anchored to C minor with long dominant and tonic pedal points. Sometimes Shostakovich prefers major 3rds to minor 3rds in chord I, and sometimes no 3rd at all. But neither the chromatic writing nor a short excursion to A minor (starting in bar 86) suggests that this is anything other than a profoundly tonal movement.

Most of section B (bars 28–49) is accompanied by a long double pedal on tonic (C) and dominant (G). This drone is played by all three lower parts, while the first violin has a falling, then rising, chromatic line. This leads to an expressive figure in bars 32^2–33 that Shostakovich modifies in various ways over the next ten bars. As the drone ceases, another reference to DSCH (cello, bar 46) marks the end of Section B.

At the start of the central C section, a simple idea introduced by the first violin (bar 50) is transferred to the second violin two bars later, and developed into a **countermelody** to the long, slow first violin theme that begins in bar 55. This begins with a quotation from the first movement of Shostakovich's fifth symphony – one of his most famous works (see *left*). This violin duet is accompanied throughout by more long pedals, this time in octaves, first on C, then on G, and finally back to C.

This section ends, like the previous two, with DSCH at its original pitch (starting in bar 79). Here the cipher is heard in rhythmic **augmentation**, harmonised with unrelated block chords of G major, E♭ minor and F major, all in root position. This is followed by a perfect cadence (bars 82–85) in which the dominant chord begins with two biting dissonances (A♭ and F♭) and in which the tonic chord again lacks a 3rd (sometimes called an 'open 5th' chord). The chord of A minor in bar 86 provides a link to the next section.

Section B^1 (bars 87–101^1) is a restatement of material from the first B section, but with a number of changes. It begins with the only extended passage in the movement to completely break free of the fateful key of C minor. Violin parts in 3rds give the music greater warmth and below them the cello plays the chromatic melody that was allocated to the first violin when it first appeared in bar 28.

Another ray of sunshine permeates the gloom with the appearance of very quiet root-position triads of C major and F major in bar 95, but chromatic lines soon return. This is the only one of the five sections of the movement that doesn't finish with a statement of DSCH at its original pitch – instead, the cipher is used to open the final section (A^1) in the second half of bar 104.

Instead of beginning with imitative entries of DSCH, as at the start of the movement, here it is played in octaves either side of a dominant pedal in the viola. This (like the first note of the cipher in the cello and second-violin parts) is sustained from the end of the previous section to provide a seamless join. The omission of the opening imitative section of the movement means that the theme from the first symphony starts in bar 106 (11 bars earlier than before), where its first note overlaps with the last note of DSCH.

The music from section A is then restated almost exactly until a brief extension (bar 114) leads to a final appearance of DSCH (bar 118^2, second violin), again leading to a perfect cadence in C minor. All of the instruments sink to their lowest notes and the second violin briefly refers to the motif from the central section (bars 122–123). On the last repetition of this, the A♭ is notated as G♯ (known as an **enharmonic** change) to form a link to the second movement, which is in the remote key of G♯ minor.

Shostakovich's life was at a low ebb in 1960 when he wrote this work. An unhappy marriage had ended in divorce the previous year, he had been diagnosed with an incurable illness (although he was to live for another 15 years) and was feeling suicidal after being forced to join the Communist Party that he so loathed.

This may help to explain the gloomy mood of this work, but can you see how it is achieved in musical terms? The instruments are used in a low register throughout, often playing on just their lowest string. The melodies are slow moving, legato and mainly conjunct, and there is no use of double-stopping, pizzicato, tremolo or other effects. The gloom of C minor is intensified by long pedals on tonic and/or dominant, with many perfect cadences in the tonic, and the dynamics are mainly very quiet, only rising in level for the homophonic statements of DSCH at the ends of sections A and C.

Exercise 4

1. Explain precisely how the letters DSCH relate to this movement.

2. What are the only two pitches played by the viola in bars 50–79?

3. Compare bars 87–92 with bars 28–33.

4. What effect do you feel the long pedal notes and low tessitura of the strong parts have on the character of this music?

5. Briefly describe some of the different types of texture used in this movement.

6. What examples would you choose from NAM 9 to show that the music is essentially tonal?

Rag Bhairav (North Indian)

Context

The classical music of northern India is like western chamber music in that, traditionally, it is presented by a few highly skilled performers to a small and attentive audience. But there are also many differences, and not just in the instruments and sounds involved. The music is improvised according to conventions that are well understood by the listeners who, like the performers, sit on a carpeted floor. They may silently tap along to the music, respond to feats of technical and artistic skill with anything from a murmur of approval to a huge round of applause, or even request their favourite pieces.

> NAM 58 (page 519)   CD4 Track 16
> Ram Narayan (sarangi)
> Chanranjit Lal Biyavat (tabla)

There are usually at least three performers, each with a specific role in the music: a soloist (either a singer or player of a melodic instrument), a percussionist, and a musician who plays a repetitive or drone-like accompaniment. Improvisations can last from just a few minutes (like NAM 58, which is unusually short) to several hours. Concerts don't normally have a fixed programme or length.

Indian musicians learn their skills during a long apprenticeship with a respected teacher (sometimes a family member) during which they listen, imitate and memorise. Notation is sometimes used in the early stages of tuition, but performances are always given from memory.

Instruments

The melody in NAM 58 is played on a *sarangi* – an instrument with three main strings that are stopped with the fingernails of the left hand and played with a heavy bow held in the right hand. There are also up to 35 additional strings that vibrate in sympathy with the bowed notes (and that can also be plucked), producing the characteristic shimmering tone. The player sits cross-legged and the instrument is held in an upright position against the chest with its base resting on the player's feet. The traditional role of the *sarangi* was to accompany singers and/or dancers, but performers such as Ram Narayan (who plays on NAM 58) have shown that it is at least as versatile as the more familiar *sitar* for solo improvisation.

The *tampura* (or *tambura*) is a large stringed instrument that is plucked to provide the simple four-note **ostinato** that runs throughout the piece, largely independent of the other parts. The pitches it plays are shown at the start of the score, but the first one is incorrectly printed as B in some editions of NAM – it should be G in the top space of the bass stave, making the notes of the ostinato *pa* and *sa*. The notes on the *tampura* are always played on open strings, but their tone can change markedly with the style of plucking.

The *tabla* are a pair of small drums that can be played with various combinations of finger and hand strokes known as *bols* (meaning 'words'). Different pressure can vary the tone, and the drum heads are mounted with a patch made from a paste of iron filings and rice flour which gives further opportunity to vary the sound.

> Technical terms in Indian music have been transliterated into English. You may find alternative spellings in other books, as well as some vowels marked with diacritics (signs such as the accents in French).

The elements of North Indian classical music

Melodic improvisation is based on a series of pitches called a *rag* (pronounced 'rahg'). These are more complicated than the scales used in western music because each has strict rules about how the notes are to be played as well as which ones to use. It is simplest to think of a *rag* as a template for melodic improvisation.

> The moods historically associated with different *raga* are those of Hindu *rasa*, listed in the margin box on page 56. However, over time such linkage has become more theoretical than practical.

Each *rag* is intended to express a particular mood and many are associated with times of the day or seasons. *Rag Bhairav* is said to suggest awesome grandeur tinged with melancholy and tenderness, and was traditionally performed early in the morning. However, these days you might well hear *Rag Bhairav* sung or played in a 'Bollywood' film or used as the basis for a popular Indian song.

The improvisation on the tabla is based around a *tal* (pronounced 'tahl') – a repeating rhythmic template, sometimes described as a rhythmic cycle, that the player embellishes.

NAM 58 uses the most common of all rhythmic cycles, known as *tintal*, which consists of 16 beats, divided into four groups known as *vibhags*. In many *tala* each *vibhag* has a different number of beats, but in *tintal* they all have four beats, making them rather like bars of quadruple metre in western music.

The improvising musicians must arrive together on the first beat of the *tal* – this is marked **X** in the score, and known as the *sam* (pronounced 'sum'). Each *tal* must have at least one contrasting *vibhag* known as *khali* (marked **0** in the score) which the player distinguishes by using just the smaller of the *tabla*'s two drums. In *tintal*, the third *vibhag* is *khali* and it helps the performers to be aware of where they are in this relatively long 16-beat cycle:

Tal (16-beat *tintal*)			
1 2 3 4	5 6 7 8	9 10 11 12	13 14 15 16
X		**0**	
sam		*khali*	
Vibhag 1	Vibhag 2	Vibhag 3	Vibhag 4

The structure of *Rag Bhairav*, which was recorded in about 1980, follows the outlines of a traditional North Indian performance, although in a compressed form. It starts with a simple exposition of the main elements of the *rag* in free time and then gradually builds in intensity, gathering a stronger sense of pulse when the *tabla* enter, and ending with sections of great virtuosity.

The introductory section is called the *alap* and Ram Narayan begins by slowly establishing the pitch *sa* (C in the score) as the principal note of the *rag*, and the one on which he will eventually end. The pitches *sa* and *pa* (the only notes played by the *tampura*) may suggest tonic and dominant, but there is nothing tonal about this music, and the precise pitches of all the notes in the *rag* differ from those used in the scales of western music.

At 3³ (the point at which the transcription moves into the treble clef) Narayan introduces a *mukhra* – a short melodic phrase that marks out different phases of the improvisation. Here it signals a move to a higher register on the *sarangi*. The *mukhra* follows the traditional pattern of a rise to *pa* (the second most important pitch after *sa*) which is then repeated:

The *mukhra* returns at 6⁹ (continuing into stave 7) to announce a return to the lower register, after which Ram Narayan shows the full range of the *rag* during staves 8 to 13. So far, the notes have been embellished with:

➤ Microtonal inflections of pitch (called *sruti*)

➤ Wide vibrato around a note (called *gamak*)

➤ Slides between notes (called *meend*).

On staves 14 and 15 Narayan introduces a more expansive form of decoration – scale-like figures called *tans* – that culminate in his highest note at the end of stave 15. In a longer improvisation, a more rhythmic section called a *jhor* (see *right*) would start at this point. However, here the *jhor* is represented only by this short passage of *tans*, which descend straight into the next appearance of the *mukhra* (starting at the end of stave 17).

The entry of the *tabla* (stave 19) provides a clear sense of pulse for a final section that gradually increases in intensity, called the *jhala*. Narayan begins this section by developing a phrase of limited range based on the end of the *mukhra* (bracketed in the example *above*). At 21⁷ he recalls the opening pitches of the *rag* before returning to the *mukrah* in the middle of stave 22 (after the second quaver rest).

The *sam* at the start of stave 23 marks a development of the opening notes of the *jhala* (i.e. from the start of stave 19), which leads to a series of brilliant *tans* beginning at 25⁸. These end with a headlong descent into the *mukrah*, which starts after the accented B in the middle of stave 28.

As the pulse gradually quickens, further returns of material from the opening of the *jhala* coincide with the *sam* at the beginning of

Listening guide

When reading the score in NAM, note the non-standard key signature, which indicates that A♭ and D♭ are the only two flats in the piece. The score is a transcription, made by writing down what is heard on the recording.

From here on, locations such as 3³ mean stave 3, note 3.

A traditional instrumental performance of a *rag* consists of three sections:

The *alap* is a slow introduction in free time, during which the soloist explores the notes of the *rag*, accompanied by a *tanpura* drone or ostinato.

The *jhor* is slightly quicker and has a greater sense of pulse, although the *tabla* do not yet join in.

The *jhala* sees the entry of the *tabla*, further increases in speed, and the use of much exciting decoration.

NAM 58 is based on the shorter structure of a vocal improvisation, in which there is no distinct *jhor* section, although it reflects the gradual increase in speed and intensity that is a feature of almost all improvisations.

staves 29, 31, 33 and 35, the last of which is decorated and then extended to form the concluding phrase of NAM 58.

Exercise 5

1. Explain how a *tal* differs from a bar in western music.

2. What is the importance of the beats marked **X** in the score?

3. Describe the ways in which the music becomes more exciting from stave 13 to the end.

4. Listen to the recording and then explain how the *tabla* part is varied during the improvisation.

5. To what does the term *jhala* refer?

6. What is a *tampura* and what role does it play in NAM 58?

7. Which one of the following terms correctly describes the scale-like figures on stave 32?
    khali   tans   gamak   alap

8. Explain the role of the *mukhra* in giving structure to this piece.

9. What musical term best describes the texture of NAM 58?

Sample questions

In Section C of the Unit 6 paper you will have to answer one of two questions about the instrumental works you have studied. Your response is expected to be an essay, written in continuous prose, and your clarity of expression, spelling and grammar will be taken into account in the marking.

Remember that it is important to give locations of each specific feature that you mention, but there should not normally be any need to write out music examples. You will be allowed to refer to an unmarked copy of NAM as you write.

Here are two essay topics to use for practice. Aim to complete each essay in 50 minutes.

(a) Compare and contrast the structures and use of melody in the three following works:

Corelli's Trio Sonata in D, Op. 3, No. 2: movement IV (NAM 15, pages 200–201)
Mozart's Piano Sonata in B♭, K. 333: movement I (NAM 22, pages 253–257)
Berlioz's *Harold in Italy*: movement III (NAM 3, pages 42–65).

(b) Compare and contrast the textures and use of instruments in the three following works:

Shostakovich's String Quartet No. 8, Op. 110: movement I (NAM 9, pages 163–166)
Cage's Sonatas and Interludes: Sonatas I–III (NAM 10, pages 166–170)
Rag Bhairav (NAM 58, pages 519–521).

Applied music

In ecclesiis (Gabrieli)

Before starting on the text below, you may find it useful to read the opening paragraphs about Giovanni Gabrieli's *Sonata pian' e forte* on page 60, and to listen to NAM 14.

The wealth of Venice, along with the echoing spaces and multiple choir galleries of its grandest church, St Mark's, provided all that was necessary for a new style of church music in which spatially separated choirs of instruments and voices echo and answer each other in **antiphony**. This dramatic new style, which developed towards the end of the Renaissance and continued into the early years of the Baroque period, is known as polychoral music.

We don't know when *In ecclesiis* was first performed, but it would have been for a major service in St Mark's, where Giovanni Gabrieli was organist, probably in about 1606. It was first published in 1615, three years after the composer's death.

Gabrieli wrote for 14 independent parts in *In ecclesiis*:

➤ Four solo vocal parts

➤ Four choral vocal parts

➤ Six parts assigned to a group of specific instruments: three cornetts, two trombones and a violin (then a new instrument, but the range of the part is closer to that of a viola).

In addition, a bass part for organ, from which the player improvises chords, runs throughout the work, although it doubles the instrumental or vocal bass when everyone is performing. This type of bass part was a new feature in music of the period although it is, of course, the origin of the figured bass part that we saw in Corelli's trio sonata. The chords can be improvised in a wide variety of ways – the score of NAM 27 offers one suggestion and the recording on CD3 offers another.

Another feature of the work is Gabrieli's idiomatic writing – the choir have relatively simple parts, the solo voices are expected to cope with more elaborate lines, while the instruments are required to play dotted rhythms and repeated notes (like those in bars 31–33) that are totally unlike vocal melodies.

The divided choirs of polychoral music, with singers placed in different parts of the building, are sometimes called *cori spezzati* ('split choirs').

Compositions of the early 17th century that combine and contrast vocal and instrumental ensembles, supported by a **continuo** bass part are often described as being in *stile concertato* (concerted style).

The combination of a solo voice and continuo accompaniment heard at the start of NAM 27 was a new type of texture in music of the period and, when used in early Baroque music, is known as monody (not to be confused with monophony).

Context

> NAM 27 (page 269)   CD3 Track 2
> Gabrieli Consort and Players
> Directed by Paul McCreesh

Resources

> A cornett is a wooden wind instrument with fingerholes and a brass mouthpiece. Its tone is like that of a soft trumpet and it was often used with trombones at this time (as in NAM 14).

> We saw that idiomatic instrumental writing was starting to appear at this time when we studied Sweelinck's *Pavana Lachrimae*, written shortly after *In ecclesiis*.

Other useful terms

Structure

A translation of the text is given on page 538 of NAM.

Bars			
1–5	A	First vocal solo	
6–12	B	*Alleluja* refrain (1)	
13–24	C	Second vocal solo	
25–31	B	*Alleluja* refrain (2)	
31–39		Instrumental *Sinfonia*	
39–61	D	First vocal duet	
62–68	B	*Alleluja* refrain (3)	
68–94	E	Second vocal duet	
95–101	B	*Alleluja* refrain (4)	
102–118	F	*Tutti* (everyone)	
119–129	B¹	extended *Alleluja* refrain (5)	

The text of *In ecclesiis* is a Latin hymn of praise divided into five sections by repeated interjections of the Hebrew word *alleluja*. Listen to the whole work and see if you agree with the following:

➤ Each of the first four phrases of the Latin text is set for one or two solo voices and has its own distinctive melody

➤ The choral interjections of *alleluja* are all similar (despite some differences in scoring), although the last one is longer

➤ The last sentence (*Deus adjutor noster in æternum*) and the final longer *alleluja* are scored in 14 parts for all three choirs

➤ There is an instrumental interlude (*sinfonia*) which divides the two vocal solos from the two vocal duets.

The result is a **rondo** structure built around the central sinfonia, with *alleluja* (B) as the refrain: A–B–C–B–sinfonia–D–B–E–B¹. The use of refrain to hold together these highly contrasting textures is typical of the new *concertato* style, but it is another of the very modern features that permeate this work. And there are more …

The new style

Gabrieli and some of his contemporaries used a number of new techniques in a style that at the time was described as the *seconda prattica* (the second practice, the first being the older polyphonic style of the 16th century). These new techniques are ones that we now associate with Baroque music.

The combination of solo voices, choir and instruments supported by a continuo group is the most obvious feature, but the **ostinato** bass that starts in bar 3, and the rhythmic repeated phrase above it are typical of the new style, as is the use of various types of **sequence** in bars 13–19. The ways in which Gabrieli takes account of the massive six-second echo of St Mark's (for instance, the total silences in the middle of bar 10 and the end of bar 102) also reflect the drama of much Baroque music.

The striking chromatic chord (an augmented triad) on the third beat of bar 31, and the strings of dotted rhythms that follow are also typical of the emerging Baroque style, but Gabrieli reserves his most dramatic effects for the final sections. In bar 102 all three choirs plus the organ are heard together for the first time, and they enter with a massive homophonic setting of *Deus* on two unrelated chords a third apart (F major and D major). They are linked by the common note A but supercharged by the **false relation** between the outer parts (F in the bass of the first chord, F♯ in the topmost cornett part in the second). The progression is then repeated a tone higher in bar 103, using unrelated chords of G major and E major, with another false relation between the outer notes. In this way, Gabrieli emphasises the most important word in the text, *Deus* (God).

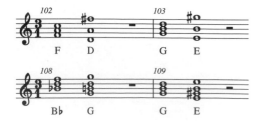

When Gabrieli repeats this effect in bars 108–109, he ratchets up the drama still further by making the entire progression fall in 3rds between unrelated chords (shown *left*). Other new ways of using harmony in this closing section include unprepared discords, such as D♮ sounding against G♯ in bar 104, and the climactic effect of a dominant **pedal** in bars 115–117.

There are, of course, more traditional techniques in the piece as well. The change to triple time for the *alleluja* sections was common in earlier music, as was the use of a **tierce de Picardie** in the final cadence (although the rather neat idea of finishing the piece with the same four chords with which it began is a more novel effect).

You should be able to spot points of imitation (for instance, in bars 10–11 and in the *sinfonia*) and the use of contrapuntal textures that contrast with the homophony. More easily overlooked are the combined **canons** that add to the brilliant tumult of sound in bars 114–117. The first is in the choral alto and tenor parts, starting with the minim E in bars 114 and 115 respectively. The second is for all four soloists, starting with the tied E in the countertenor of bars 114–115 and imitated at an interval of two beats by the other soloists. The third is between the two cornetts in bars 115^4–117.

Exercise 6

1. How does the solo vocal part in bars 26–31 differ from the solo vocal part in bars 7–12?

2. Look up the terms **melisma** and **syllabic** in the glossary and then give an example of each type of word-setting in this piece.

3. Explain what is meant by monody and give an example of its use on page 271 of NAM.

4. Why does the harmony sound so dramatic in bars 108–109?

5. With what type of cadence does *In ecclesiis* end?

6. Look up the word cornet in a music dictionary and then explain how it differs from a cornett.

7. Make a brief list of all the features in NAM 27 that would have seemed new to listeners in the early 17th century.

Pulcinella Suite: Sinfonia, Gavotta, Vivo (Stravinsky)

This was a set work in 2010, so you will find a discussion of it on pages 65–72 of this guide. Remember to complete the exercise on page 72 before continuing.

> NAM 7 (page 139)   CD1 Tracks 7–9
> Academy of St Martin in the Fields
> Conducted by Neville Marriner

Passport to Pimlico: The Siege of Burgundy (Auric)

The French composer Georges Auric may seem a surprising choice as the composer of scores for several of the most famous 'Ealing comedy' films, in which a distinctly British sense of humour is exploited to the full. However Auric had a reputation as a composer of light, witty music, dating back to the 1920s, when he had been the youngest member of *Les Six*, a group of urbane and satirical French composers which included Milhaud, Poulenc (composer of NAM 19) and Honegger. Auric had also written film scores for the avant-garde film director Jean Cocteau, as well as much theatre and ballet music.

This 1949 comedy is about the residents of Pimlico in central London. An unexploded bomb left over from the Second World War blows up and in the debris they find an old document decreeing that Pimlico is part of the ancient French province of Burgundy.

Context

> NAM 42 (page 369)   CD4 Track 1
> Royal Ballet Sinfonia
> Conducted by Kenneth Alwyn

> The Ealing comedies were made at Ealing studios in west London. Auric's other scores for these films include *Hue and Cry* (1947), *The Lavender Hill Mob* (1951) and *The Titfield Thunderbolt* (1952).

Quickly seizing their opportunity, the residents of Pimlico declare the area to be independent of the rest of the country and set about dispelling the gloom of post-war Britain by abolishing licensing laws and the food rationing that was then in place.

The music of NAM 42 ('The Siege of Burgundy') accompanies a scene in which British government officials retaliate by partitioning off 'Burgundy' with a cordon of barbed wire, setting up customs barriers and cutting off water and electricity. Other Londoners come out in force to throw food over the barricades to the besieged folk of Pimlico. Like most film scores, the structure of the music is dictated by the screenplay and doesn't follow any conventional musical form.

Commentary

Auric captures the humour of the busy scene in a musical collage of rapidly-changing ideas that often resemble the circus music frequently imitated by French composers of his generation. He does this with:

➤ Short, repeated motifs based mainly on scale and tonic triad figures (bar 1–4, bar 5)

➤ Frequent and surprising changes of key (E major in bars 1–8, plunging straight into G major at bar 9)

➤ Rapid changes of texture and instrumentation (bars 13–20)

➤ Witty chromatic writing (bassoon theme, bar 22)

➤ Harmonies that enliven simple chords with added notes (such as the perfect cadence at the end of bar 12 in which E is added to the D^7 chord and passing notes decorate the bass)

➤ Mainly quaver and semiquaver rhythms at a fast tempo.

The headline 'Burgundy is bombarded with buns' is accompanied by a bright opening fanfare in E major. Loud trills on tonic and dominant capture the exhilaration of the scene. The descending horn scale in bar 1 is repeated in 3rds in bar 2 and, to intensify the excitement, it appears in free **diminution** in bars 3 and 4.

The motif which enters at bar 5 shows how Auric achieves a bustling, breathless mood. It is based on the tonic chord of E and is immediately repeated in bar 6. Cellos and basses use the same rhythm in bar 7 and the whole package is neatly wrapped up with contrary motion scales and a quick perfect cadence in bar 8. The music then dives straight into G major at bar 9 for a decorated repeat of the previous four bars.

Auric enhances the fun with many witty orchestral effects – the consecutive 5ths between flutes and tinkling glockenspiel in bars 5–6, busy semiquaver scales in 3rds from the accompanying strings, and joyous trills and leaps from clarinets in bars 9–10.

A short link (bars 13–14) features an inverted tonic **pedal** on G spikily offset by a brass entry on F♯. The scale-based motif in bar 15 introduces a new texture (bare octaves) and new keys (B minor, then B major). Strings and wind alternate in **antiphonal** exchanges to illustrate the noisy debates in Hyde Park and Trafalgar Square.

The music slows as the 'government yields to public pressure' and in bar 20 Auric underlines the point by concluding the political debate with a charmingly old-fashioned but very definitive cadence in B major ('so there!' the music seems to say).

The jolly bassoon motif in bars 21–23 is yet another idea based on the tonic triad of E major – this time decorated with accented **chromatic** auxiliary notes (marked * in the example, *right*). The music drops a semitone at bar 27, the treasury being treated to some suitably luxurious harmonies. Bar 33 sees yet another new key (this time, C major) and a varied repeat of the bassoon motif, which is now transferred to high woodwind.

Presents from other Londoners are seen arriving in bar 39 and so Auric reuses the music from the similar scenes on the first page of the score. There is a clever reversal of sections, though – this time bars 9–12 are heard first (transposed from the original G major to E♭ major in bars 39–42) and then the music winches up a semitone so that in bars 43–46 we can hear bars 5–8 in their original key of E major, but with fuller scoring.

> In bar 41 'con sord.' is an abbreviation of *con sordino*, meaning 'with mute'.

A fanfare in bars 49–50 is prematurely interrupted by a 'suspense motif' (a classic device in film music to suggest horror or surprise) as the talks suddenly deadlock. Auric's suspense motif (bars 52–53) consists of a mysterious low tremolo on divided violas, below which cellos and basses play a distorted version of the theme from bar 5. Relief comes almost immediately in the form of an airlift and so the dominant harmony of bars 49–50 is resumed in bar 54.

The final section stays entirely in C major, despite the F♯ which wickedly infiltrates the final cadence in bar 64. With considerable tongue in cheek, Auric depicts the arrival of a helicopter with a dainty little tune, delicately scored for piccolo doubled by celeste, and accompanied by pizzicato strings.

> A celeste (or celesta) is a keyboard instrument with hammers that strike metal bars. When listening to CD4, compare this doubling of piccolo and celeste with bars 23–25, where the piccolo is doubled by a glockenspiel (an instrument with metal bars that are struck directly by the player, using a pair of beaters).

This tune starts with a one-bar motif in bar 55 which is given two varied repeats and rounded off with a cadential figure to make a four-bar phrase. Its second four-bar phrase begins with another reversal of previously heard material – bar 59 is a varied repeat of bar 57, and bar 60 is a varied repeat of bar 56 (both filled-out with extra parts). A final statement of the tune by the horn in bar 63 is cut off after only one bar as trumpets lead to a perfect cadence in C major, undermined by an F♯ that might well remind you of Stravinsky's deliberate weakening of cadences in *Pulcinella*.

Exercise 7

1. What is antiphony and where does it occur in this extract?

2. Contrast the textures of bars 19 and 47 by giving each its precise technical term.

3. How should the upper strings play bar 23? How should the violas play bar 52?

4. The eight bars starting in bar 55 are entirely diatonic. What does diatonic mean?

5. Explain how Auric creates a sense of comedy and busy activity in this extract. As a starting point use the list opposite, but try to find *different* examples of each technique you mention.

Inspector Morse: Morse on the Case (Pheloung)

Context and style

Barrington Pheloung was born in Australia in 1954 and studied at the Royal College of Music in London, after which he settled in Britain. He has composed music for advertising campaigns by companies such as Rover, Andrex and Sainsbury, ballet and film scores, and music for both television and multimedia projects.

> NAM 46 (page 433)   CD4 Track 5
> Conducted by Barrington Pheloung

NAM 46 is taken from an episode of *Inspector Morse*, a series of television detective mysteries first broadcast between 1987 and 2000. The title and incidental music was written by Pheloung, who faced two unusual challenges. The first was the very large amount of material needed over the course of 33 two-hour episodes. The second was the inclusion of a great deal of diegetic music by other composers – that is, music experienced by the characters on-screen, rather than background music for the benefit of the audience.

In the case of Morse, the diegetic music ranges from classical CDs that the detective plays while brooding over a mystery to operas and concerts that he attends as part of his investigations. To avoid detracting from this music and to distinguish the diegetic extracts from his own underscore, Pheloung adopts an unintrusive style based on slow-moving lines, thin textures and single notes to reflect Morse's complex intellectual reasoning. In particular, he avoids the clichés of film music: for example, instead of up-beat rhythms for an exciting car chase, his music reflects the fact that Morse suffers from vertigo and has a horror of fast driving.

Pheloung also entered into the spirit of the mysteries. The theme music (not part of NAM 46) starts with the rhythm of the word 'Morse' spelled out in Morse code on the note E – the initial of the detective's first name (which itself remained a mystery until almost the end of the series). In a 1993 documentary Pheloung indicated that sometimes he even included Morse-code 'clues' about the identity of the suspect in his background music.

In NAM 46, which comes from an unidentified episode, Pheloung uses the understated textures and ambient sounds characteristic of much Postmodernist music. Unlike the short, repetitive ideas of Minimalism he avoids obvious rhythmic and melodic patterns, and instead focuses on texture and timbre. The meditative, sensory mood is further enhanced by quiet dynamics and long, sustained notes that change in unexpected parts of the bar, offering no obvious sense of pulse, despite the constant $\frac{4}{4}$ metre.

Structure and tonality

The structure of the music would have been determined by the images that it accompanies, but it falls into three main sections, determined by instrumentation and tonality:

> You can find the aeolian mode by playing an octave of white notes on the piano, starting from A. The notes A and E are its main pitch centres.

➢ Bars 1–52 for horns, piano and upper strings, entirely **diatonic** in the aeolian mode and overlapping with the start of …

➢ Bars 49–97 for oboe, piano and upper strings, in which the **chromatic** notes F♯ and A♭ appear

➢ Bars 98–112 for all nine instruments, which gravitate towards C major but retain a persistent dissonant F♯, like an unsolved clue niggling away in Chief Inspector Morse's mind.

The extract begins with a thin, two-part texture. The opening intervals played by the piano are each reversed in direction by unison muted strings – the piano rises a 4th, the strings fall a 4th; the piano falls a 3rd, the strings rise a 3rd.

The strings continue this very slow pattern of descending 4ths and rising 3rds below the piano fragments in bars 8–12. Horns enter on an A in bar 12 and descend a tone to G in bar 15. The first violin again responds by reversing the direction of this major 2nd, moving *up* a tone from C to D in bar 18.

Meanwhile, at the very end of bar 17 the piano announces a three-note melodic cell (D–E–A), followed by just its first two notes played harmonically (the major 2nd on D and E in bars 22–24). Again the first violin responds by reversing the direction of the original rising interval, once more falling a major 2nd from D to C in bar 24, while the second violin returns to the rising 4th with which the extract began (now on G–C).

Bar 26 sees the return of our three-note figure (D–E–A) in the piano, now shrunk to semiquavers, its outer notes also serving as the left-hand accompaniment. Meanwhile the third horn is playing an **inversion** of this figure (A–G–D) in much longer note values. The next appearance of D–E–A is expanded to four much longer notes (A–D–E–A) in the right-hand piano part of bars 32–35. Pheloung then uses just the two outer notes of the original motif (D–A) in bars 36–38, doubled in major 9ths by the left hand.

This slow manipulation of tiny melodic cells is accompanied by an almost imperceptible thickening of texture as instruments are added and the string writing expands from unison at the start through two parts from bar 14 to three from bar 29. Notice also how the bass (played by the viola) very slowly descends over 52 bars, starting on E in bar 1 and eventually arriving on D a 9th lower.

The first section dies away to the sound of falling major 2nds (inversions and transpositions of the first two notes of D–E–A), ending with an open 4th on D and G in bars 49–52[2].

Commentary: Bars 1–52

The entry of the oboe in bar 49 introduces a new timbre for this section, but melodically the oboe continues slowly to explore different versions of the three-note cell that dominates the work (G–A–D until bar 60 and then A–D–E). The piano's F♯ in bar 52 clashes with the oboe's G, although the differences in pitch (almost two octaves) and timbre take the edge off the dissonance.

The texture has by now reduced to two parts and then becomes **monophonic**, allowing the ear to focus purely on the tone of the oboe, which dies out in bar 60 to be followed by the only complete silence in the extract.

From the end of bar 64 the piano introduces a new version of material from bar 8 and the upper strings return, at first in unison and then in two parts. Pheloung continues merely to hint at ideas rather than to state them directly. For example, chords are often suggested by just their outer notes – G[7] (bar 82), F/A (bar 85) and A minor (bar 87). In each of these bars, notes change later than expected: a semiquaver after the first beat of bar 82, a quaver after

Bars 49–97

the first beat of bar 85 and a dotted quaver after the first beat of bar 87. Both features result in an ambiguity that adds to the sense of mystery in the music.

It is a feature of the *Morse* stories that the viewer is never sure if the inspector is following up the right lead – there is often a note of uncertainty, and this time that note is the A♭ sounded by the piano in bar 92 against A♮ and B in the strings. As the piano tone dies away the same pitch is taken over by the oboe and sustained until the strings give up and fade out.

Bars 98–112   The oboe's fall from A♭ to E signals the start of the final section, in which Pheloung continues to revisit earlier material. Compare, for instance, the piano part in bars 98–99 with that in bars 26–28. The pattern in bar 99 is then reused in bars 108–109, but it is now metrically displaced so that it appears a quaver later in the bar. Other variants of this tiny idea occur in bars 102–105 (violins). Similarly, new versions of the three-note idea are developed and extended to six notes by the harp, starting in bar 101.

This final section is marked out by new timbres: all four horns in unison (indicated by 'a 4' in bar 98), harp and (at last) the entry of the low strings. The use of the full ensemble allows slightly thicker textures, although the instruments are used very sparingly and never all play together (and the oboe is silent after bar 101).

Pheloung restricts most of his instruments to a very narrow range – horns never exceed a 5th, the strings are muted and used only in their lower register, and cello, bass and harp are silent until this final section. The pianist rarely plays more than two notes at a time and the dynamics are very restrained – the f in bar 107 marks the point at which the harp introduces the final reference to the three-note pattern (here extended to four notes) from the first section.

Chief Inspector Morse's cases often end enigmatically, and so does Pheloung. Bars 102–112 outline an extended VII⁷–I progression in C major, despite the piano sometimes clouding the first chord with a dissonant C, but the recurring F♯ adds a note of nagging doubt. The music settles on the none too conclusive sound of a C-major triad in bar 110, but the horn note vaporises, leaving the final chord without its 3rd. Mystery solved … or not?

Exercise 8

1. What special effect are the violins and violas instructed to use from bar 1 onwards?

2. How does the viola part relate to the violin parts in bars 1–13?

3. Compare the piano pitches in bars 31–35 with those in bars 26–28.

4. Compare the oboe part in bars 49–60 with the horn part in bars 25–35.

5. Auric's use of harmony in NAM 42 can be described as functional (meaning that it uses chords and cadences to define keys). How would you describe Pheloung's use of harmony in NAM 46?

6. Briefly explain how 'Morse on the Case' is based on the slow evolution of tiny melodic cells.

Agbekor dance (traditional Ewe)

In west Africa, societies such as the Ewe people of Ghana have a traditional musical heritage that is rich in rhythmic complexity. European music, for all its harmonic sophistication, often seems rhythmically dull to African musicians, who strive for the inter-action of several markedly different rhythms played at the same time. Simultaneous layers of opposing rhythms produces a texture known as **polyrhythm** and it is this that gives the music its sense of vitality. The exciting rhythmic style of African music spread via the slave trade to the Caribbean and the southern states of America, from where it had a direct influence on many of the jazz and pop music styles of today.

In many parts of Africa drums have special significance as symbols of political or religious power, and are often associated with tribal chiefs and royal families. African musicians do not refer to playing their instruments, but to teaching them to speak – they do not like playing drums from other regions because these 'don't speak the same language'. This link between language and music is important. The relative pitch of spoken words affects their meaning in most African languages and these inflexions can be imitated by the 'talking drum' to communicate messages, as explained *below*.

The performance is directed by a master drummer who, on this recording, is Mustapha Tettey Addy (born 1942). He comes from a large family of drummers just outside the city of Accra in Ghana. Addy is one of the leading scholars and practitioners of west-African drumming. In 1988 he founded the Academy of African Music and Arts in Ghana, where traditional skills in drumming continue to be taught and demonstrated.

The *agbekor* is a ritual war dance which was originally intended to be a preparation for battle, although nowadays it is performed for entertainment at social gatherings and cultural presentations. The dance is presented in platoon formation (with the dancers in one or more lines) and it features stylised movements to represent such features as reconnaissance, surprise attack and hand-to-hand combat. The main part of the dance is, of course, fast-paced, as illustrated by the music of NAM 62.

Each of the three instruments has a fixed and unchanging role in the performance. The *gangkogui* consists of two bells joined by one handle and struck with a wooden beater. The bells are made of iron and in NAM 62 are roughly an octave apart in pitch. The main function of the *gangkogui* is to play a repeating pattern called a time line – a rhythmic **ostinato** which acts as a reference point for the other performers, including the dancers.

The *atsimevu* is the master drum. It is a tall narrow drum (about 1.3 metres high) that is leant against a wooden frame. The head is about 28cm in diameter and the drum is open at the bottom. The *atsimevu* can be played with one stick, two sticks or with the hand, and a variety of muting effects are possible, as explained at the head of the score. The variety of pitches possible through the use of different drum strokes can emulate the tonal and rhythmic inflec-tions of speech (giving rise to the expression 'talking drum') and

Context

> NAM 62 (page 532)   CD4 Track 20
> Mustapha Tettey Addy

The dance

The instruments

this property can be used to communicate directions to the other players and dancers, or to incorporate statements of praise to the tribal chief on ceremonial occasions. The master drummer will also sometimes indicate cues by playing the *gankogui* pattern on the side of the drum. Can you see where this happens in NAM 62?

The *sogo* is a barrel-shaped drum about 75cm high, closed at the base. It is played in a sitting position, with the drum resting on the ground between the player's knees. It plays its own rhythm against the time line, and sometimes adds variations and improvisations.

Commentary

Divisive rhythm:

Additative rhythm:

Although the time signature indicates that the very fast pulse falls into units of 12 quavers, they are not articulated as four groups of three, as normally occurs in $\frac{12}{8}$ time, in which regular subdivisions are known as a 'divisive' rhythm. Instead, they are articulated as an 'additive' rhythm in a pattern of 2+3+2+2+3 quavers (shown *left*) – one of the most common rhythms in African drumming.

The syncopation of this pattern is not obvious at the start, where the *gankogui* begins alone – in fact, it sounds as if the *atsimevu* part is syncopated when it first enters. Before we have time to register a common pulse, the *sogo* enters with a device found in much African music. It plays patterns that are the same 12-quaver length as the other parts, but they are staggered so that each starts one quaver after the metrical pattern of the bell. At the end of bar 13 the master drummer uses this device in the opposite direction – the *atsimevu* patterns enter one quaver *before* the bell.

The *sogo* continues to plays its own rhythm against the time line – the basic pattern heard at the start attracts two variants (bars 12^2–13^1 and 26^2–27^1) both of which alternate with the original version in the second half of the piece.

The master drummer, as befits his status, has a much wider variety of patterns than the other two players, enhanced by the different pitches and tonal effects marked in the score. As the piece proceeds the master drummer introduces increasingly complex patterns, including the syncopations of bars 25–26 and 35, and triplets in bars 41–42. The resulting interaction with the other parts produces a **polyrhythmic texture**, with frequent **cross-rhythms**, that is the most characteristic feature of west-African drumming.

If possible, try performing this dance on whatever percussion instruments you have available. Even at a slow pace it will require the utmost concentration.

Exercise 9

1. What type of dance is the *agbekor*?

2. What is an *atsimevu*? What role does it play in NAM 62?

3. Describe what is meant by a time line. Name the instrument that plays the time line in NAM 62 and show how the part it plays relates to the $\frac{12}{8}$ time signature in the transcription.

4. Explain the meaning of cross-rhythm and give an example of one from NAM 62.

In Section B of the Unit 6 paper you will have to answer two questions (from a choice of three) on pieces from the Applied Music area of study. Here are three to use for practice.

You can write in continuous prose or short note form. You will be allowed to refer to an unmarked copy of NAM, and you should give the location of each specific feature that you mention. Aim to complete each question in 20 minutes.

(a) *In ecclesiis* by Giovanni Gabrieli (NAM 27, pages 269–287) was probably composed to be performed during a service in St Mark's, Venice. Identify features of the style, texture and vocal writing that make it particularly suitable for this purpose.

(b) The three dances from Stravinsky's *Pulcinella* suite (NAM 7, pages 139–159), were first heard as ballet music in 1920. Comment on features of their melody, rhythm and instrumentation that audiences at the first performance might have found particularly attractive.

(c) *Morse on the Case* (NAM 46, pages 433–439) was written to accompany a television sequence from a detective mystery. Discuss the ways in which Barrington Pheloung creates a mysterious sound world from the controlled use of dissonance and slowly evolving melodic cells.

Glossary

Note that some of the terms in this glossary may apply to set works that you are not studying.

Accented passing note. A dissonant note sounded on the beat and filling the gap between two harmony notes. In NAM 22 the notes F and A in the right hand of bar 53 beat 4 are accented passing notes, clashing with the underlying C^7 chord. *See also* **Appoggiatura** and **Passing note**.

Acciaccatura. An ornament printed as a small note with a slash through its stem and flag (♪) that is either played as short as possible, or is played with the main melodic note and immediately released. It often forms a discord with a harmony note, as is the case with the acciaccaturas in the second half of bar 15 in NAM 37.

Alberti bass. An accompaniment pattern in which the notes of a chord are repeatedly sounded in the order low, high, middle and high again. It is named after an obscure Italian composer who was addicted to the device. See NAM 22, bars 71–80 (left hand).

Anacrusis. One or more weak-beat notes before the first strong beat of a phrase, as in bar 5 of NAM 52 and bar 8 of NAM 53. Often called a 'pick-up' in jazz and pop music.

Anticipation. A note played immediately before the chord to which it belongs. The anticipated note is often the tonic in a perfect cadence, as in bar 426 of NAM 1, where the semiquaver G at the end of the bar anticipates the tonic in the final chord of the movement.

Antiphony. The alternation of different groups of instruments and/or singers. There is a short antiphonal exchange between wind and strings in bars 47–49 of NAM 17; a longer example occurs between the two instrumental groups at the start of NAM 14.

Appoggiatura. A dissonant non-chord note, often approached by a leap, that resolves by moving to a chord note. It is like a **suspension** but without the preparation. Appoggiaturas are sometimes written as small notes, like ornaments, as in bar 12 of NAM 37, where C♯ in the vocal part clashes with B in the accompaniment before resolving on the same note.

Arco. An instruction for string players to resume bowing after using some other technique, such as **pizzicato**, as seen in NAM 3, bar 53.

Articulation. The degree of separation between notes. In NAM 23 the slurs in the first piece indicate that it should be articulated smoothly (legato). Most of the notes in the second piece are marked with staccato dots, indicating a detached style of articulation. At the start of the third piece, the combination of slurs and staccato dots indicates mezzo-staccato – notes that should be only slightly detached.

Atonal. Western music without a note that acts as a home pitch to which all other notes are related. This means, in particular, that atonal music avoids major and minor keys (and also modes). NAM 8 is atonal.

Augmentation. A proportionate increase in the note-lengths of a melody. The last bar of NAM 32 is an augmented version of the previous bar. The opposite of augmentation is **diminution**.

Augmented-6th chord. A chromatic chord based on the sixth degree of the scale (the flattened sixth degree if the key is major) and the note an augmented 6th above it. The chord also contains a major 3rd above the root and may include a perfect 5th or augmented 4th above the root. An augmented-6th chord can be seen on the last beat of bar 80 in NAM 22 (left hand), where the key is G minor and the augmented 6th is formed by the notes E♭ and C♯. The chord resolves when the two notes forming the augmented 6th move outward by a semitone to the dominant, as occurs on the first beat of bar 81 in the same piece.

Auxiliary note. A non-chord note that occurs between two harmony notes of the same pitch. In bar 6 in NAM 22 the second semiquaver (C) is an upper auxiliary and the fourth semiquaver (A) is a lower auxiliary. The harmony note in B♭ in both cases.

Avant-garde. A term referring to composers or works seen as breaking new ground, such as the music of NAM 11.

Backbeat. A term used in pop music to describe accenting normally weak beats (e.g. beats 2 and 4 in $\frac{4}{4}$ time). In bars 3–4 of NAM 51 the backbeats in the drum part are marked with accents.

Balanced phrasing. *See* **Periodic phrasing**.

Baroque. A term referring to music written in styles typical of the period 1600–1750, such as NAM 1, 15 and 21.

Bend. *See* **Pitch bend**.

Binary form. A two-part musical structure, usually with each section repeated, as in the first piece in NAM 23. In longer binary forms the first section often ends in a related key and the second modulates back (perhaps through other related keys) to the tonic. This can be seen in the two dances of NAM 21, and in NAM 15, where the first sections end in the dominant key (A major) and the second end in the tonic key (D major). Binary form is often represented as ‖:A:‖:B:‖ but there is not normally any contrast in mood or theme between its A and B sections as there is in the ABA structure of **ternary form**. *See also* **Rounded binary form**.

Bitonality. The use of two different keys at the same time, as in bars 4–6 of NAM 31, where the choir parts outline E♭ major but the accompaniment outlines C major.

Blue note. A term used in jazz and blues-based music for a note (usually the third, fifth or seventh degree of a major scale) that is made more expressive by slightly lowering its pitch. In the vocal part of NAM 52 the note G♮ is the blue 3rd of E major and the note D♮ is the blue 7th.

Break. A term used in pop and jazz for an instrumental solo within a song, as occurs in bars 33–44 of NAM 57.

Cadence. The last notes of a phrase, suggesting a point of repose. If harmonised, the chords can define the degree of completion more exactly. *See* **Perfect cadence**, **Imperfect cadence**, **Interrupted cadence**, **Plagal cadence** and **Phrygian cadence**.

Cadential $\frac{6}{4}$. A triad in second inversion is called a $\frac{6}{4}$ chord because its upper notes form intervals of a 6th and a 4th above its bass note. A cadential $\frac{6}{4}$ refers to chord Ic used before a perfect cadence (Ic–V$^{(7)}$–I) or as the first chord of an imperfect cadence (Ic–V). It is one of the most characteristic sounds of the Classical style and can be found in NAM 22, where a perfect cadence in F major is formed by the progression Ic–V^7–I in bars 57–59.

Canon. Music in which a melody in one part fits with the same melody in another part even though the latter starts a few beats later. The device occurs in the type of song known as a round. In NAM 34, the entire first soprano part in bars 43^3–50 is sung in canon by the second soprano three beats later. *See also* **Counterpoint**.

Chamber music. Ensemble music intended for only one performer per part, such as NAM 16. The term originally referred to music that was suitable to be played in a room (or chamber) of a private house.

Chromatic. A word meaning ‘coloured’, used to describe notes outside the current key or mode. They are added for colour and do not cause a change of key. Accidentals are not necessarily chromatic. Bars 1–8 of NAM 15 are in D major and the G♯ in bar 4 is chromatic because it does not belong to that key – G♮ returns in the very next bar. However, the G♯ in bar 9 has a different effect. It is part of a modulation to A major which, unlike the previous example, is confirmed by a cadence in this new key in the next bar. The music from here until bar 19 is in A major and the G♯s used in this section are not chromatic – they are **diatonic** notes in the new key of A major. *See also* **Tonality**.

Circle of 5ths. A series of chords whose roots are each a 5th lower than the previous chord. In practice the series would soon drop below the lowest note available on most instruments, so the bass usually alternates between falling a 5th and rising a 4th, producing the same series of pitches. NAM 39 starts with a circle of 5ths in bars 1–9.

Classical. A term often used for any sort of art music, but more specifically referring to music written in styles typical of the period 1750–1825, such as NAM 16, 17 and 22.

Coda. The final section of a movement. In tonal music the coda will often consist of material to confirm the tonic key. For example, the coda of NAM 2 (bars 122–133) contains three perfect cadences in the tonic key of D major.

Codetta. A little **coda**. The final section of part of a movement.

Comping. Improvising a jazz accompaniment, as in bars 7–42 of the piano part of NAM 48.

Conjunct. Movement to an adjacent note (a tone or a semitone away) in a melody, also known as stepwise motion. In the first 12 bars of NAM 13 the top part is entirely conjunct. The opposite of conjunct is **disjunct**.

Consonance. Harmonious sound, lacking tension. The opposite of **dissonance**.

Continuo. Abbreviation of *basso continuo*. A continuous bass part of the Baroque period played on one or more bass instruments. It also provides the foundation for improvising harmonies on chordal instruments such as the harpsichord, organ and lute. Such improviation was done in accordance with the conventions of the time, guided by any **figured bass** given in the part (*see* NAM 15). The term is also used to mean the instrumental group that plays the continuo part.

Contrapuntal. A texture that uses **counterpoint**.

Contrary motion. Used to describe simultaneous melodic lines that move in opposite directions. In the first piece in NAM 23, the melody and bass move in contrary motion throughout the first six bars – when the melody rises, the bass falls, and vice versa. *See also* **Oblique motion, Parallel motion** and **Similar motion**.

Countermelody. A melody of secondary importance heard at the same time as (and therefore in **counterpoint** with) a more important melody. In NAM 17 the horn melody in bars 250–253 is combined with a cello countermelody.

Counterpoint. The simultaneous combination of two or more melodies with independent rhythms. There may be some **imitation** between the parts but counterpoint can also be non-imitative. A whole movement may be contrapuntal, such as the gigue in NAM 21, or the music may alternate between contrapuntal and other textures, as in NAM 18, where a section of **fugal** counterpoint begins at bar 67. The term is often used interchangeably with **polyphony**.

Cross-rhythm. A passage in which the rhythmic patterns of one or more parts runs counter to the normal accentuation or grouping of notes in the prevailing metre. The effect of 'two-against-three' in bar 3 of NAM 39 is an example of a cross-rhythm.

Development. The central section of **sonata form**. The term is also used more generally to describe the manipulation and transformation of motifs and themes in any sort of music.

Dialogue. A texture in which motifs pass between different parts. In NAM 35, the falling 3rd in bar 1 is exchanged in dialogue between pairs of parts throughout the first four bars. This is not imitation, because there is no overlap between these motifs.

Diatonic. Pitches of the prevailing key and music which contains only those pitches. The first two complete bars of NAM 37 are purely diatonic. Bars 3 and 6 are not diatonic as they contain **chromatic** notes which colour the harmony but do not establish a new key. The D#s in bars 15–21 are diatonic because the music is in E major here, and D# is part of that key.

Diminished-7th chord. A four-note chord made up of superimposed minor 3rds (or their **enharmonic** equivalents), creating an interval of a diminished 7th between its outer notes. In the first piece in NAM 23, the notes C#–E–G–Bb in the second half of bar 1 form a diminished-7th chord.

Diminution. A proportionate reduction in note-lengths. In the melody of NAM 22 the first two notes of bar 3 occur twice in diminution in bar 5. The opposite of diminution is **augmentation**.

Discord. *See* **Dissonance**.

Disjunct. Melodic movement by leaps rather than steps between adjacent notes, as in NAM 8. The opposite of disjunct is **conjunct**.

Dissonance. Two or more sounds that clash, producing a discord. The perception of what sounds discordant has varied over time. Before the 20th century it was normal for the tension produced by on-beat discords to be 'resolved' by means of the dissonant notes moving to a concord. In the final bar of NAM 22 the left hand outlines notes of the tonic chord of Bb major, but Eb and C in the right hand clash with this. This dissonace is resolved when these two right-hand notes drop to notes of the tonic chord in the second half of the bar. Since about 1900 dissonance has often been used as an effect in its own right.

Dominant preparation. A passage focused on and around the dominant chord to create an expectation that the tonic key will return, often at the end of the development section in **sonata form** (as in bars 87–93 of NAM 22).

Double-stopping. The performance of a two-note chord on a string instrument, as occurs in the first-violin part of NAM 16 at bar 41.

Échappée. A non-chord note that moves by step from a harmony note and then leaps in the opposite direction to another harmony note. The first Ab in the first-violin part of NAM 16 is an échappée.

Enharmonic. A term to describe the same pitch notated in two different ways. The final note of NAM 9 could have been written as Ab, but it is enharmonically notated as G# because it functions as a link to the next movement, which is in a sharp key and therefore uses G♯ rather than A♭.

Episode. A contrasting section in **rondo form**, or a passage in a **fugue** that does not contain either the subject or answer (e.g. NAM 25, fugue, bars 15–20).

Exposition. The first section in **sonata form** or in a **fugue**.

False relation. The simultaneous or adjacent occurrence *in different parts* of a note in its normal form and in a chromatically altered form. In NAM 35 a false relation occurs in bar 56 between the F♯ and the F♮. In NAM 41 an example of a simultaneous false relation between E♮ and E♯ occurs on the third beat of bar 14.

Figure. A clearly-defined melodic fragment such as the six notes heard in the ripieno violin 1 part in bars 14–15 of NAM 1. This is repeated in sequence in the next six bars. When a figure such as this is repeated exactly, varied, or used in sequence the result is called figuration. *See also* **Motif**.

Figured bass. Numbers and other symbols below a basso **continuo** part to indicate the harmonies to be improvised by chordal instruments, as in NAM 15.

Fill. A term used in pop music to indicate that a passage which is embellished or filled out in performance is not notated in full in the score, as occurs in bar 44 of NAM 54 or in the section starting at bar 17 in NAM 51. The term is also used for a brief improvised flourish (often on drums) to fill the gap between one section of a pop song and the next.

Fugal. In the style of a **fugue**, as in the opening of NAM 15.

Fugue. A type of composition based on a melody that initially enters in succession in each of several parts. This is called the subject (or the answer if it is transposed). While each subsequent part introduces the subject, the previous part continues with a new idea called the countersubject that fits in **counterpoint** with the subject. The first part of a fugue, known as the **exposition**, ends after each part has introduced the **subject** or answer. Further entries of the subject are separated by sections called **episodes**, usually based on similar material, and towards the end there may be a **stretto**.

Functional harmony. Progressions of chords, particularly V$^{(7)}$–I, that define the key(s) of a piece of music. In NAM 1, the progression I–V–I is heard four times in the first 12 bars, firmly establishing G major as the tonic key.

Genre (pronounced jon-ruh). A category or type of composition, such as the piano sonata, the string quartet or the madrigal.

Ground bass. A melody in a bass part that is repeated many times and which forms the basis for a continuous set of variations. The $\frac{3}{2}$ section of NAM 36 uses a ground bass.

Harmonic. On string instruments (including the harp and guitar), a very high and pure sound produced by placing a finger lightly on a string before plucking or bowing. Harmonics are indicated by small circles above the harp notes in bars 108–109 of NAM 5.

Harmonic rhythm. A term used to describe the rate at which chords change. There are two chords (I and V^7) in bar 1 of NAM 16, but in bars 9–12 the harmonic rhythm is much slower – chord V lasts for two bars and then chord I lasts for two bars.

Hemiola. A rhythmic device in which two groups of three beats ('strong–weak–weak, strong–weak–weak') are articulated as three groups of two beats ('strong–weak, strong–weak, strong–weak'). See the example printed on page 104.

Heterophony. A texture in which simple and elaborated versions of the same melody are heard together, as in bars 26–39 of NAM 2, where the oboe melody is accompanied by a decorated version of the same tune in the first-violin part.

Hexatonic. Music based on a scale of six pitches. The vocal melody of the chorus in NAM 57 (bars 25–32) is hexatonic – it contains six of the seven pitches in C major, but avoids the leading note (B). The accompaniment to this tune, though, is not hexatonic. *See also* **Pentatonic**.

Homophonic. A musical texture in which one part (usually the uppermost) has the melodic interest, and that the other parts accompany (as opposed to a polyphonic or contrapuntal texture, in which all the parts are melodically interesting). The last five bars of NAM 30 are homophonic; since they consist entirely of block chords, the texture in this passage could also be described as **homorhythmic** or chordal. The opening of NAM 39 illustrates a different type of homophony, often referred to as 'melody-dominated homophony' or, more simply, 'melody and accompaniment'.

Homorhythmic. A type of **homophonic** texture in which all of the parts move in the same rhythm, such as in the first four bars of NAM 38 or bars 79–81 of NAM 9.

Imitation. If a motif in one part is immediately taken up by another part while the first part continues with other music, the motif is said to be treated in imitation. The imitation is usually not exact – some intervals may be modified, but the basic melodic shape and rhythm of the opening should be audible. The imitative entry often starts at a different pitch from the original. NAM 15 begins with imitation in all three parts. If the parts continue in exact imitation for a number of bars, they will form a **canon**.

Imitative point. A motif that is used as the subject for **imitation**.

Imperfect cadence. Two chords at the end of a phrase, the second of which is the dominant, as in NAM 37, bars 3^6–4.

Impressionism. A style particularly associated with late 19th- and early 20th-century French music. Just as Impressionist paintings often blur objects and explore the effects of light, so Impressionist music frequently blurs tonality, using chords primarily for the atmosphere they create rather than as **functional harmony**, and exploring unusual and delicate tone colours. NAM 5 is typical of the Impressionist style in music.

Interrupted cadence. Two chords at the end of a phrase, the first of which is the dominant and the second being any chord other than the tonic (most often chord VI, as in bar 26 of the third movement of NAM 23, where the cadence is V^7–VI in the key of E minor).

Inversion (1). An interval is inverted when its lower note is transposed up an octave while the other note remains the same (or vice versa).

Inversion (2). A chord is inverted when a note other than the root of the chord is sounding in the bass. In NAM 2 the first chord in bars 9–12 is the tonic chord of D minor in root position, but the second chord in each of these bars is the dominant chord in first inversion (A major, with its third, C♯, in the bass).

Inversion (3). A melody is inverted when every interval is kept the same but now moves in the opposite direction (e.g. a rising 3rd becomes a falling 3rd). The alto part in bars 5–6 of NAM 32 is an exact inversion of the soprano part above it.

Lied (plural Lieder). The German for song, used more specifically to refer to 19th-century settings of German poetry for solo voice and piano, such as NAM 38. Its French counterpart is the **mélodie**.

Melisma. Several notes sung to one syllable, as in bar 22 of NAM 39.

Mélodie. The French for melody, used more specifically to refer to 19th-century settings of French poetry for solo voice and piano, such as NAM 39. Its German counterpart is the **Lied**.

Metre. The organisation of a regular pulse into patterns of strong and weak beats. For example, alternate strong and weak beats are known as duple metre, while the recurring pattern 'strong–weak–weak' is known as triple metre.

Minimalism. A musical style of the late 20th century characterised by static or slowly changing harmonies and the interaction of short patterns that repeat and change over a considerable length of time, as in NAM 12. *See also* **Postmodernism**.

Modernism. A term used to describe styles of the 20th-century century that are experimental and/or atonal, such as NAM 8, 10 and 11. *See also* **Postmodernism**.

Modes. These are usually taken to mean seven-note scales other than the modern major and minor scales (although some people refer to the latter as the major mode and minor mode). For example, the aeolian mode starting on A consists of the notes A–B–C–D–E–F–G–A. It differs from A minor in having G♮ rather than G♯ as its seventh degree. All of the notes in the last four bars of NAM 32 belong to the aeolian mode transposed down a 4th to start on E (E–F♯–G–A– B–C–D–E).

Modulation. The process by which music changes from one key to another. NAM 1 begins in the key of G major. The introduction of C♯s from bar 15 onwards indicates the start of a modulation to the dominant key of D major. This new key is then confirmed by a succession of I–V–I progressions in D major, starting in bar 23.

Monophonic. A texture that consists of a single unaccompanied melody, as in the first phrase of NAM 32.

Monothematic. A movement in which the music is based on a single theme, such as NAM 16.

Monotone. A single pitch repeated a number of times. The vocal part in bars 60–65[1] of NAM 52 is sung to a monotone on E.

Mordent. An ornament (⁓) consisting of a rapid move from a main pitch to an adjacent note and back again, as in bar 1 of NAM 21.

Motif. A short but memorable melodic fragment that is subject to manipulation through techniques such as **sequence**, **inversion**, extension. For example, the motivic material in the first two bars of NAM 16 forms the basis of almost all the thematic material in the entire movement. *See also* **Figure**.

Neapolitan 6th. The first inversion of the triad on the flattened second degree of a scale. In the key of E minor, this is a chord of F major in first inversion, as on the first beat of bar 155 in NAM 1.

Neoclassical. An early 20th-century style that combined forms and techniques from the 18th century with a more modern approach to elements such as rhythm, harmony and instrumentation. NAM 7 and NAM 19 both show the influence of Neoclassicism.

Oblique motion. A term used to describe the relationship between a melodic part that remains on a single pitch while another part either moves away from it (as at the start of the third piece in NAM 23, where the melody remains on B while the bass moves down chromatically) or towards it (as at the start of NAM 30, where the bass remains on C and the soprano moves down towards it). *See also* **Contrary motion**, **Parallel motion** and **Similar motion**.

Ostinato. A melodic, rhythmic or chordal pattern repeated throughout a substantial passage of music. For example, the four-note pattern starting in bar 163 of NAM 31 is played 31 times in succession by pianos, harp and timpani. In popular music and jazz a melodic ostinato is known as a riff. A **ground bass** is a type of ostinato.

Parallel major and **parallel minor**. Keys that share the same tonic, such as D major and D minor are known as parallel keys. The two keys can also be described as the tonic major and tonic minor. The main key of NAM 2 is D minor, but at bar 100 it moves to the parallel major key (D major) for its final section.

Parallel motion. A type of **similar motion** in which the parts move in the same direction *and* maintain the same or similar vertical intervals between notes, as in the opening of NAM 24 and in the parts for women's voices in bars 26–29 of NAM 41. *See also* **Contrary motion**, **Oblique motion** and **Similar motion**.

Passing note. A non-chord note that most commonly fills the gap between two harmony notes a 3rd apart. In the third bar of NAM 1 the second quaver in both recorder parts is a passing note between harmony notes belonging to the chord of G major. *See also* **Accented passing note**.

Pedal (or 'pedal point'). A sustained or repeated note against which changing harmonies are heard. A pedal on the dominant (NAM 16, bars 16–28) tends to create excitement and the feeling that the tension must be resolved by moving to the tonic. A pedal on the tonic anchors the music to its key note (NAM 16, bars 107–111^1). A pedal on both tonic and dominant (a double pedal) is used at the start of NAM 3. If a pedal occurs in an upper part, rather than the bass, it is called an inverted pedal.

Pentatonic. Music based on a scale of five pitches. You can find one such scale by playing the five black notes on a music keyboard. In NAM 57 the vocal melody in bars 5–12 is pentatonic because it uses only the pitches C, D, E, G and A. However, the accompaniment to this tune is not pentatonic because it includes the other two pitches of C major (F and B). *See also* **Hexatonic**.

Perfect cadence. Chords V and I at the end of a phrase, as in the last two chords of NAM 15.

Periodic phrasing. Balanced phrases of regular lengths (usually two, four or eight bars) – a style particularly associated with music of the Classical period. The introduction to NAM 37 consists of a four-bar statement ending on the dominant, balanced by a four-bar answer ending on the tonic.

Phrygian cadence. A type of **imperfect cadence** used in minor keys. It consists of the progression IVb–V, as in bars 15^4–16 of NAM 33.

Pick-up. *See* **Anacrusis**.

Pitch bend. A term used in pop and jazz for an expressive short slide in pitch to or from a note, particularly a **blue note**. In NAM 51 pitch bends are indicated by curved lines in the score, for example in bars 9–10 of the lead-guitar part.

Pizzicato. An instruction to a player of a bowed string instrument to pluck the strings instead of bowing them, as seen in the violin and cello parts at bar 32 in NAM 3. *See also* **Arco**.

Plagal cadence. Chords IV and I at the end of a phrase. For example the last two chords of NAM 38 are IVc–I in B minor, with a major 3rd in the final tonic chord that creates a **tierce de Picardie**.

Polarised texture. A term referring to Baroque music in which there is a wide gap between the bass part and the melody line(s), as in NAM 15. In performance, this is filled by improvised chords played on a **continuo** instrument such as an organ, harpsichord or lute.

Polyphony. The simultaneous use of two or more melodies. The opening of NAM 26 is polyphonic. Nowadays, the term is often used interchangeably with **counterpoint**, although it is more common to use polyphony when referring to Renaissance music.

Polyrhythmic. A texture based on the simultaneous use of two or more conflicting rhythms, as occurs throughout most of NAM 62.

Postmodernism. A term used to describe musical styles of the late 20th and early 21st centuries that have features such as familiar scales and modes, and that often avoid extreme dissonance, unlike the earlier atonal styles of **modernism**. Examples include NAM 32 and NAM 46. Many people regard **minimalism** (as seen in NAM 12) as a type of postmodernism.

Progression. A series of chords designed to follow one another.

Quartal harmony. Chords built from superimposed 4ths, rather than on 3rds as they are in triads. The use of quartal harmony can be seen in bars 23–28 of NAM 24.

Recapitulation. *See* **Sonata form**.

Refrain. A passage of music that returns at intervals throughout a work, especially in **rondo form**, although the term is also used to refer to the chorus of a song in verse-and-chorus form.

Register. A specific part of the range of a voice or instrument. For example, the first-violin part in NAM 18 starts in a low register, but climbs to a high register in bars 135–137.

Renaissance. A term referring to music written in styles typical of the period 1400–1600, such as NAM 26 (c.1528) and NAM 34 (published 1598).

Retrograde. Moving backwards. In movement 3 of NAM 10, the left-hand pitches of bars 19–21 are repeated in reverse (or retrograde) order, starting on the last note (F) of bar 21.

Rhythm and blues. A style of popular music that first developed among African-Americans in the late 1940s. It combined driving rhythms from jazz with the slow blues and, as it came to be used as dance music, louder instruments were introduced, including electric guitars, saxophones and drum kits. Rhythm and blues was an important element in the development of rock and roll in the 1950s and its influence on rock music continued for some years to come. NAM 51 is a rhythm-and-blues song, and can be compared with NAM 52, which is an example of early rock and roll from the same period.

Riff. *See* **Ostinato**.

Ritornello form. A structure used for large-scale movements in the late-Baroque period, such as NAM 1. An opening instrumental section (called the ritornello) introduces the main musical ideas. It is followed by a contrasting texture, although usually based on similar material, that features one or more soloists. Sections of the ritornello, often in different keys, then alternate with solo textures until the complete ritornello (or most of it) returns at the end in the tonic key. The fragmentary nature of most of the ritornello sections gives the form its name – ritornello means a 'little return'.

Romantic. A term referring to music written in styles typical of the period 1825–1900, such as NAM 3, 18, 23, 30, 38 and 39.

Rondo form. A musical structure in which a **refrain** in the tonic key alternates with contrasting **episodes**, creating a pattern such as ABACA or ABACABA. NAM 16 is a rondo.

Rounded binary form. A common type of **binary form** in which material from the opening returns towards the end of the second section, transposed to the tonic key if necessary. This structure, which could be represented as ‖A‖BA^1‖, is used in the first movement of NAM 21 and in the first two movements of NAM 23. Rounded binary form differs from **ternary form** (ABA) in having a B section that does not provide a clear contrast and that leads without a break into the abbreviated repeat of the opening material.

Rubato literally means 'robbed' and refers to shortening some beats and lengthening others in order to give an expressive, free feel to the pulse. The use of rubato is particularly associated with piano music of the Romantic period, such as NAM 23.

Secondary dominant. A chord (with or without a 7th) used as the dominant of a *chord* (other than I) rather than as the dominant of a key. In NAM 49, the C^7 in bar 54, is a secondary dominant because it is the dominant of the chord that follows. There is no modulation to F major because Eb appears almost immediately, turning the second chord into F^7 and thus making it another secondary dominant (of the chord of Bb^7 in bar 55).

Sequence. The *immediate* repetition at a different pitch of a phrase or motif in a continuous melodic line. A series of such repetitions is frequently used in the spinning-out of Baroque melodic lines, as in bars 69–75 of NAM 1 (where recorders perform an ascending sequence based on the initial three-note figure).

Serial music. Music based on manipulations of a chosen order for the 12 degrees of a chromatic scale, as in NAM 8. Other musical elements, such as note lengths and dynamics, are occasionally treated in a similar way.

Similar motion. A term to describe simultaneous melodic lines that move in the same direction. In bars 67–70 of NAM 3 the two clarinet parts move in the same direction. *See also* **Contrary motion**, **Oblique motion** and **Parallel motion**.

Slide. An ornament consisting of two or more short notes, printed in small type, that rise rapidly to the main note, as shown in bar 15 of NAM 37.

Sonata form. The most common structure for the first movement (and also often other movements) of sonatas, symphonies, concertos and **chamber music** in the **Classical** period and later. The essence of sonata form is the use of two contrasting tonal centres (tonic and either the dominant or another closely related key such as the relative major) in a first section called the exposition; the use of a wider range of keys to create tension and excitement in a central section called the **development**; and a recapitulation in which the music from the exposition is repeated in the tonic key. *See* NAM 22 and *see also* **Subject**.

Sprechgesang. German for 'speech-song'. A type of vocal production halfway between singing and speaking, used in NAM 40.

Stepwise movement. *See* **Conjunct**.

Straight quavers (or straight eights). In jazz and pop music, quavers that are played evenly rather than being played as **swing quavers**.

Stretto. The telescoping of imitative parts so that entries come closer to each other than they originally did. At the start of NAM 15, the first-violin melody is imitated by the second violin two bars later, and the bass joins in after a gap of a further

two-and-a-half bars. When the inverted form of this melody appears in bar 20, it is treated in stretto, each of the lower parts entering after a gap of only one bar.

Strophic. A song that uses the same music for every verse (such as NAM 37), as opposed to one which is **through-composed** (such as NAM 38).

Subject (1). One of the sections in the exposition of a movement in **sonata form**. Bars 1–10 of NAM 22 contain the first subject of this sonata-form movement.

Subject (2). The melody upon which a passage of imitation is based, such as the opening of the cello part in NAM 9.

Substitution chord. A chord that functions in a similar way to the simpler chord that it replaces. For example, in NAM 57 Fm^7 is substituted for the simpler chord of F in the second half of bars 13, 15 and similar places.

Suspension. A device in which a note is first sounded in a consonant context (the preparation) and is then repeated (or held) over a change of chord so that it becomes a dissonance (this is the suspension itself). Finally, there is a resolution when the suspended note moves by step (usually downwards) to a consonant note. All three stages can be seen in the violin 2 part of NAM 15: the note A is prepared in bar 17 (it is part of both chords in that bar), it then sounds against the B in the first-violin part at the start of bar 18 (creating the actual suspension) and it resolves by falling to G# (thus forming part of the prevailing chord of E major) in the second half of that bar.

Swing quavers. Also known as swung quavers. In jazz and pop music the division of the beat into a pair of notes in which the first is longer than the second. Swing quavers may be notated as ♪♪ or as ♪. ♪ but are performed closer to ♩ ♪ in both cases. They are indicated by instructions above the time signature at the start of NAM 51 and NAM 52, but in NAM 41 the ♪. ♪ rhythms are swung on the recording to reflect the style of the song, even though there is no specific instruction in the score. If pairs of quavers are to be played evenly in places where they might otherwise be swung, they are described as **straight quavers**.

Syllabic. Vocal writing in which all (or most) of the syllables are set to single notes, as in NAM 34.

Syncopation. Off-beat accents or accents on weak beats. In bar 1 of NAM 33 the note on the word 'fall' is syncopated by a leap to a high note on the weak fourth beat and by the suppression of the next strong beat through the use of a tie.

Ternary form. A three-part structure consisting of a middle section flanked by two identical or very similar passages. The form can be represented by the letters ABA or, if there are differences in the A section when it returns, ABA[1]. NAM 18, 19, 25 (prelude only) and 30 all make use of ternary structures. *See also* **Rounded binary form**.

Tessitura. The part of the pitch range in which a passage of music mainly lies. For example, the lead vocal in NAM 55 is entirely in a high tessitura, especially obvious in bars 25 and 43.

Texture. The effect resulting from the relationship between the various simultaneous lines in a piece of music. Specific textures include **monophonic**, **homophonic**, **homorhythmic**, **polyphonic** (or **contrapuntal**), **heterophonic** and **polyrhythmic**.

Through-composed. A song with mainly different music for each verse (such as NAM 38) rather than one which is **strophic** (such as NAM 37).

Tierce de Picardie. A major 3rd in the final tonic chord of a passage in a minor key. For example, NAM 33 is in A minor, but the C♯ in bar 24 is a tierce de Picardie that makes the last chord A major.

Timbre (pronounced tam-bruh). Tone colour. The clarinet has a different timbre from the trumpet, but it also has different timbres in various parts of its range. The timbre of an instrument can also be affected by the way it is played, for example by using a mute or plucking a string instead of using the bow.

Tonality. The use of major and minor keys in music and the ways in which these are related. Not all music is tonal – some is modal (based on one or more **modes**) and some (like NAM 59) is based on non-western scales. Western music that uses neither keys nor modes, such as NAM 8, is described as **atonal** (without tonality).

Tonic major and **tonic minor**. *See* **Parallel major** and **Parallel minor**.

Transcription. The notation of music that was previously not written down or that existed in some other type of notation. The scores of popular music, jazz and world music in NAM are all transcriptions from recordings. The term is also used in the sense of 'arrangement' to describe music that has been adapted for different performing resources. In NAM 20, bars 1–16, 33–48 and 82–98 are free transcriptions of the three eight-bar phrases in NAM 33.

Tremolo. The rapid and continuous repetition of a single note, as in the violin and cymbal parts of the last four bars on page 385 of NAM, or the rapid and continuous alternation of two pitches, as in the E♭ clarinet part in the same bars. The same page shows how these two types of tremolo are normally notated. Further examples can be seen in the string parts on page 116 of NAM.

Triad. A three-note chord formed by two superimposed intervals of a 3rd, such as A–C–E.

Trill. An ornament, indicated by a *tr* sign, that consists of rapid alternation of two notes a step apart, as seen in bar 37 of NAM 22. The same symbol is also used for a roll on a percussion instrument, even though this doesn't involve different pitches, as can be seen in bars 74–76 of the timpani part in NAM 4.

Tritone. An interval of three tones, such as B to the F above, as occurs between the outer parts on the last beat of bar 16 in NAM 34. Other examples occur at the ends of bars 10 and 13 in this piece.

Turn. A four-note ornament that can be indicated by the symbol ∾. It usually starts a step above the written note, drops to the written note, falls to the note below and then returns to the written note. The vertical stroke through the symbol in bar 62 of NAM 22 indicates an inverted turn, in which the order of notes described above is reversed.

Turnaround. In popular music, a short passage at the end of a section designed to lead the music back to the tonic key for a repeat of an earlier section. For that reason, it usually ends on chord V^7 of the home key, as in bars 33–34 of NAM 53.

Tutti. 'All' – the full ensemble, or a passage of music intended for the full ensemble. In bar 89 of NAM 1 the word 'tutti' signifies the entry of the full orchestra following the violin solo in the previous six bars.

Unison. A term to describe two or more people performing the same note or melody at the same pitch. In NAM 2 the bassoon plays in unison with the cellos for the first eight bars. In a wind part, the instruction 'a 2' (seen in bar 1 of the oboe part in the same score) means that both instrumentalists should play the same notes in unison. The term is also often used to describe women and men (or boys and men) singing the same melody, as in bars 11, 13 and 14 of NAM 32, although this is more accurately described as singing in octaves.

Vibrato. Small but fast fluctuations in the pitch of a note to add warmth and expression. The technique is not possible on instruments that produce notes of fixed pitch, such as the piano or harp, but is used by most other instrumentalists and trained singers. The speed and width of vibrato depends on the context and style – in Baroque times, vibrato was regarded as a type of ornament to be used with discretion, while in Romantic music it was often used as frequently as possible. The clarinet solo in NAM 48 and the saxophone solo in NAM 49 both show how a wide vibrato was a standard technique in early jazz.

Virtuoso. A performer of great technical skill. The term is also used to describe music which requires a high level of technical skill.

Vocalising. Singing to vowel sounds rather than real words, as in the parts for women's voices, starting at bar 26 in NAM 41.

Walking bass. A bass part that maintains the same note-lengths throughout a substantial passage, as in much of NAM 52, starting at bar 14.

Whole-tone scale. A scale in which there is a whole tone between all adjacent notes. It occurs in the clarinet and flute solos in bars 32–33 of NAM 5.

Word-painting. The musical illustration of the meaning or emotion associated with particular words or phrases, such as the use of the highest note in the song for 'Happie' in NAM 33.

For further help on technical terminology, consult the *Rhinegold Dictionary of Music in Sound* by David Bowman. It provides detailed explanations of a wide range of musical concepts and illustrates them using a large number of specially recorded examples on its accompanying compact discs. The *Rhinegold Dictionary of Music in Sound* is published by Rhinegold Publishing, ISBN 978-0946890-87-3.

Index of works